The Telegraph
BOOK OF CHAMPIONS

The Telegraph
BOOK OF CHAMPIONS

AN ANTHOLOGY OF THE GREATS THROUGHOUT THE SPORTING YEAR

EDITED BY MARTIN SMITH

Aurum
Press

For my mother

CONTENTS

INTRODUCTION

The certificate is around somewhere. Top-quality parchment paper. Unframed. My name on it. Winner of the junior school second-year 60-yard race; ahead of Christopher Geggus, Christopher Reynolds, Trevor Richmond and Andrew Harding. I say ahead of, but as the headmaster commented as he handed over the certificate, I was so far in front at the tape that I had time to turn around and watch everyone else trail home in my wake. Suddenly people were starting to sit up and take notice. My head went up several cap sizes almost instantaneously. Did we have a future sporting champion in our midst? The PE teacher, Mrs Wallen, turned up a pair of spikes for the upcoming district athletics championships in which I was to represent the school on a 'proper' track at Hornchurch Stadium. If I had known of him at the time I would have been dreaming of becoming Britain's first Olympic 100 metres champion since Harold Abrahams, some forty years earlier. If everything went to plan then you would never have heard of Allan Wells and Linford Christie, and Carl Lewis would by now have been a long-forgotten long-jumper.

Mine, I am sure, is a tale typical of many young boys and girls who once had a modicum of sporting promise, no matter how fleeting. How many of us have dreamt of winning an Olympic gold medal, or holding aloft the World Cup trophy? A fortunate few do go all the way to enter the pantheon of sporting champions; most of us don't. Is it down to luck or perseverance, determination and motivation, tunnel vision and the mental strength that some of us didn't show when we were subsequently outrun by a peer?

This book is a celebration of those boys and girls who didn't let setbacks defeat them as they climbed the greasy pole to success in their chosen sport. Through their words and deeds contained here, maybe we can learn how and why they crashed through the glass ceiling that contains the rest of us, and earned the nomenclature of sporting champion.

A few ground rules first. This is very much a personal selection, a mixed bag of the great and good, and there is no apology for that. The one hundred articles chosen from the *Telegraph* archives had to meet the criteria that, where possible, they shine a light into the deep recesses of the minds of our champions. They should give an idea of the route they took to reach the summit of achievement, or explain what motivated them. The articles have to be incisive. Where obvious candidates for inclusion have been omitted, it is probably because what was written about them didn't meet that criteria, not that their careers are without merit. Additionally, I have been determined not to repeat articles that have appeared in previous *Telegraph* anthologies I have compiled.

Each article represents a moment in the subject's career, sometimes at the end, occasionally at the beginning, often in the middle. To underline their achievements, past, present and future of that frozen moment, a brief statistical summation of their championships has been appended. These should not be considered comprehensive but a snapshot from the headline section on their sporting curriculum vitae.

To keep the selection focused, varied and hopefully interesting, it has followed the annual calendar of sporting events (taking in the four-yearly cycle of global events where appropriate). So the book starts early in the New Year at the smoky, beer-fuelled sporting arena that is the Circus Tavern in Purfleet, Essex, home of the PDC World Darts Championship, and ends one December out in the sunlit (and beer-fuelled) sporting arena of the MCG in Melbourne with England winning an away Ashes series for the first time in nearly quarter of a century. It passes through snow, sun, showers and floodlights, grass, mud, clay and canvas, with other esoteric surfaces and climatic conditions in between.

The live reports included are contemporaneous and usually written against deadline for the following day's newspaper, often without the benefit of action replays of the significant moments. The interviews were generally conducted around or during an event and the articles are largely as they appeared, though some have been tweaked appropriately when they moved too far from this book's *raison d'être*.

If there is one anecdote to explain graphically the difference between us and them, the champions and the never-weres, it is probably embodied in Daley Thompson's assertion that he would train on Christmas Day – sometimes even twice. In those far-off days of the 1970s and 1980s, 25 December was crossed out in most sportsmen's diaries as a well-earned day off. Not in Thompson's. He used the fact to give himself a psychological advantage over his opponents who he suspected were tucking into a second helping of Christmas pud and brandy butter along with the rest of the population.

Steve Redgrave, the champions' champion, says he never switched off. Ever. During a training camp in darkest Bulgaria at the height of their powers, his pairs' partner Matthew Pinsent explained: 'When it hurts, you think of the other guys around the world. You think, "I wonder where the Australians are training today? I wonder what the French are doing? I wonder if the Germans are getting a quick pair together?"' Redgrave responded to Pinsent's ponderings: 'You can be sure they're working, right now, on a plan to try to beat us.' As interviewer Michael Calvin noted: 'The urgency of his words exposed a champion's cocktail of perfectionism and paranoia.'

For that brief moment on top of the podium, hearing the National Anthem play in your honour, as Thompson and Redgrave did on so many occasions, years and years of unremitting practice have gone in. Redgrave and Pinsent estimated that they would train for thirty-four hours for each of the 240 strokes they required to complete the Olympic course. They would lift more than six million kilograms during weight-training sessions in the four years between Games. Their rivals in Australia, Germany and France would be doing the same. Any slight advantage, whether mental or physical, would be important.

A common thread running through the articles in this book is the refusal of the true champion to accept defeat, as Brough Scott puts it in a memorable insight into the multi-medalled swimmer Michael Phelps during the 2008 Olympics: 'It is why he accepts the early mornings, the impossible training sessions, the carbo-loaded diet, the unrelenting routine, the feeling that without winning there cannot be air to breathe or eyes to see . . . he is a champion because he has an ingrained rage against the possibility of defeat.' Scott notes: 'You see it with them all, just as much with Rafael Nadal in tennis as with A.P. McCoy in the racing game.'

Scott, a jump-jockey-turned-journalist, is spot-on about McCoy. The champion jockey every season since 1995–96, is obsessed with winning. A long-standing *Telegraph* columnist and tipster, in a piece he penned after he rode his 4,000th career winner, McCoy said: 'Essentially I am a dreamer. I have been dreaming all my life. When I started I dreamt I would be champion because it is a sport that is all about the people who win the most and I have a fear of not winning.' Despite the inherent dangers in a National Hunt jockey's line of work, he revealed he loved what he did, adding: 'If I was ever granted one wish it would be to come back as another person and be able to start this all over again.'

The need to find the winning edge has unfortunately, though inevitably, in some cases led to doping. Where there is money and aggrandisement available, there will always be those willing to flout the rules. Arguably the biggest cheat of them all is Lance Armstrong, sadly just one of too many two-wheeled pedlars of deceit. Brendan Gallagher's profile contained in these pages marked Armstrong's seventh and final Tour de France 'win'. It walks a legal tightrope between celebrating a champion and conjecture that all might not be as it seems. The fire could not yet be discerned for the smoke. Prophetically, Gallagher revealed that at a presentation the previous year Armstrong's team-mates had held up six fingers to denote his tally of successes; Armstrong put up seven. He knew he would win in 2005. He knew he couldn't be beaten: his drugs were better than anyone else's drugs. But if he looks in the record books now – following a belated investigation into the accusations that had been around all his career – he will realise it would have been more appropriate for him to have joined together his thumb and forefinger. So not a champion anymore, but included here as a warning of how the all-consuming desire to win, for whatever reason, can topple over into the dark side.

Michael Schumacher, whose reign of dominance in Formula One ran concurrent with Armstrong, was also not averse to a little chicanery to reach the chequered flag first. Other drivers were shunted off the track, his own car used as a road block on one famous occasion, and every stunt pulled to gain himself an advantage. David Coulthard, a rival and sometime victim, calls him 'the perfect pantomime villain'. In the immediate aftermath of Schumacher's life-threatening skiing accident, and with the benefit of hindsight, Coulthard revised his own somewhat jaundiced views on the seven-time world drivers' champion. He wrote: 'Michael was the reference point for me. I can see that now. If I beat him to a win or a podium, I knew I had done a very good job. He gave my career credibility.' He also recognised there were two Michael Schumachers: the track bully and the family man. To that can be added 'the consummate professional'.

Like Schumacher, his present-day heir, Sebastian Vettel, is a product of the Graf Berghe von Trips kart club in Kerpen, the magnet for precocious Formula One wannabes. Schumacher went there aged six, Vettel at eight. Motorsport correspondent Tom Cary visited the club and learnt about the inter-family rivalry that forged a champion's mentality. 'Once,' wrote Cary, 'Vettel became angry when his sister Stephanie went quicker than him in the family kart. He refused his lunch and stayed out [on the track] until he had set a better time.'

Vettel had been given a 60cc kart by his father at the age of three. This book is littered with examples of toddlers being given equipment by their parents and taking to the sport like the proverbial ducks. In many cases it is as an extension of the parents' own sporting interests; in a few the adjective 'pushy' can be inserted for apposite alliteration. Steffi Graf's father and mother, for instance, were regular tennis club members and it was natural to include their daughter from the age of four. Ben Ainslie's parents purchased his first boat, a little wooden Optimist dinghy, for Christmas when he was eight. Steve Davis's dad had a 6-foot junior table in the kitchen that begat his son's future career. Nicole Cooke would go on family cycling tours around parts of the West Country.

All of these were innocent introductions to the sports that would dominate their offsprings' lives. However, the award for pushy parent *in extremis* must go to Earl Woods. Shortly after Tiger had won the first of his four Masters titles, James Mossop delved into the background of the twenty-one-year-old golfing superstar in the making. He discovered that Woods senior had planned his son's career almost from conception. By the age of eleven months, we are told, little Eldrick (Tiger) was swinging a miniature club perfectly. By the age of four he was spending eight hours a day on the golf course. His mother Tilda took his astrological chart to Buddhist monks. Mossop says they revealed that her son had wondrous powers and that if he went into politics he would become a president or a prime minister. In the military he would be a general. Instead he would reign over the fairways and greens for more than a decade and a half. His father took it further and said out loud that, in Mossop's paraphrasing, 'Tiger would transcend the game, bring to the world a humanitarianism it had never known before and that God Himself had decided that Earl was the man to nurture this treasure'. In a direct quote, Earl Woods described Tiger as 'The Chosen One': 'He will have the power to impact nations. Not people. Nations. The world is just getting a taste of his power.' The sportsman as deity: the son could not afford to fail with that sort of build-up.

This book also recognises the champion as team. There are paeans to sporting champions in the plural, groups of individuals moulded to perform in unison, who have reached a peak at the right moment to carry off the spoils. Forty years of hurt later, Alan Ball takes us through the build-up and reasons for England's World Cup triumph in 1966; there are the Rugby World Cup-winning performances of England and South Africa; Sri Lanka overcoming the odds in the Cricket World Cup and, dotted throughout, of England overcoming Australia to win Ashes series plural. There is also a peek inside the mind, methods and longevity of the multi-title-winning Sir Alex Ferguson at Manchester United.

Ferguson aside, just about every poll carried out to discover the Sportsman of the Twentieth Century was topped by Muhammad Ali. He certainly adorned the front of the *Daily Telegraph's* sports supplement going into the new millennium on 1 January 2000, just as the classic photograph of him standing over the crushed George Foreman has been chosen to illuminate the cover of this book. The Rumble in the Jungle: Donald Saunders was there in Kinshasa in 1974 to see Ali reclaim his world crown after a gap of six years, only the second fighter to do so. Saunders was moved to call him 'the greatest heavyweight of my time' in his report reproduced here.

But it was not just as a boxer that Ali should be remembered, though that would be enough for most pugilists, most sportsmen. No, as Saunders saw first-hand in the aftermath of the most famous fight in boxing history, it was as a role model for the disadvantaged of the world that lifted Ali above the rest: 'Ali is not just a superb athlete. He is a symbol of hope to millions of less privileged and less gifted members of his race. Surely no one else from any sport, with the possible exception of Pelé, could bring a city to the fever of excitement he inspired in Kinshasa.'

On the subject of overcoming life's vicissitudes, what can be more inspirational than our paralympians? In the 1970s the Sports Council's motto was Sport for All, and nowhere is that better highlighted than in paralympic sport of which the *Telegraph* has been a longstanding supporter. The case of Ellie Simmonds, poster girl for the 2012 Paralympics in London, shows not only her vitality and determination, but the sacrifices of her family. Lee Pearson's integration into the able-bodied world was so complete that when he went to his first Games in 2000, he found himself disappointed by what he found. 'I'd always liked to think that I was unique,' he said, 'and there I was, suddenly surrounded by hundreds of athletes with far more severe problems than me.'

Oscar Pistorius became the ultimate pin-up for the Paralympic movement when he fought a long campaign to have disabled athletes allowed to compete against the able-bodied, continuing to break down barriers in 2012 when he ran in both the Olympic and Paralympic Games in London. Paul Hayward's assessment of the Blade Runner came as he was arrested in 2013, charged with the murder of his girlfriend. A lurid court case during 2014 cast a shadow over his character, if not his sporting achievements.

All the sportsmen and women in this book provide evidence of how they reached the top – their rigorous training regimes, paranoiac levels of practice, practice, practice and, of course, the all-important element of luck. Side by side in this line-up they remind us of why sport is so compelling, and why winning big is only for the few.

Anyway, you've read the paper, now read the book.

There is a veritable phalanx of people who should climb on to the podium to collect gold medals for their part in helping this book across the finishing line. Step forward: Robin Harvie, Lucy Warburton and Emily Kearns, my hard-working editors and task-masters at Aurum Press; Cerys Hughes, publishing manager at Telegraph Media Group, who has been a rock throughout; Gavin Fuller, Lorraine Goodspeed and the rest of the *Telegraph* library, who have facilitated my research and kept me amused during my visits; Keith Perry, Phil Shaw and Andrew Baker, for their guidance and support at crucial times; the writers, who watched, interviewed and tried to get inside the heads of the sporting champions included in the following pages – and then wrote beautifully about them; and the production staff, who handled their copy with due care and diligence. You are all champions to me.

Martin Smith
April 2014

PREFACE

AN INGRAINED RAGE AGAINST DEFEAT

Deep inside a true champion there is a will that refuses to accept defeat. It is why he accepts the early mornings, the impossible training sessions, the carbo-loaded diet, the unrelenting routine, the feeling that without winning there cannot be air to breathe nor eyes to see. You see it with them all, just as much with Rafael Nadal in tennis as with A.P. McCoy in the racing game. In press conferences, Michael Phelps smiles and speaks serenely of noble things like 'taking the sport of swimming to where I would like it to be'. But right at the core he is a champion because he has an ingrained rage against the possibility of defeat.

Brough Scott on Michael Phelps

JANUARY

PHIL 'THE POWER' TAYLOR – PDC WORLD DARTS CHAMPIONSHIP

BRISTOW'S PROTÉGÉ ON TARGET TO UPSTAGE THE MASTER

Giles Smith, 27 December 1997

No one can pretend the last few years have been a Champagne phase for darts. Rendered cash-conscious and image-sensitive by its television-led boom in the 1980s, the sport seemed to spend much of the next decade in a state of panicked introversion. There were endless campaigns for a leaner, cleaner darts: no smoking, drinking or fighting on the oche. But at what cost to the essential nature of the game? As Martin Amis anxiously observed, as long ago as 1988: 'It is now accounted a "victory for darts" when a thin player beats a fat one.' Darts was eating itself – and a more painful, more gruelling spectacle it would be hard to imagine.

It did not help when a tiresome and credence-sapping boxing-style split broke the sport's governing body in two. This left, on the one hand, the Professional Darts Council, who set up shop with Sky Sports at the end of 1993, absorbing nearly all the game's most popular figures and commencing the annual PDC World Darts Championships in the bellowing Circus Tavern at Purfleet in Essex; and on the other, the British Darts Organisation, whose Embassy World Professional Darts Championship, held at

Frimley Green in Surrey, cannot help but seem strangely sallow by comparison with the lights, heat and smoke of Purfleet.

Yet, ironically, amid this chaos – and to no small extent obscured by it – the sport has happened upon a prodigy, a living darting legend. Phil 'The Power' Taylor is not a thin player. At thirty-seven, he has an ample, landlord's waist. He also has unfashionable hair and a moustache. His forearms are like Popeye's: ham-shaped, tattooed. Yet if darts needs 'an ambassador' (the eternal cry), then who better than The Power; world champion five times over, a feat matched only by Eric Bristow; the winner of some 180 of the 200 worldwide professional tournaments he has entered in his nine-year career; a performer of almost hilarious consistency in a sport which mocks the very idea; the man television's Voice of Darts, Sid Waddell, calls 'the greatest darts player that's ever drawn breath'?

The Power heads for Purfleet where, if past form is any guide, he will be wearing one of the most horrible shirts you have ever seen. (He used to get them from Stagewear Unlimited, who were well named; now a friend makes them.) Also he will be racking up the 180s and the ton-forties in quantities which seem to defy probability. And he will be pushing towards that sixth world title which will place him in a darting zone all his own. In the event of which, he will weep copiously and be unable to utter a single coherent word into the microphone which Sky Sports, with indecent haste, will thrust under his nose. Choking is a feature of Taylor's post-championship celebrations in a way it is distinctly not a feature of his darts.

One lunchtime recently I visited The Power to see how his preparations for Purfleet were going. He runs a modest but cosy pub – inappropriately, the Cricketers Arms – nicely situated by a green in Stoke. Its walls boast darts trophies the way other pubs' walls boast horse-brasses. We talked in the flat upstairs, where there were comfy chairs, more darts trophies, some of Taylor's four young children, a large television and an Alsatian the size of a Shetland pony. Taylor said: 'A pub's a twenty-four-hour job and yet you want to give one hundred per cent to your darts . . .' You could see the difficulty.

Outside, some testament to his profile, sat the six-berth van with giant darts painted on it, which houses the Phil 'The Power' Taylor Exhibition Show. 'Normally a dart exhibition is very boring,' Phil conceded. 'People just standing there, playing darts.' But Phil has modelled his exhibition nights on the Radio One Roadshow: a stage, some flashing lights, lots of dry ice, a tape of Monty Python's 'Always Look on the Bright Side of Life'. 'We'll do a musical quiz with a prize for the winner,' Phil says, 'and we have a game of *Bullseye* like you have on the TV. And we finish off with a bit of disco music until the landlord switches the electric off on us.' An unlikely compere for disco-frenzied pub nights, Taylor is a gently spoken man, instantly friendly and likely to refer to you at any time as 'duck'. As long as you are not playing him at darts. 'He's a bully,' says Sid Waddell. 'He's a pussy cat off the oche, but he's a killer up there.' Or as Taylor puts it: 'If I see the winning post, I tend to kick and really go for the jugular. I keep scoring heavy. It's like a boxer: if somebody keeps hitting you with a left hook, you're going to go down eventually.'

Taylor did not start playing darts until he was twenty-six, and then only one day a week, in a little Stoke club and at the urging of his father. 'But I was very good,' he said. 'A natural player.' After a year he was playing at super-league level, and within three months of that he had been picked to represent his county. In 1988 he was playing for Staffordshire at The Crafty Cockney, Eric Bristow's darts club, now defunct, when Bristow spotted his potential and offered to sponsor him. Bristow, of course, had been the most famous darts player in the land and was awarded an MBE in the years of his pomp. But when he made his offer to Taylor, the former world champion was deep into his now legendary bout of 'dart-itis', which saw the near-terminal desertion of his nerve. 'I think it was a terrible time for him,' Taylor says. 'I think he was brave to go on at all. Most people would have packed up. He was going on TV and couldn't let go of his darts. Very embarrassing – for somebody who was world number one.' Bristow thought his career was finished and he decided to live vicariously through Taylor. He paid for hotels, air fares and entry fees. 'If I won, I paid him back,' Taylor says. 'It was a loan, but I could have lost him money. I think he stumped up about £10,000 in all. Nobody had ever done that in darts. Now young lads are asking me to do the same. I suppose one day I will – take someone under my wing and take them round the world with me. When I see the right person.'

Taylor had been living in a two-bedroomed, terraced house in Stoke and earning £250 a week as a turner in a ceramics firm. With Bristow as a backer, he now took voluntary redundancy and set off to make his way in darts. Waddell says: 'Bristow physically bashed Taylor to be the player that he is.' Certainly results came rapidly: after one year, Taylor was in the world top ten and the following year, 1990, he was selected for the first time to play in the Embassy World Championships. He won. Now, Bristow may well watch his hand-picked successor wipe him from the record books – a sight which will bring him mixed pleasure, according to Waddell. 'Eric will be the sickest guy in the Circus Tavern. No one should go near him for an hour.'

'You've got to get your opponents frightened of you,' Taylor says, 'and that's what I've got now. People are frightened to play me. You'll get players who try antics: pulling the darts out slow, walking directly towards you on the way back. But as soon as someone starts doing that, I know I've got them. My forte is on stage, for TV. Because the cameras are on there and that's when I'm at my best.'

The day we met, at around 3 p.m., Taylor changed and went downstairs for his daily two hours of practice. The pub does not open until six, so Taylor and his friend Mick had the bar to themselves. The object of the exercise they unsmilingly set themselves was to complete a two or three-dart finish for every number between eighty and 180. Most of us could probably spend a fractious month working on this. For Taylor, it was the business of less than an hour. He was using his made-to-commission darts, the grips of which have the texture of iron files. He stood absolutely side-on to the board, the folds of his chin squashed against his shoulder. The atmosphere grew dutifully concentrated and the conversation took on an intermittent and random nature. At one point Taylor looked out at the snow falling thickly across the car park and said, meditatively: 'If you were an Eskimo, you'd have to go out in that and find something to eat.' Other topics included the virtues or otherwise of the pop star Robbie Williams and the bloke who comes in the pub quite regularly who, according to Taylor, wrote Stevie Wonder's 'Isn't She Lovely'. I was going to mention that, as far as I was aware, it was Stevie Wonder who wrote Stevie Wonder's 'Isn't She Lovely', but Phil was shaping up to throw and somehow the moment passed.

Increasingly, though, the only sounds to be heard were the crackle of the fire and the thud of tungsten on cork – or just occasionally, the clatter of tungsten on pub lino. For even The Power clips the wire every now and again. Nevertheless, 'I'm very confident,' Taylor had said earlier, referring to Purfleet and in a manner which did not incline you to doubt him. 'If I get my head right, I'll take a lot of beating.'

Sporting Champion: Phil 'The Power' Taylor – 14 PDC World Champion-ships (1995, 1996, 1997, 1998, 1999, 2000, 2001, 2002, 2004, 2005, 2006, 2009, 2010, 2013); 2 BDO World Championships (1990, 1992).

HENRY COOPER – BRITISH HEAVYWEIGHT BOXING CHAMPIONSHIP

COOPER THRASHES LONDON FOR THE TITLE

Donald Saunders, 13 January 1959

Henry Cooper, the young man from Bellingham, who tried, tried and tried again, is the British and Empire heavyweight champion. He earned those proud titles at Earls Court after outboxing and outpunching Brian London over fifteen of the most bitterly contested rounds I have ever watched. At the end of a contest that must surely consolidate Britain's newfound prestige among world heavyweights, both warriors looked as though they had been fighting with meat axes. Cooper was bleeding from cuts above and below his left eye and from a gash over his right eye. London's right eye was a grotesque sight – a mere slit of bruised and bleeding flesh. Both men were almost too weary to stand. Yet when this bitter personal feud, which began several years ago when Cooper's brother Jim was savagely mauled by London, had come to an end, these one-time enemies clasped each other's shoulders and let everyone know that as far as they were concerned honour had been well and truly satisfied.

For Cooper this victory is the climax of a story as full of ups and downs as the most imaginative boxing fiction written. A few months ago his future as a heavyweight looked like being confined to the smaller halls of Britain. Three times he had tried to win a title – from Joe Erskine, Joe Bygraves and Ingemar Johansson. Each time he had met with humiliating defeat. In September 1958 this courageous young man was given another chance – in a British title eliminator against the tough, hard-punching Welshman Dick Richardson. Cooper got up off the floor that night to win a memorable victory. A month later he again hauled himself from the canvas and went on to outpoint the American Zora Folley.

Again, here Cooper had to overcome adversity that would have defeated many a lesser man before he received the award that had so long eluded him. After six rounds of bruising boxing it looked as though London was going to keep his title and that Cooper was going to suffer the fate many had predicted for him – a summary defeat caused by eye injuries. The tender skin round Cooper's eyes had already begun to show signs of wear and tear. His left eyebrow had been grazed in the fourth round and was bleeding freely by the sixth. By the seventh the wound had worsened and Cooper was further handicapped by another, deeper cut under the same eye.

At the end of the seventh, the referee, Mr Ike Powell, went over to Cooper's corner and asked him if everything was all right. Bravely, Cooper replied: 'Yes, I'm all right.' Then back he went into battle. Mercilessly the now supremely confident London hammered him around the ring, throwing punches from all angles with those long, well-muscled arms. I doubt that anyone among the 18,000 spectators would have given much for Cooper's chances of success at that moment. But Cooper himself had clearly decided that he just would not be beaten. Though he still could not keep out London, he did at least succeed in jolting him frequently with left jabs to the face. At first the blows seemed a mere annoyance to London, but slowly they began to show their effect. London was no longer barging in with quite the same fury, nor was he showing his opponent the contempt that had been plain earlier on. Moreover his right eye had now begun to puff. And that small swelling soon grew large.

Then, in the tenth round, Cooper at last saw blood trickling from the champion's right eyebrow. Immediately he made that wound the target for his copybook left jabs. And Cooper's aim was so much more accurate that London's had been. Punch after punch ripped through London's guard and widened the gash. But whereas Cooper's second had skilfully succeeded in staunching the blood – at least from the cut under his left eye – London's corner was powerless to stop the flow that handicapped the champion. Boxing on with confidence, Cooper's grip on the fight grew tighter. The only question left to be answered was whether the champion still had the power to pull the fight out of the fire with one big punch. Soon he knew he hadn't. Cooper's other eye was cut, but even that could not rekindle the fire in London's weary fists. He was so bewildered at the end of the fourteenth round that he attempted to hold aloft Cooper's hand in a token of victory.

Only when he returned to his corner did he discover that three long minutes remained. Bravely and wearily he heaved himself out of his stool for the fifteenth time and went forward gamely, wearily and bleeding to what he knew was inevitable defeat. Mr Powell hardly needed to hold up Cooper's hand. All of us knew that the British copybook style of boxing had rarely scored a more convincing victory. Later, London disclosed that he had injured his right hand early in the fight, but he admitted that Cooper had fairly and squarely proved himself the better man.

Sporting Champion: Henry Cooper – British Championship (1959–67, 1970–71); Commonwealth Championship (1959–71); European Championship (1964, 1968–69, 1970–71).

TONY ALLCOCK – WORLD BOWLS CHAMPIONSHIPS

ALLCOCK STEPS ASIDE AND LEAVES
BOWLS TO THE BOYS

Robert Philip, 24 February 2003

Be it as a boy soprano in the concert hall, or trotting round the show ring at Crufts with his prize-winning Cavalier King Charles Spaniel puppy, or on the bowling green, Tony Allcock has become accustomed to being crowned champion. Described as 'the greatest all-round bowler in the history of the sport' by world number one David Gourlay, Allcock has retired from the so-called 'old man's game' at the youthful age of forty-seven to devote his seemingly boundless energies to a variety of alternative pursuits. 'Secretly, I intended to quit twelve months ago,' he says, nodding at the 2002 world indoor singles trophy partly hidden by the forest of good luck cards on the antique cabinet in his home in the Gloucestershire countryside, 'but then I went out and won that thing so I decided it would be only fair to stick around for another year and defend my title. In reality, at the top level, bowls is a young man's game and I now find myself the oldest member of the circuit. I rode horses at a very high level and, when I got frightened looking at a five-bar gate, I knew my time had come – so my time has come in bowls. That said, I don't think it's fair to pooh-pooh bowls as an old man's game because we're all going to be old one day and there's not too many sports at club level where someone of seventy, say, can compete against a thirty-year-old.'

It was as a thirty-year-old in 1986 that Allcock won the first of his fifteen world titles (indoor and outdoor, singles and pairs, he was the master of all), much to the chagrin of many in the bowling community who regarded the pipe-smoking David Bryant as the boss of the rink. Who was this slim-hipped young whippersnapper with the David Gower curls and tight white flannels? 'David was a god but we were actually very close friends despite our different images and close rivalry. When Steve Davis was winning everything he was never as popular as he is today. That's the mentality of the British public – knock 'em down and then when they're down pick 'em up again. And so when I won the mixed and men's pairs titles at this year's world indoors, they were highly popular victories and the crowd made it a very emotional experience. Tina Turner blasted out "Simply the Best" and I was accorded two standing ovations. I said my farewells in the middle of the rink and thought, "Wow, what a fantastic end to a career". Reluctantly – very reluctantly, I have to say – I then agreed to compete in the Welsh Masters, which is a world-ranking event where I surprised everyone – not least myself – by beating David Gourlay in the final. All the press boys were saying, "Look, we've written the script and yet it's going on and on".'

Perfectionist that he is, Allcock ensured he did not bow out of major singles competitions without providing a dramatic PS to the tale. 'I won the first set and David needed two maximums from the last two ends to draw level. His third ball nestled sweetly on the jack and, with the last bowl I ever delivered in a world-ranking event, I nudged David's ball out and rested on the jack myself. Instead of delivering his own last bowl, David turned to me, shook my hand and gave me a hug. That was a gesture which meant a lot to me and proved yet again that even in a highly competitive sport like bowls, thank God, there is still room for good old-fashioned sportsmanship.'

Curiously, for a man who exudes self-confidence in all walks of life, Allcock can display an endearing streak of vulnerability, such as his preparations for the 2002 world indoor singles at Norwich. 'I'm a psychologist's nightmare because I've always had a strategic plan for the negative result which isn't in the accepted identikit of any champion. Looking at the draw, I knew I would probably get through the first round but packed my suitcase for only a four-day stay; four pairs of underpants, four shirts, two pairs of trousers. I spent a hell of a lot of money in the launderette and, by the end of the fortnight, had also bought a whole new wardrobe, which ate up quite a chunk of the £25,000 first prize. I also made sure the car was always filled up with petrol so I could make a fast getaway when I lost. It was the sweetest of all my victories coming, as it did, fifteen years after my previous world indoor title at Coatbridge in 1987.'

Allcock has embarked on a new career as chief executive of the English Bowling Association at their headquarters in Worthing, but he is too much of a diplomat to admit that beating long-time rival Richard Corsie, of Scotland, 8–3, 9–4 in the final represented a double dose of sweetener. 'Let's just say there was a lot of history between us,' he says. Still ranked number six in the world, Allcock's decision to retire at the top has surprised friend and foe alike, yet he professes no regrets. 'I'm embroiled in so many things, I realised I just wasn't putting in the same effort. My heart wasn't in it anymore and I've always followed my heart; I don't do things I can't do well. I set myself very high standards in everything and if I'm not making a very good job of it, I pull out immediately.'

Allcock was born with a cowl of skin covering his head and keeps it in a drawer to this day as a good-luck charm. 'My mother, who wasn't particularly superstitious, told me the cowl meant I'd never want for anything and that if I was ever in danger of drowning, I'd be saved by a sailor. Poppycock? A few years ago in Florida I got into trouble when I was swamped by a huge wave while swimming and this lad in a boat suddenly appeared from nowhere to pull me out with a rope. It was a miracle. I've always struggled with religion but to all intents and purposes I have to believe there's something out there.'

Whether the mystical powers of the cowl are responsible or

merely the hand fate has dealt him, Allcock has made a success of almost every venture he has undertaken. 'Luck, desire, call it what you will, but I've always been an achiever; at twenty-four I was principal of a school for the mentally handicapped. I came from a very humble background – of which I'm fiercely proud – but taught myself about opera, art, antiques. I run a successful boarding kennels and dog welfare centre. I'm the top breeder this year of Japanese Chins, and one of my Cavalier King Charles Spaniels won the Top Puppy title at Crufts in 2002.' Is there anything he's not good at? 'Yeah, relationships,' admits Allcock, twice divorced and now content in bachelorhood.

Regarded as a loner during his early years on the circuit – 'When I was number one in the world in the 1980s, I was totally focused. I didn't want to talk to the press, I didn't want to talk to the players, I wouldn't have an after-match drink' – Allcock has emerged as the consummate 'team man'. As performance director of England's 2002 Commonwealth Games squad in Manchester, he inspired his charges to the nation's best medal haul: three golds, one silver and a bronze from six events. On top of which, he also guided sixty-nine-year-old Ruth Small to victory in the partially sighted event. 'To work with someone visually impaired wasn't a humbling experience, it was fascinating; and in its own way every bit as emotional as my victory at the world indoor earlier in the year. Here was a woman of nearly seventy who'd gone to the gym four or five times a week, followed a nutritious diet, consulted a sports psychologist, practised for hours on end and eventually won the gold-medal play-off 15–0. Oh, did I shed some tears.' For a seemingly simple game, bowls is a highly complex sport and Tony Allcock one of its greatest and most complex champions.

Sporting Champion: Tony Allcock – 3 World Indoor Singles Championships (1986, 1987, 2002); 2 World Outdoor Singles

Championships (1992, 1996); 8 World Indoor Pairs Championships (1986, 1987, 1989, 1990, 1991, 1992, 1997, 2003); 1 World Outdoor Triples Championship (1980); 1 World Outdoor Fours Championship (1984).

SERENA WILLIAMS – AUSTRALIAN OPEN

SERENA JOINS THE SLAM ELITE

Clive White, 26 January 2003

The roof over the Rod Laver Arena had to be closed when the Australian Open's 'extreme heat policy' came into effect as early as 9.35 a.m. But while temperatures outside soared to 47°C, the heat was rising inside, too, irrespective of air conditioning, as the incomparable Williams sisters scorched the Rebound Ace surface with their shots in what was arguably the finest Slam final the pair have contested – and they have contested a few. Their mother, Oracene, could bear to watch it no longer, leaving her ringside seat at the end of a first set in which her two girls had slugged it out, toe-to-toe, for one minute short of an hour. She returned, one hour and twenty-three minutes later, to take a snapshot of the younger daughter celebrating her place in tennis history as only the fifth woman to win four consecutive Slams.

Whether or not it was because of that record, or because of the criticism that their all-too-frequent meetings have attracted, this was one of those finals when one believed both of them really cared. In fact, one is almost tempted to say there was no love lost. Serena, twenty-one and normally impervious to emotions, had to fight back tears as she received the winner's trophy, following a desperately narrow victory over Venus, 7–6,

3–6, 6–4. 'I never get choked up, never,' she said, 'but I'm really emotional right now. I'm really, really happy.' And you know, for once, you believed her.

This was the closest of any of their eleven meetings – which Serena leads 6–5 – and the first time that Venus had taken a set off her in the Slams since Serena began her 'Grand Slam quest' at Roland Garros in May 2002. By winning this Australian Open – or Serena Slam, as it has come to be known – she joins all-time greats like Maureen Connolly, Margaret Court, Martina Navratilova and Steffi Graf, who all won four consecutive Slams, though Navratilova's and Graf's, like Williams's, were not in a calendar year. Needless to say, that is her next target.

Serena seemed genuinely moved by her achievement and humble about it, too. 'I just can't believe I can now be compared to these women because they're such greats and I've really been able to look up to them,' she said. There have been times in this championship, though, when it seemed she might not get her wish. The unseeded French woman, Emilie Loit, was a break up against her in the final set in the opening round, while the Belgian, Kim Clijsters, had two match points, at 5–2 in the third, in the semi-finals. But each time she showed her champion's pedigree by refusing to accept defeat. There were moments in the final when it seemed that her sister might dash her hopes, too, but Venus's nerve was found wanting on the big points – unlike her sister.

Venus clearly had the majority support among the 15,000 crowd – which she diplomatically said she never noticed – but was unable to make it work for her. So awesome was the strokeplay at times that the crowd sat mesmerised, the silence broken only by the tweeting of birds trapped under the closed roof. The first set could have gone either way until it came to the tie-break, and then there was only going to be one winner. Venus took the second set convincingly enough, after squandering three break points in the sixth game before she finally won it. And she had a break point against Serena in the opening game of the third set but let the advantage slip from her grasp. In the next game, in which she was broken to love, she appeared to stop playing at one stage, when one of her shots was contentiously called long when it was in, and Serena glowered at a line judge. 'Don't be scared of her,' called out one spectator to the quivering line judge. Easier said than done when you have just had a close-up view of the not-so-serene Serena hurling her racket in the direction of her chair on losing the second set.

Even Serena had to smile, though, when in the next game Venus broke back, having stood her ground at the net with a triple-volley return before smashing a forehand down the line. Games then went with service until Venus's suspect second serve was exposed again, for the final time, in the tenth game. 'She wasn't going to go away,' Serena said. 'Usually she has a double fault or something. She hit so many big serves and honestly I didn't think I was going to be able to pull it out and I just said, "Serena, fight, fight".'

No brother or sister likes to lose to a younger sibling, as John McEnroe will testify, but Venus's take on the matter is quite exceptional: 'I'm just trying to be just like her,' she said as she collected her fourth consecutive runners-up prize. There surely never was a better loser, which may be part of her trouble. Certainly, Serena would never have accepted defeat so honourably. But one sensed there was a new resolve about Venus. 'I think she was probably just a little mentally tougher out there than I was,' she said. 'I think maybe that's the main thing that's dropped off in me. I'm going to work on it. I'm going to fight and I'm going to concentrate.'

Sporting Champion: Serena Williams – 5 Australian Opens (2003, 2005, 2007, 2009, 2010); 5 Wimbledons (2002, 2003, 2009, 2010, 2012); 5 US Opens (1999, 2002, 2008, 2012, 2013); 2 French Opens (2002, 2013); 1 Olympic Games (2012).

NOVAK DJOKOVIC – AUSTRALIAN OPEN

DJOKOVIC WINS BATTLE OF ENDURANCE

Simon Briggs, 29 January 2012

The unquenchable spirit met the unbreakable here when Novak Djokovic faced Rafael Nadal on Rod Laver Arena. It was certainly the longest, surely the hardest and arguably the greatest Grand Slam final in history. The bare facts are that Djokovic won the Australian Open 5–7, 6–4, 6–2, 6–7, 7–5 in a match that lasted five hours and fifty-three minutes. A marathon match for sure, except that this went far beyond that, into Iron Man territory. One could only marvel at the players' endurance and athleticism. Remember that Djokovic had invested four hours and fifty minutes in the tricky business of subduing Andy Murray in the semi-final. To go back to the well after less than forty-eight hours' rest was a mind-boggling achievement. Goodness knows what his feet looked like the next morning.

Just because a match is long, it does not necessarily follow that the quality has to be high. The John Isner–Nicolas Mahut epic at Wimbledon in 2010 was unfailingly one-dimensional. But this final was full of pulsating points, including one breathless thirty-two-stroke rally, at 5–4 in the final set, which drew a standing ovation from the crowd. What will linger in the mind is the courage and the commitment of these two men. They are the masters of the anti-choke – that rare and admirable ability to strike the most penetrating shots when on the verge of defeat. This explains why their past two Grand Slam encounters have been so bewilderingly changeable. The US Open final in 2011 was a minor classic, running to four hours and ten minutes. But you could take the drama of that night at Flushing Meadows, square it, and still not come close to what we saw here.

The first set was the least memorable of the five. Djokovic did not quite have his forehand calibrated in those early exchanges, allowing Nadal to break him twice. Still, as they sat down to prepare for the second set, the match clock was already ticking round towards the eighty-two minutes that it took Victoria Azarenka to win the women's final twenty-four hours earlier. The argument for equal pay has rarely looked so shaky. In the second and third sets, Djokovic showed why he had beaten Nadal in their previous six meetings. He found his rhythm, and his peerless service return. The serve sits up higher on Melbourne's Plexicushion courts than it does anywhere else, and no one is better at ramming it back at his opponent's feet than Djokovic. Time and again, Nadal was forced to take his second shot on the half-volley. 'His return probably is one of the best in history,' said a disbelieving Nadal after the match. '[He makes it] almost every time.'

Djokovic cruised through the second and third sets, then moved to 4–3 in the fourth. He was bestriding the court, striking one shot in three from within the baseline, whereas the equivalent figure for Nadal – who was being forced so far back that the line-judges needed steel toecaps – was one in twenty. But the narrative had more twists left in it. At 0–40 down and facing three break points – effectively championship points – Nadal seemed to find a red button somewhere deep inside his psyche. He pressed it and went into overdrive, forsaking all caution and ripping winner after winner with that haymaker of a forehand. The meek figure of the previous two sets evaporated, and he began swinging his big left arm like a 500 lb gorilla. Djokovic's break points were quickly swept away, and Nadal snatched the tie-break to set up a final set. As he went down on his knees to celebrate, the Australian Open was already half an hour into its third week. Babysitters across Melbourne must have been holding their employers to ransom.

At this late phase, the players could have been forgiven for shanking a few shots, or declining to chase the wide balls. Instead they were producing Hollywood tennis, each stroke so powerful and well-aimed. The only sign of strain was the grimace etched on Nadal's face. Djokovic remained outwardly calm, although he could not help collapsing to the ground after losing that thirty-two-shot rally late in the final set. He was cheered on by a vocal group of patriots, who held up an oil painting – done in the style of the Serbian Orthodox Church – of their hero as a saint.

Would Djokovic's nerve crack? Hardly, for it must be made of titanium. He lost his serve to concede a 4–2 lead, then broke straight back when Nadal did the unthinkable, missing an easy backhand put-away down the line. This is the frightening thing about playing Djokovic: miss just one opportunity and you know he will make you pay. Here is a man who has no technical weaknesses, makes hardly any errors and will never back down mentally. The challenge is stark: play a perfect game, or expect to lose. And Nadal did lose, as Djokovic broke him again, then served out the match, staving off one final break point with a huge inside-out forehand. The champion had defended his title, and he ripped his shirt off and clenched his biceps like a weightlifter on Muscle Beach.

All that was left was an excruciatingly prolonged awards ceremony, in which the sponsors droned on so long that someone thoughtfully produced a pair of chairs for the players halfway through. Djokovic sat half-slumped, his features blank and his eyes staring glassily into the distance. It was the face of a man who had exhausted all his inner reserves. But inside you knew he was satisfied. He had just delivered one of the greatest sporting performances of the age.

Sporting Champion: Novak Djokovic – 4 Australian Opens (2008, 2011, 2012, 2013); 1 Wimbledon (2011); 1 US Open (2011).

FEBRUARY

JOE MONTANA – SUPER BOWL

MONTANA STAGES A NEW COMEBACK

Ian Chadband, 26 October 2013

Joe Montana would like it to be known that reports of his death have been greatly exaggerated. Greying, yes, but otherwise alive and very well, and able to reflect on the weirdness of how an internet hoax a couple of months before led to wildfire rumours that he had died in a car accident. 'We were on a boat in the south of France when I heard about my death,' he smiles. 'A couple of people called to see if it was true and were kind of relieved to find it wasn't!' Trust him to remain an oasis of unflappable cool amid a global panic over his own demise. No wonder the man famed throughout American football as the Comeback Kid for his habit of overturning impossible odds can chuckle: 'Perhaps this could be my best comeback of all so far!' Actually, what sports hero ever seemed more imperishable? He runs you through the ailments of a battered fifty-seven-year-old quarterback – an arthritic, bone-scraping knee, a very dodgy back and a neck held together by two operations – but all you see is the presence of gleaming, indestructible sporting greatness.

He enjoys his anonymity in London. At his local farmers' market back in downtown San Francisco, he sighs: 'People can't wait to take a picture of you picking up a piece of fruit. Er, I'm not sure what's so exciting about that. We try to be normal but most of the time people don't allow you to be.' That is because, to America, he can never be any ordinary Joe.

There may have been more agile quarterbacks. Ones with a more powerful, deadlier arm. Faster, bigger, stronger athletes, too. Yet if you wanted one to deliver a throw for your life, it had to be Montana.

Even when trying to pull off some totally improbable fightback, he never seemed to falter. Four Super Bowl triumphs and no losses; the only man to win three MVP awards in the grandest show of all. All achieved with seemingly preternatural serenity. 'Maybe if I'd concentrated more in the first part of the game, I wouldn't have had to concentrate so much at the end of the game,' he says, clearly enjoying debunking his own mystique. He reckons his real secret was simply being able to remember that 'football is just a stupid game' while at the same time never losing his almost pathological detestation of defeat.

He guides us back to 1989 and Super Bowl XXIII in Miami. The 49ers trail Cincinnati by three with just three minutes and twenty seconds on the clock and, with the tension suffocating, all eyes turn to him in the huddle. Inspirational, game-turning oratory or blinding tactical wizardry are awaited. Instead, Montana turns to his uptight, perennially worrying team-mate Harris Barton and points to the stands: 'Hey, look, that's John Candy over there.'

'Harris loved celebrity spotting so I thought he'd appreciate it. Only he looked at me like I was crazy! I think he appreciates it a bit more today.' Of course. Nine passes later, Montana had delivered him a Super Bowl ring. 'You have to believe that, when it comes down to it, there's nobody better than you. And that if it comes to that one final pass, you have to make sure you're that guy. And you have to relish it.'

Montana is self-effacing but press him on which quarterback he would want to throw a ball to save his life and you get the true gauge of his self-confidence. 'I'd pick myself first!' he smiles. 'Who wouldn't?' Montana's mystique has probably become even more powerful because, of all the great modern American sports megastars, perhaps none has kept a more dignified, lower-key profile after retirement. While others hogged the spotlight in the media or coaching, his one spell as a television analyst ended swiftly, he says, because 'all they really wanted was for you to be argumentative, definitive and loud – and that wasn't me'.

These days, he does a bit of motivational speaking, real-estate development and acts as an NFL ambassador, with his next task to help spread the grid-iron gospel to China. 'Life's been a lot of fun,' he says, before conceding, 'but not anywhere near as much fun as when I played.' He searched for years to find a replacement thrill. 'In vain,' he says. The only thing that has truly come close to replicating any given Sunday, he swears, is watching a couple of promising young quarterbacks called Montana. He and wife Jennifer have travelled thousands of miles watching their sons, Nate and Nick, play. Nate, twenty-four, has tried out with the 49ers and Joe is still smiling at having just seen twenty-one-year-old Nick defy injury to pull off a trademark Montana last-gasp comeback for Tulane University in New Orleans. Joe won a Super Bowl in the Superdome there, but this felt just as sweet. 'I honestly get more pleasure out of seeing them than I did with my own career. I wouldn't miss a game. No matter what.'

Whether or not they make the pro grade, imagine the impossibility of having to follow Dad. No wonder they avoid wearing Joe's hallowed San Francisco number sixteen. 'I think they just wish they could be judged on themselves and not on me. The hardest part has always been that expectation,' says Joe. 'Even when they were eight, people always expected me to be at home with them, teaching them how to read defences. But we just let them be boys and find their own way. I'm proud of how they've handled things.'

There are only tiny flashes of his ferocious competitiveness, like when asked about Steve Young, the quarterback who, during his injury absence, famously usurped his job at San Francisco, an indignity which eventually prompted him to move to Kansas City. Does he think he was a better quarterback than Young? 'I don't think so,' he says. Then comes the tell-tale grin. 'I know so.' Yet Montana seems comfortable in his skin, happy to have put his family ahead of everything – he is just as proud of his two daughters, lawyer Alexandra and actress Elizabeth – after his nonpareil career.

So, what would he like to best remembered for? That unreal off-balance throw which led to the legend of 'The Catch' from Dwight Clark which won the NFC Championship in 1982? 'No, my greatest achievement? You know the portable goalposts the kickers use. Well, at the very top of the post, it's hollow so every day before practice, the quarterbacks would get a roll of used tape and see who could throw most into the top. I wouldn't ever let anybody beat me.' His eyes twinkle with mischief. Whether it be the tape-chucking championship of Candlestick Park or the Super Bowl, it never did make any difference to Montana. There is, it is grand to relate, plenty of life yet in the ultimate winner.

Sporting Champion: Joe Montana – 4 Super Bowls (1982, 1985, 1989, 1990).

RHONA MARTIN – WINTER OLYMPIC GAMES

THE COOLEST MUM

Simon Hart, 5 February 2006

When Britain's curlers gathered for their Olympic send-off back in 2002, a single photographer from the Scottish Institute of Sport took one picture and then went away. This time Rhona Martin was required to pose for more than an hour at Glasgow's Braehead curling rink, and still the men with the cameras weren't satisfied. The Winter Games are here again. The ice queen is back.

Martin, a quietly spoken, thirty-nine-year-old Ayr housewife who wears her ordinariness with pride, is an unlikely sporting heroine. Martin and her curling team-mates won the gold in Salt Lake City in 2002 on a night of high tension at the Ogden ice sheet when, with the final stone of the match, Martin withstood suffocating pressure to deliver the perfect winning shot. Six million British television viewers stayed up beyond midnight to share her moment of glory and, for a day or two, curling was all the rage. Most of us have long since forgotten the finer points of laying and sweeping, but not the drama of what became known as Martin's 'stone of destiny'. Debbie Knox, the only other 2002 team member to be selected for the 2006 Games in Turin, says she never had any doubt Martin would make the shot because of her extraordinary powers of concentration. 'She knew what she had to do and although I felt sick, I also felt confident she would play the shot. She is completely blinkered when she's on the ice.'

Martin admits one of her biggest weapons is her ability to focus on her game – so much so that she was completely oblivious to the importance of that final stone. 'It wasn't the hardest shot I've ever had but I only had six inches to play with, so there wasn't a lot of room for error,' she recalls. 'It was our thirteenth game and we were pretty mentally tired by that stage, and I think I just felt relief I had a shot to win the game. I never for one moment thought, "This is for the Olympic gold medal". Even when we won, I just thought, "OK, we've won the competition". It didn't occur to me we were Olympic champions.'

Winning an Olympic curling gold medal is more about mental than physical endurance, which is why the all-Scottish men's and women's squad travel with two sports psychologists in harness. During the Games, Martin and her colleagues play nine round-robin matches to qualify for the semi-finals and final. 'Each game lasts for two and a half hours, so you have to be mentally very fit to deal with the tactics of the game and the changing ice conditions,' says Martin. 'Over the years I think it's something I've become good at. I can switch off all the distractions around me and focus on what I've to do on the ice.'

That ability to blot out extraneous thoughts has had therapeutic benefits. Martin broke up with her husband in 2005 because of financial problems and, with debt collectors hovering, was forced to sell the family home and move out with her two children, Jennifer, thirteen, and Andrew, ten. She now has to rely on the DSS to pay the rent. Head coach Mike Hay is certain curling has provided Martin with an opportunity to escape from her problems. 'She is a quiet girl but there is a lot of underlying strength and resilience,' he says. 'She's had a lot of things going on leading up to the Olympics. She's had to cope with them and she's very determined. She put her curling first and made a fantastic effort to get into the squad, so good luck to her. She obviously enjoys the sport because if she didn't, she certainly wouldn't have had the drive to go through what she has and turn up here and be selected. It was no foregone conclusion that she would be selected. In fact, a couple of years ago people were saying there was no chance because her form wasn't good, her team weren't doing well and she hadn't represented Scotland for four years. But out of adversity she has shown her qualities to come through.'

After the triumph in 2002, the talk in the media was how Martin and her girls would cash in on their success. Martin never believed the hype and, whatever the outcome in Turin, she does not expect to earn a penny. In fact, she will be worse off on her return to Scotland because her pre-Olympic funding will cease. So is she bitter that her success failed to translate into money? 'Not at all, not at all,' she replied. 'It wasn't an Olympic sport when I started playing. It was just a hobby and, OK, it's turned into a lot more and it takes up a lot of my life, but I've never been in it for money. Even when we won the gold I never thought for a minute that I would make money out of it.'

Wealth may have eluded her, but there have been quite a few other perks. 'Some of the experiences I had were just unbelievable,' she says. 'I would never have dreamt that I would make it to the Royal Box at Wimbledon and I still can't believe some of the things I get asked to go to – and just for winning a curling competition. Even now, when I'm in a room with people like Steve Redgrave and Kelly Holmes, it feels weird when they talk to me. I have to remind myself that I also won an Olympic gold medal.'

Martin laughs when she thinks about her double life – one minute a celebrity, the next a mother struggling to make ends meet. 'One day we went down to Buckingham Palace to get our MBEs, but when I got home my son was moaning that there was no food in the fridge and could I go to the supermarket. You just switch. One moment you're doing something really, really exciting and meeting famous people and then suddenly you're a mother and you've got to get on with the washing and ironing. Your other life is forgotten.'

Now it is time for her curling life to take precedence again, to recapture that feeling of empowerment when she took aim four years ago and sent her stone gliding towards its target. Circumstances may have conspired against her in her personal life, but on the ice Martin is in total control. 'She's a great leader,' says Knox. 'When she's on the ice, there's no doubt who is in charge.'

Sporting Champion: Rhona Martin – 1 Olympic Games (2002).

AMY WILLIAMS – WINTER OLYMPIC GAMES

FORGOTTEN GOLDEN GIRL SLIDES BACK INTO PUBLIC'S AFFECTION

Ian Chadband, 15 December 2010

Arthur has been in intensive care and Amy Williams cannot wait for the reunion. 'I'm picking him up this week from the sled hospital,' she smiles, thinking of the gleaming old friend who transported her into Olympic history. 'Be nice to have him back.' Arthur was mangled something rotten when Williams piloted him towards gold at nearly 90mph through all the violent G-forces, the bumps and the buffeting down the fastest ice chute in the world at the Vancouver Winter Games in February 2010.

'When we stripped Arthur down, opened him up for his post-Olympic MOT, lots of the stainless steel inside had bent, twisted and buckled from the sheer force of those Olympic runs,' she explained. Emergency treatment was needed. Back at sled hospital – AKA the Southampton front room of engineering student Rachel Blackburn – this veritable Ferrari among skeleton bobs has been lovingly rebuilt. Which begs the question: if Arthur was beaten up that badly, what did those same forces do to a slip of a woman like Williams herself? It was not difficult to appreciate her toughness and courage in Whistler, but it is not until this particular afternoon at the University of Bath, watching her grimace through her weight training, that the true magnitude of her Olympian spirit is made clear.

A throwaway remark from her physical trainer about how she is having to modify her training gives the painful game away. For Williams, it can now be revealed, has a serious long-standing, degenerative back problem which years ago even made her question whether to give up the sport. She won the Olympics while on painkillers, it transpires, just a few days after the disc problem flared at the worst possible time. 'I've had a real bad problem, stemming from a bulging disc in my lower back, probably ever since I had a bad crash in my second year in skeleton,' she shrugged, explaining that she had never publicly talked of her trouble before because she did not want anyone to think she was trying to offer a sob story. 'But it has been a massive problem over the years and I was at a point when it was that bad six or seven years ago that I thought, "Do I continue?" It won't get better; the pain's just there, an occupational hazard. I just get on with it. Even now, it hurts. It makes you tired because a constant level of pain is wearing. I've had loads of injections over the years and, ideally, I think the doctors would want me to stop, but I know what I can and can't do.'

She says constant physiotherapy and regular doctors' checks, not to mention careful precautions such as strapping a hot water bottle against her back to combat the freezing temperatures, kept her 'in one piece long enough to get to the Olympics'. Yet a temperamental back, subject to the unnatural forces imposed by her lightning slides and explosive starts pushing a sled half her weight, can seize up at any point. 'Just a movement a little bit wrong and it can flare up again like it did just a few days before Vancouver. I was on painkillers but couldn't have injections so as not to dull my reactions.' That is why her performance, not just in becoming the first British woman to win an individual Winter Olympics gold since Jeannette Altwegg fifty-eight years ago, but also destroying her opponents by a massive margin of more than half a second, was so staggering. And it felt even more astonishing to see Williams having to rely on a machine wheeled out of a vast shed on a university campus to simulate her push starts. Yes, welcome to the land with no bob track! It reminded you why her Austrian coach, Mickey Gruenberger, likened her achievement to a bloke born and bred in Innsbruck scoring a century at Lord's.

How quickly we forget, though. The rarity value, daring and courage of her golden slides on the world's fastest track, which had left all competitors living on their nerves in Whistler following the death of luger Nodar Kumaritashvili on the eve of the Games, feels so long ago that, almost scandalously, Williams barely scraped on to the BBC Sports Personality of the Year shortlist. The day we met, she had been booked to switch on the Christmas lights in Bath with Camilla, Duchess of Cornwall. It is one of many of the faintly 'surreal' things to have happened since her success, from being sent a vast box of Curly Wurlys from Cadbury in honour of her nickname, to several marriage proposals addressed to 'Amy Williams, Bath'. On stage, the television presenter host tells the local heroine: 'Of course we'll all be rooting for you at London 2012, Amy!' Oh dear.

Therein lies the problem. There is no 2012 for Williams; amid London Olympic fever, will there only be indifference towards the forgotten ice maiden until the defence of her crown in Sochi, Russia, in 2014? It is why it was such an odd, mad year after Vancouver. Everything and nothing had changed. She has loved doing the celeb circuit, roaring round the track with the Stig and nattering with Cilla at Royal Ascot. She even let herself go by eating the odd Curly Wurly and, shockingly, 'sometimes going to bed after 9.30 p.m.'. Yet she also notes that, apart from one deal with BMW which meant she did not have to catch the bus anymore, her financial situation hardly altered a jot. She seemed no different, still as grounded and attractively chirpy as you hope your Olympic heroes would be.

When Williams has not been in Prague seeing her boyfriend, Slovakian sledder Petr Nárovec, she has been doing her best to be a one-woman advert for her sport. The sliding itself, she admits almost sheepishly, has slid down her priority list. 'I'm taking a bit of time out because I have to completely re-evaluate everything. Suddenly I've achieved my ultimate goal so there is a touch of "so, what now?!"' She could have skipped the entire winter's World Cup season and nobody would have blamed her. But she could not trust herself. 'If I had, I might never have come back,' she pondered. 'How are you going to know?' Now she thinks she does know. She did not expect to be at her sharpest, mentally and physically straight away, but then perked up: 'I've still got aims – I've never won a World Cup race, a world championship – there's plenty to target.' Suddenly, you can see the old flash of ambition and determination flare in her eyes. I remembered it from St Moritz before the Olympics when, having explained I was there to interview her big rival Shelley Rudman, she gave me a killer look which said: 'You've picked the wrong one, chum.' For Williams was the right one, a rare champion. Her dodgy back went again four weeks ago, but like her Arthur, the old steel is just being reinforced. 'Oh, I've still got a lot to give,' she said. 'I'm not done yet.'

Sporting Champion: Amy Williams – 1 Olympic Games (2010).

MARCH

ARKLE – NATIONAL HUNT FESTIVAL, CHELTENHAM

ARKLE SIMPLY TOOK THE BREATH AWAY

Brough Scott, 29 February 2004

Best Mate is a fantastic horse. He is the best-balanced steeplechaser I have seen and his record of twelve wins and four seconds shows that he has been a star throughout his life. But Arkle, with a steeplechasing record of twenty-two wins, two seconds and two thirds? Well, he was a freak. Forty-odd years since Arkle's first Gold Cup, that unforgettable defeat of the 1963 winner Mill House, Best Mate attempts to become the first horse since Arkle to win the Gold Cup three times running. The *Racing Post* completed the biggest reader poll to find the most popular racehorse of all time. Arkle was first, Best Mate fourteenth. Arkle's are big shoes to fill.

I remember exactly where I was when I first saw him: standing by the last fence at Cheltenham for the Honeybourne Novices' Chase on Saturday, 17 November 1962, Arkle's first race over fences. I was a nineteen-year-old amateur rider already seriously affected by the racing bug and had no defence against the image in front of me. We had been warned the Irish thought this lean, greyhoundy, long-eared thing was a bit special, but what happened at the finish just took the breath away. There were decent horses against him, but Arkle just skipped the fence and sprinted twenty lengths clear as if he was another species altogether. Perhaps he was.

It was all the more remarkable because when Arkle had first appeared at Tom Dreaper's stables two seasons earlier he had not been that impressive. 'His action was so terrible behind,' recorded Pat Taaffe in Ivor Herbert's excellent Arkle biography, 'that we thought he would be a slow coach – a slob.' Compare that with Best Mate as a four-year-old, already so perfect that Terry Biddlecombe was instantly smitten on that first point-to-point day in County Cork in February 1999. Best Mate ended his opening campaign running an unlucky second in the Supreme Novices' Hurdle at the Cheltenham Festival, Arkle finished off running fourth in a moderate handicap at Fairyhouse with 10 stone 5 lb. Best Mate was better than Arkle – over hurdles. Over fences, Arkle was something else. As his body matured into its frame, he developed first an athleticism, and then a presence that I have never seen before or since. By the time he came back to Cheltenham for the equivalent of the Sun Alliance Chase at the Festival, he was kicking all other novices out of the way. But when he returned for the Gold Cup next season, it seemed he might have found his match in the massive 1963 Gold Cup winner Mill House, who had given him 5 lb and a beating in the Hennessy the previous November. What happened on that cold, clear March day in 1964 became one of the defining moments in jumping history. You have to remember that we were hailing Mill House as the greatest English-trained chaser since the War, a giant of a horse whose spring-heeled leaps used to bring gasps from the crowd as if they were watching hammer blows from a heavyweight. The Irish were insisting that Arkle had slipped at Newbury, but none of us believed them. Then as they turned for home and we waited for Willie Robinson on Mill House to put the upstart in his place, we saw the unthinkable, a horse not just as good as Mill House, but quite emphatically, brutally his superior.

I was a young jockey by then, a twenty-one-year-old

undergraduate down from Oxford getting ready to ride in the Cathcart two races after the Gold Cup. In the weighing room we couldn't believe what our eyes had told us. I remember poor Willie Robinson sitting on the bench just as shattered as if he had been taken out by the young Cassius Clay, who had turned over Sonny Liston a month earlier. Willie had thought Mill House unbeatable. He was wrong.

There was a sense of awe around the place which never left us whenever Arkle ran. For he didn't just win; he used to destroy his opponents or attempt seemingly impossible tasks in handicaps. In truth, his subsequent Gold Cups were little more than exhibition rounds, the most memorable moment when he completely ignored the fence in front of the stands on the first circuit in 1966. It was what Arkle did in handicaps conceding two, sometimes nearly 3 stone, which has seared itself in the memory.

Best Mate, since his first Gold Cup, has run in just five races, all level weights or conditions events. At this stage Arkle had run eleven times after his Gold Cup, six of them in handicaps, winning the Irish Grand National with 12 stone, two Hennessys, a Whitbread and the Gallaher Gold Cup at Ascot with 12 stone 7 lb. Most remarkably of all, he finished a close third in the Massey-Ferguson at Cheltenham in December 1964 with 12 stone 10 lb, giving 32 lb to the winner, Flying Wild, and 26 lb to the equally talented second, Buona Notte. I can see Arkle now, still fighting back, refusing to be anchored by the extra lead. He couldn't do it, but he nearly did.

By then Arkle had developed the most astonishing presence about him. He used to walk round the paddock with his neck very upright and those astonishing long ears scanning the crowd, the emperor of all he surveyed. On the track he was utterly dominant, sometimes just carting Taaffe to the front, often throwing extravagant leaps just for the hell of it, once or twice landing on the fence rather than over it. We couldn't take our eyes off him. We used to race back to see him unsaddle. We felt we were treasuring something beyond compare. We were right. Completely unfair to start using any of this to denigrate Best Mate. The current champion is a wonder of our times; a brilliantly handled, immensely attractive, beau ideal of the jumping horse. But he is not Arkle. How could he be?

Sporting Champion: Arkle – 3 Cheltenham Gold Cups (1964, 1965, 1966); 1 King George VI Chase (1965); 1 Irish Grand National (1964); 2 Hennessy Gold Cups (1964, 1965); 1 Whitbread Gold Cup (1965).

DESERT ORCHID – NATIONAL HUNT FESTIVAL, CHELTENHAM

I'LL NEVER FORGET THE DAY I RODE THE LEGEND IN A GALLOP

Lucinda Green, 14 November 2006

It never entered my head that Desert Orchid would ever die. So much about him was legend and legends do not die. But he has. The most loved and respected horse in the country will never again set his determined foot on Cheltenham racecourse to lead the parade before the Gold Cup. Never again will he be fascinated by the bagpipes at the Highland Show, which made him intent on closing the gap between him and the nervous piper. Never again will he be able to cheer sick people, whose illness he could discern, making him especially gentle with them. Fifteen years of making people smile and tingle – and that was after his racing days.

His three jockeys, Colin Brown, whose retirement let in Simon Sherwood and Richard Dunwoody, who took over after Sherwood hung up his saddle, all agree Desert Orchid's principal qualities were his immense intelligence, his bravery and his durability. He was never lame and he ran away with everyone on the gallops – except trainer David Elsworth's aptly named head lad, Rodney Boult, who could settle him.

With this in mind, when I was given the honour of being allowed to ride him on the gallops for an article I was writing for *The Daily Telegraph*, I did not try to hold him. He took me up at a reasonably strong canter, but he did not, however, stop at the end. His power and balance were evident and brakes or not he made you feel so safe. Those tight pricked white ears encompassed the view and between them his brain was clearly clocking the situation. 'Dessie planned his own races,' remembered Sherwood. 'He burst off at the beginning to lose the riff-raff and then gave himself a breather – he needed to, he had to carry so much weight. Then he'd battle it out with the few that stayed with him.'

The great grey's owners and breeders, the Burridge family, shared Desert Orchid with the world, just as Jim Lewis shared triple Gold Cup winner Best Mate, for his all too short time on this earth. The horse crossed the country to perform public functions, sometimes with his devoted stable lass, Janice Coyle, and often for charity and no financial reward. Desert Orchid travelled everywhere in a little blue horsebox inscribed with his name. It had the effect on other drivers that a siren and a blue light generally do. Waved through like royalty, Desert Orchid was king of his sport and of the hearts of those who loved his immortal qualities.

Sporting Champion: Desert Orchid – 1 Cheltenham Gold Cup (1989); 4 King George VI Chases (1986, 1988, 1989, 1990); 1 Irish Grand National (1990); 1 Whitbread Gold Cup (1988).

WALES – SIX (NÉE FIVE) NATIONS CHAMPIONSHIP

WALES' CROWNING GLORY

Richard Sharp, 18 March 1979

Wales have done it again! Playing with immense flair and skill, the Welsh finally overwhelmed England 27–3 in Cardiff to win the Triple Crown for the fourth successive time and the Championship for the second year running. What a magnificent win this was. With twenty minutes to go Wales were leading by only seven points to three and sadly their inspiring captain J.P.R. Williams had to leave the field with a leg injury. Many sides might have weakened at that stage, but not this Welsh fifteen. They produced in that final quarter a display of sheer irrepressible magic and ran in four brilliant tries of breathtaking quality to which England, quite simply, had no answer. When J.P.R. appeared in the stand at the end of the game to bid farewell to the many hundreds of supporters and admirers who had been calling for him, Welsh joy was complete.

Even the most partisan in the English camp would wish to pay tribute to the Welsh team in their moment of triumph. They were, unquestionably, the better side and thoroughly deserved their crushing victory by three tries, two goals and a dropped goal to a solitary penalty goal. The outstanding players in this Welsh victory were J.P.R. himself, Fenwick in the centre, Davies and Holmes at half-back, and Quinnell and Ringer who were quite magnificent in their back row. Roberts and Phillips, too, who came in as late replacements, had every reason to be pleased with their performances.

Perhaps it was at half-back that the Welsh supremacy was most apparent. I have always believed that Davies and Holmes would make a fine pair of international halves, and here they both played with great distinction. Holmes, immensely strong and resilient, provided a superb service to his partner and also found the energy to get through an immense amount of running and tackling. Outside him, Davies played with the skill and composure which we have come to expect from international fly-halves. His dropped goal gave Wales the all-important first score and later his accurate kicking to the corners ensured that the Welsh pack were continually going forwards while the English were on the retreat. Fenwick, goal-kicking apart, had a tremendous game in the centre and his influence was particularly important in the last quarter after his captain had been forced to leave the field. Not only did he hold the Welsh midfield defence together at the critical moment, but he also cleverly masterminded some of the best Welsh attacks.

England, after an heroic win against France, must have come to Cardiff with high hopes, but on the day they never looked like winning. Although Scott and Horton won some good balls in the line-out there were few moments when England really threatened the Welsh defence. On such a day, against a side of the quality and character of this Welsh fifteen, steadiness and courage is not enough and the English were unable to raise their game to a higher level.

The match began in glorious sunshine and conditions were perfect for rugby with the ground soft but not muddy. Fenwick, normally so effective with his kicking, missed several penalty chances and there were handling errors by both sides. One such error, by Cardus in front of his own posts when he dropped Fenwick's attempted penalty kick, led directly to the first Welsh score. From the ensuing set scrum, Davies neatly dropped a goal. After half an hour Wales scored again. A fine surging run by Quinnell was followed by a long rolling kick to the corner by Davies. Wales won the line-out, J.P.R. came into the line and gave a perfectly timed pass to Richards, who scored. Fenwick missed the conversion, but from the restart, the Welsh forwards were penalised and Bennett kicked England's penalty goal from 35 yards.

The pattern in the early part of the second half remained much as it had been in the first. The Welsh continued to play with the greater skill and both sides continued to waste scoring chances. Ironically, the departure of J.P.R. Williams and the arrival of Griffiths as his replacement saw the start of the final Welsh onslaught. Once again it was Davies's rolling kick to the corner which created the scoring chance. England won the ball at the line-out near their own line, but it was untidily won and Roberts plunged over for the try. Minutes later Ringer scored after clever play by J.J. Williams and Fenwick, and it was J.J. Williams himself who scored a thrilling try. Fenwick switched the direction of attack in midfield and gave a perfectly timed pass to Richards who sent the speedy Welsh winger racing away to the corner. Martin was called up to take the conversion and he produced a magnificent kick from the touchline. Incidentally, this was a fine advertisement for the old-fashioned toe-kick which one sees so rarely now.

To compound England's woes, Wales scored their final try, the most glittering of them all, in injury time. Griffiths brilliantly picked up a pass off his toes and raced away down the right before sending Rees away for the try. At last Fenwick succeeded with a kick at goal, thus equalling the record of thirty-eight points in an international season, and the Welsh success was complete.

Sporting Champions: Wales – 15 Five Nations Championships (1911, 1922, 1931, 1950, 1952, 1956, 1965, 1966, 1969, 1971, 1975, 1976, 1978, 1979, 1994); 4 Six Nations Championships (2005, 2008, 2012, 2013); 11 Grand Slams (1908, 1909, 1911, 1950, 1952, 1971, 1976, 1978, 2005, 2008, 2012); 20 Triple Crowns (1893, 1900, 1902, 1905, 1908, 1909, 1911, 1950, 1952, 1965, 1969, 1971, 1976, 1977, 1978, 1979, 1988, 2005, 2008, 2012).

SCOTLAND – SIX (NÉE FIVE) NATIONS CHAMPIONSHIP

SCOTLAND SLAM THOSE OF LITTLE FAITH

John Mason, 19 March 1990

Scotland, whose forthright and prickly challenge was hugely under-estimated by those with England sympathies, head for New Zealand as worthy winners of the Grand Slam, the Triple Crown and the Calcutta Cup – after beating England 13–7. The All Blacks will pay them every respect. A delighted Ian McGeechan, Scotland's coach, whose mild manner is a beguiling disguise for a character of steely resolve, exclaimed with mock horror after the Murrayfield triumph that he was afraid New Zealand would be taking the 1990 champions of Europe extremely seriously. They travel secure in the knowledge that their single-minded endeavours in the Five Nations' season, aided by the meticulous planning of McGeechan, Jim Telfer and the selectors, have justly earned themselves a place of honour in Scottish sporting history.

As an example of how tight matches should be played, this victory, by a try and three penalty goals to a try and penalty goal, would have been difficult to improve upon. England were challenged constantly at the source of their strength and, harried into error, lofty calm deserted them. The poise and control that brought England twenty-three points against Ireland, twenty-six against France and thirty-four against Wales surfaced only occasionally. Not even the sweetest of tries by Guscott could save previously unbeaten England from the defeat that hurt the most. As English promised faltered and faded in the face of aggressive defence, the Scots, mostly unsung elsewhere in Britain, savoured the joys that accompanied the sound of English bodies continually slipping up on a host of banana skins. It was not the slightest consolation to England's players to know that they were not alone. While mindful that Scotland would have attended to their homework earnestly, because McGeechan, the leading coach in Britain, would not allow otherwise, I did not think England's forwards, the power base of the side, would be overcome.

From the moment that David Sole, already a leader of imposing stature after a handful of matches, led out Scotland, doubts began to invade English hearts. The team did not run on to the pitch, they did not march – they walked, a stately, dignified stride more eloquent than a thousand words or the absurd posturing of Willie Anderson at the start of the Ireland–New Zealand match in November. This, as each step of the fifteen players rammed home the message to the startled England team, who had run on in the standard manner, is our patch. If you want glory today, you have to take it from us by force. This is the gauntlet: pick it up. Add two thunderous verses of 'Flower of Scotland', and England were already partly homeward 'tae think again', as the stirring song insists. Yet impressive, daunting even, as all this was, that was no reason for a well-prepared England team, who had been playing well, not to respond in kind.

I cannot agree that it was more a case of England losing the match than Scotland winning it. But I do accept that England were depressingly inept when pinned down by Scottish methods that cannot have come as the slightest surprise to anyone. The ability of the Scots to get a man between the ball and an England player was masterly. The sustained, hard, bruising work of John Jeffrey, the match's outstanding player, was extraordinary. As Finlay Calder was scarcely a pace away either, Scotland's flankers eclipsed the England pair. Even when White, Scotland's number eight, went off because of injury, the effectiveness of the back row did not lessen. Turnbull went to the flank and the tireless Jeffrey continued his splendid machinations at number eight.

Without too much control, a minimum of quality possession and some repetitious schemes that did not work, England struggled. There was a marvellous try for Guscott following a thrusting break by Carling – about the only time Scotland's defence faltered. By then, Chalmers had kicked two penalty goals because of England's indiscipline. Shoddy scrimmaging directly after half-time let Scotland off the hook. Gavin Hastings swept down the short-side and, with England turning to cover his acutely placed kick, Stanger, stretching high, was first there for the try. England, while appropriately complimentary to their rivals, did mutter about the refereeing of David Bishop, the New Zealander, afterwards. Though some of his decisions relating to collapsed scrums when Scotland were in dire straits in the first half, made little sense, I thought it was swings and roundabouts in the end.

The Scottish forwards took England on, Armstrong sniped and snarled at their heels – his best match by far for Scotland – and Chalmers did everything asked of him. Not even the excellent Andrew could disturb his composure. If Scotland missed two tackles all afternoon that would have been it. The offside line was plain for all to see and Mr Bishop saw that justice was done in that respect, too. Hungry Scotland did the job they had set their hearts on. There can be no grumbles.

Sporting Champions: Scotland – 5 Five Nations Championships (1925, 1929, 1984, 1990, 1999); 3 Grand Slams (1925, 1984, 1990); 3 Triple Crowns (1925, 1984, 1990).

SWINDON TOWN – FOOTBALL LEAGUE CUP

WILTSHIRE LADS PUT JOY BACK INTO SOCCER

Donald Saunders, 17 March 1969

As Don Rogers strode majestically through the mud and sand at Wembley to score the second of his two superb goals, Swindon not only clinched their rightful place among the League Cup winners by a 3–1 margin against Arsenal, but demonstrated that British soccer has not yet lost its soul. Swindon's victory was as bold and handsome as were the goals of Rogers. And those are adjectives one has rarely been able to employ in reports of football matches in this country during recent years.

So much of soccer, indeed of major sport, is as absorbing to the paying spectator nowadays as a lecture on elementary mathematics. Textbooks, tactics, technique and statistics, reinforced by the endless jargon of the professors and those who worship mindlessly at their feet, are relentlessly strangling the life out of what used to be an uncomplicated form of mass entertainment. Swindon and Rogers reminded us forcefully just what we have been missing. They re-emphasised that sport is not merely a matter of well-practised proficiency. It is about people, their strength and frailties, their courage, character, comradeship, endeavour and natural physical gifts.

No doubt, the analysis will drily pronounce that Swindon were able to rise so nobly to the occasion because they had nothing to lose. I prefer to suggest that this Third Division team gave the best performance seen at Wembley since England triumphed in the World Cup final because they realised they had something to win. Too many British clubs, especially in the First Division, go on to the pitch thinking only of tomorrow. Always they are seeking to edge a little nearer the top of the League table or into the next round of a cup competition, so that ultimately they will arrive in Europe – where they start the dreary process all over again. Yet, Europe is no longer an unconquered soccer Everest. Celtic and Manchester United have already been to the summit and as others, inevitably, follow, public interest will decline and the financial rewards will be diminished. When that stage is reached, clubs and their players will be forced to come back to one of the basic principles of sport – to go out and seek victory at all times by playing to the limit of their ability. That is what Swindon did here. Consequently, they gained the prize they so richly deserved and brought unexpected reward to thousands who had begun to despair of ever again seeing a really entertaining big football match.

It was delightful to watch a lad who was said to have been cutting a bit of a dash down in Wiltshire, leap on to soccer's most demanding stage and stop the show with an impudent exhibition of exciting, natural talent. What a joy it was, too, to see a team eagerly seeking, and scoring, another extra-time goal when most of their contemporaries would have been cautiously protecting what seemed to be a match-winning lead. It did not matter that this was the final of a competition which the elite feign to disdain, being decided on a pitch that was a disgrace to the headquarters of English football. Swindon played exhilarating soccer that few First Division clubs could have matched.

To suggest that Arsenal played badly would be unjust to them and their conquerors. For a long time they produced the all-round efficiency that had raised high hopes of their becoming League champions. Indeed, had the match ended at ninety minutes with Swindon winning 1–0 – as once seemed likely – Arsenal rightly could have claimed they were a little unlucky. For much of the first half they contained Swindon's eager forwards without great difficulty and, with Sammels and McLintock at last coming to terms with conditions they hated, were beginning to assume control as the interval approached. Then, in the thirty-fifth minute, Arsenal met with disaster. Ure and Wilson got themselves into a dreadful tangle, the persistent Noble hit the ball forward and it rebounded somewhat uncertainly off the goalkeeper's body through the mud, for Smart to prod into the net.

Those who later accused Arsenal of playing without heart clearly had forgotten how resourceful Bertie Mee's men faced up to this adversity. Though their defence was stretched to the limit by a now supremely confident Swindon after the interval, they held on grimly and, with half an hour to go, started to surge forward. Eight times in a matter of four minutes Arsenal forced Swindon to concede a corner kick. Had they possessed the marksmen they have lacked so often this season, they must have scored three or four goals. Ultimately, four minutes from time, Arsenal were only too happy to settle for the equaliser, headed home by the rugged, industrious and, hitherto, luckless Gould.

That goal should have knocked the stuffing out of Swindon and sent Arsenal, reprieved so late in the day, happily roaring on to victory in extra time. Instead, from the moment the game was restarted, this final belonged to Swindon. Though their midfield general, Smith, had limped off to be replaced by Penman, they tore great gaps in the Arsenal defence, who had lost much of their steadiness once the injured Simpson had changed places on the bench with Graham. A Swindon goal seemed inevitable. When it came, seconds before the extra-time interval, it was a beauty. Penman's corner kick bounced nervously among the flying boots until it came to Rogers, who calmly checked it, dragged it round a defender's legs, then hammered it into the roof of the net.

That was a good enough goal to bring any final to a rousing climax. But Rogers had not yet finished. With seconds remaining, this arrogant young man raced over the halfway line on to a pass from Smart and took the ball into Arsenal's penalty box. He paused cheekily before walking round Wilson, then drove the ball into the net with a flourish that demonstrated quite clearly what he thought of First Division giants. As the crowd rose to their new idol, I was left with two chastening thoughts – the price on the head of this inexperienced youngster will now inevitably soar beyond £150,000 and poor Frank McLintock has another Wembley loser's medal to put alongside the three he already possessed.

Sporting Champions: Swindon Town – 1 Football League Cup (1968–69).

SRI LANKA – WORLD CRICKET CUP

AUSTRALIANS COME UNSTUCK AFTER RANATUNGA GETS TACTICS RIGHT

Christopher Martin-Jenkins, 18 March 1996

The two final ironies of the World Cup were these: Sri Lanka, against the state-of-the-art professionals of world cricket, were tactically cuter and altogether more efficient on the big night; and they were fresher and sharper than their distinguished opponents to a considerable extent because those same opponents had refused, albeit for entirely understandable reasons, to play them in the preliminary round. Although legal repercussions will persist, the bitterness created by the Australian decision not to play in Colombo, and any lingering resentments from Sri Lanka's tour Down Under, will be forgotten in the afterglow of their stylish, confident and utterly deserved victory over Australia in the sixth World Cup final. That it was really only a small upset is indication of how far and how quickly Sri Lanka have travelled since they were considered one of the two weakest of the nine Test nations.

They won by seven wickets, with twenty-two balls to spare, a huge margin in limited-overs cricket. Aravinda de Silva followed Clive Lloyd and Viv Richards as only the third man to score a century in a World Cup final and his innings was in the same class as the memorable ones at Lord's by those great West Indians in 1975 and 1979. De Silva's batting has always been touched by genius. Now, on the biggest occasion of his life, he played with quite wonderful judgment too. His 107 not out was scored off only 124 balls, but he limited himself to thirteen fours and a six. It is not easy for someone who, when the force is with him, can hit any ball almost anywhere he pleases to pace an innings to such perfection.

There could have been no more appropriate opponents than Australia; no more deserving partners in the cool swallowing-up of Australia's score than the two durable left-handers – Asantha Gurusinha, a stalwart for so long, whose sixty-five off ninety-nine balls included six fours and an astonishing, bludgeoned six over long-off from Shane Warne, and Arjuna Ranatunga, Sri Lanka's Napoleon. It was Ranatunga, already at a mere thirty-two the longest surviving international cricketer without any serious interruption to his career, who scored the winning runs with a reprise of the delicate offside tickle with which he had also hit his first ball, with supreme confidence, for four.

Sri Lanka's fortune on the day was limited to the fact that Australia, having lost the toss, were obliged to field and bowl in a foggy dew. The shrewd planning lay in the Sri Lankan decision, by the captain Ranatunga and his advisers, Duleep Mendis and Dav Whatmore, to put Australia in after a practice session under the lights had shown them how soaking wet the outfield would get when the sun set. Most uncharacteristically, Australia had practised only by day, their coach Bobby Simpson, who usually misses not a single trick, having decided, reasonably enough up to a point, that they had played enough night cricket. Perhaps weariness from two tough games in succession, and two more overall than Sri Lanka, played a part in this potentially fatal decision to leave something to chance. It was academic in a way because Mark Taylor lost the toss and was given first use of a lovely pitch for batting, but he would have batted anyway if the coin had spun the other way and that would have been as wrong as Azharuddin's decision to field in the Calcutta semi-final.

Sri Lanka deserved reward for their boldness – all five previous finals had been won by the side batting first – but even more for the way that they recovered in the field after a commanding innings from Taylor had left them dangerously exposed. It was astonishing that having reached 137 for one in the twenty-seventh over, Australia should have been limited to 241 for seven. The spinners, Muralitharan, Dharmasena, de Silva and Jayasuriya, did the trick, supported by fielding of peppery keenness. Pulling with relish and great power, often to balls barely short of a length, Taylor hit seven fours and a six in his fifty off fifty-two balls, mainly at the expense of Chaminda Vaas. Although Muralitharan suffered too as the quick-footed Rick Ponting lent his captain ideal support, the game changed from the moment that Taylor swept de Silva to deep backward square leg. Ranatunga read the tea leaves and brought his best slow bowler back, the other spinners supported well and in twenty-five overs Australia managed a single boundary: this on a quick outfield, despite overnight rain, and with a boundary of no more than 70 yards. Michael Bevan stayed calm and made what he could from the later overs, but the Sri Lankans know his game inside out, as they do every other Australian's, and they did not give him room to make more than a couple of those clean strokes over extra cover or the bowler's head.

Australia in the field were not so tight. They made some brilliant stops, certainly, and their tall fast bowlers, Glenn McGrath and Paul Reiffel, both bowled particularly straight to an ideal length, but there were chances missed and many a fumble on the slippery surface. Jayasuriya was a little unluckily ruled out by little more than millimetres on the evidence of several inconclusive replays after a fine throw from third man by McGrath, and in the same over Kaluwitharana was late on a pull from Damien Fleming. From the moment, however, that stocky little Aravinda, bright-eyed as a squirrel, stroked his first ball past the bowler off the full face of his bat, only one side was going to win. The support and skill of the two left-handers kept him company until the job was done, the money won and the new power in the world established. The image will long remain; one of the most romantic in the continuously evolving history of cricket. Half past ten on a misty night in Lahore as the rain begins to fall. Arjuna Ranatunga, a tubby little thirty-two year old in a dark blue shirt and trousers, holds up a huge silver trophy: a monument to a little nation's marvellous sporting achievement.

Sporting Champions: Sri Lanka – 1 World Cup (1996); 1 ICC Champions Trophy (2002 – shared with India when final washed out).

CHRIS HOY – WORLD TRACK CYCLING CHAMPIONSHIPS

KING OF TRACK IS OUT OF THIS WORLD
Robert Philip, 13 February 2008

The teenage Nick Faldo was moved to take up golf after happening upon television coverage of the 1971 Masters tournament while idly channel-hopping. Andy Murray queued outside Wimbledon as a six-year-old in the hope of securing Andre Agassi's autograph. As a small lad on the terraces at Goodison, Wayne Rooney idolised Everton's Swedish winger Anders Limpar. Every hero, it seems, needs a hero. So which cyclist, one wonders, can claim credit for capturing the youthful imagination of Chris Hoy? Who was it that inspired the Edinburgh schoolboy to first climb into the saddle? Which of the sport's legends – Jacques Anquetil, Eddy Merckx or Bernard Hinault, perhaps – can take the credit for the emergence of our multiple Olympic, World and Commonwealth champion? 'It was E. T. actually,' reveals Hoy, who was a wide-eyed tot of six when Steven Spielberg's tiny alien visitor first waddled across our cinema screens in 1982. 'The BMX scenes were fantastic so I pestered my dad into taking me along to the local track at Danderhall where I saw all these kids having terrific fun. That was it, I was hooked and it all sort of spiralled from there.'

Even so, from performing bunny-hops and triple-tailwhips like Elliot and his youthful gang, to standing on top of the podium at Athens 2004 requires a giant leap of the imagination. What transformed Hoy from two-wheeled daredevil into an Olympic track champion? 'When the Commonwealth Games came to Edinburgh in 1986, I saw the velodrome on TV and that sparked my curiosity. In particular, I remember watching Eddie Alexander win the bronze-medal ride-off for Scotland, which was really exciting. But I didn't experience an epiphany or anything like that; I certainly didn't think to myself, "One day I'll ride on a track like that and win a gold medal", but it did have an appeal which is why I swapped my BMX for a racing bike.'

Like Hollywood's cute extra-terrestrial, Hoy almost lost his way on a couple of occasions – having to choose between rowing and cycling as a teenager, then deciding between the wild life of a student at St Andrews University and the relatively monastic life of a dedicated athlete. 'I got into rugby and rowing at school [the fee-paying George Watson's College which boasts rugby star Gavin Hastings and Olympic Alpine skier Martin Bell among its former pupils] but felt cycling offered me the greatest scope for advancement. It was a difficult choice because I loved participating in them all, but by the time I reached sixteen or seventeen I realised it was cycling that I was most serious about. I still miss the camaraderie of the dressing room and the boathouse and watch both sports whenever I can. Having been in a boat, albeit not anywhere near their level [he did, however, win a British Junior Championships silver medal in the coxless pairs], it does give you a little bit of an inkling what Steve Redgrave and Matthew Pinsent had to put themselves through time and time again on the nation's behalf.'

Hoy, too, puts himself on the rack every time he climbs into the saddle; did not three-time Tour de France winner Greg LeMond famously say that come the end of every stage 'even my eyelashes ache'? 'Doing a seven-hour slog through the mountains is a different thing entirely to what I do. On the track, it's primarily in the legs that you feel it. A sprinter's pain is far more intense because it tends to be concentrated in the legs, but what the road racers go through, in terms of both physical and mental suffering, is truly horrendous. Two years ago I completed a mountain stage of the Tour for charity – at a fairly leisurely pace – which gave me a slight idea of the agonies that these guys live through hour after hour. Our pain is sharper – it's hard to describe just how bad it is; like an acid burn I suppose – but we don't suffer for nearly as long. You can always back off, but you won't win any medals that way. The more it hurts, the faster you go.'

It has to be said that Hoy hurts himself more than most in pursuit of medals and records. In La Paz in May 2007, he covered the last 150 metres in a state of growing unconsciousness and could only breathe with the aid of an oxygen mask for over half an hour, after failing to break the 1,000 metres world mark. I say 'failing', but Hoy's time of 58.880 seconds was five 1,000ths of a second outside the record set by Frenchman Arnaud Tournant at the same high-altitude venue six years earlier. 'It's not something I would rush to do again. At 12,000 feet above sea level you really are pushing the body to its outer limits. I was aware of the risks involved but it was the only place on Earth I could have beaten the record. I went into the attempt knowing that, yes, there would be pain, but that any pain would only be temporary. You can't allow yourself to be frightened by the prospect of pain. Although it was Arnaud's record I was chasing, I'm in cycling to see how far I can push myself, not to challenge other people. Although I dreamt of becoming Olympic champion I didn't set out with that goal in mind. But as soon as I became Scottish champion, I wanted to be British champion, then European; every time I achieved something, I would aspire to the next level.'

Having achieved almost every ambition, does he look back on his Bolivian adventure with a feeling of deep regret? 'No, frustration yes, fondness even, but regret no. It was something I had to do and I've got some great memories of the attempt. The bottom line is that I did the very best I possibly could on that day and in those conditions. A lot of things went wrong and if one thing – just one thing on that long list – had gone right, then I might have broken the world record. That said, Arnaud probably encountered exactly the same problems, so it was an amazing performance.'

Hoy is one of the fittest men on the planet but, at the age of thirty-one, how long can he go on depriving himself of life's pleasures in the rush for gold? 'It's not as an ascetic existence as you might think. You've got to have a balance in your lifestyle. Being happy is the most important thing whether you're an architect or an athlete and if you're happy when you're on the back of a bike it'll show in everything you do. You need the occasional treat, although I probably won't touch alcohol for four, maybe five months leading up to the Olympic Games. Like anyone, I had a few drinks over Christmas and New Year but this is the Olympics we're talking about and I'll do everything I possibly can to win another gold medal. I don't want to find myself standing on the podium with a silver round my neck and thinking, "Maybe if I hadn't gone out that one night, maybe if I hadn't had those beers or eaten that lamb Madras I wouldn't have been second . . ."' And if he had never seen *E. T.*? 'Now that's a question to which there's no answer.'

Sporting Champion: Chris Hoy – 11 World Championships (2002 – 2, 2004, 2005, 2006, 2007 – 2, 2008 – 2, 2010, 2012); 6 Olympic Games (2004, 2008 – 3, 2012 – 2); 2 Commonwealth Games (2002, 2006).

ANTONY ARMSTRONG-JONES – BOAT RACE

THE DAY SNOWDON WON HIS DEADLY
DUEL ON THE RIVER

Sue Mott, 30 March 2002

'I'm in a bad mood,' said the Earl of Snowdon, opening the door of his house in such a leafy and gorgeous pocket of London that parking costs 20p for four minutes at the meters. This did not augur well. I had come to discuss the 1950 Boat Race in which the man who would marry The Queen's sister ten years later caused an absolute, raving sensation while coxing for the Cambridge crew. But how do you bring up controversy with a member of the Royal Family in a bad mood? Fortunately, Lord Snowdon's black temper was indistinguishable from exquisite politeness and kindness. He served me a glass of Semillon–Chardonnay from a typical bachelor pad fridge (more wine than food) and we settled in the study to contemplate his scooter.

'What's your balance like?' he said, eyeing the electric contraption his son, David, had bought him as an unlikely mode of in-house transport. I confessed not good enough to go for a spin. He said his wasn't either. But apparently some of his guests do go for jaunts up and down the terracotta tiles of his basement. It was a pretty loose connection with the sporting world – indoor scooting – but as good an introduction as any to that 'unprecedented incident' (*The Times*) in the Boat Race more than half a century ago.

'Gosh, it was a long time ago,' he said wistfully, turning the pages of a leather-bound scrapbook in which he had recorded every newspaper cutting, card, reminder and keepsake from his former life as A.R.C. Armstrong-Jones, of Eton and Jesus College, Cambridge, aged twenty, biker, student architect and controversial coxswain. It was all there in the old, yellowing newsprint. April

Fool's Day 1950, and the banks of the Thames were teeming. Vera Lynn was there, the Prime Minister Clement Attlee, the Crazy Gang, including Bud Flanagan, and scores and scores of people in hats. It was a huge event. A defining moment of the sporting year. The crews bobbed on the start line, rushing with adrenalin and pure loathing. 'You had to build up a hatred,' said Lord Snowdon definitely. 'You had to build it up like the war, you know. You thought of Oxford as Germans.'

He sat, immaculate, in the stern of the Cambridge boat, a young man with no sports credentials whatsoever about to yell himself into notorious posterity. But what was he doing there, he who had been so uninterested in sport at Eton that his only activity on the famous playing fields was to bring out the buns on a tray to the rugger team? At sixteen, he contracted polio and spent a year in the Liverpool Royal Infirmary. Any incipient sports prowess withered and died forever. And yet there he is in all the pictures, a serious-faced boy in pale-blue jacket with piping and hopelessly inefficient blanket trousers. 'They were incredibly heavy. If you fell in or got wet they weighed a ton. They weren't practical. They weren't warm either. Totally useless now I come to think of it.'

Why on earth had he been chosen as the Cambridge cox? 'Oh, I was the only one around,' he said vaguely. There would be more to it than that. Possibly the post-race party thrown by his uncle, the stage designer and artist Oliver Messel, who lived in a gorgeous house in Pelham Place which nearly collapsed when one of the crew members, staggering with celebratory cocktails, leaned on a false pillar which wobbled and threatened an interior earthquake. In other words, A.R.C. Armstrong-Jones was a great source of social entertainment. His idea of pre-race training on one occasion had been to buy a motorbike and gust airily into London with a large rower riding pillion and panniers sloshing with Champagne. He and his friend were on a date with two young ladies. 'But they didn't come. We sat drinking the Champagne in Hyde Park in the dark and eventually decided it was time to go back. But my passenger fell asleep as I was going round a corner in Baldock and we drove straight into a lamp-post. I flew one way and he flew the other and we lay in the gutter until a lorry driver stopped to help us.' Despite the twin inconveniences of concussion to himself and a broken arm sustained by his friend, the two students managed to re-enter the confines of Jesus College without alerting the authorities. 'I had a key cut to the dustbin lift,' confided Lord Snowdon, who had unfortunately not been able to apply the same ingenuity to his degree course.

'I was studying architecture. But not much of it. In fact, I was asked to go down for a year. There is a subtle difference between being asked to go down and being sent down. It's slightly politer. There was this awful little twerp, my college tutor, who said, "I wouldn't ask you to go down if you'd done more for college rowing rather than the university rowing". You see, Jesus was very autonomous. They hated anything to do with the university. To row for Cambridge was a form of betrayal.' So rowing, the only sport with which Lord Snowdon has actually had any truck, was his doom as an architect. His mother sent him a telegram. It said: 'On no account are you to consider changing careers.' He changed it immediately and set up a photographic studio in London.

But before that and the marriage to Princess Margaret in 1960 which thrust him to celebrity, came his early dice with fame in the Boat Race. 'In those days, it was all so different. The training was very lackadaisical and amateurish. I, of course, didn't have to train. All I had to do was get off weight. I got down to 8 stone 4 lb shovelling malt in a brewery. You could lose about a stone in three hours.' He made one or two technological contributions to the Cambridge campaign. He designed a rudder made of aluminium and wood laminated together to act more efficiently in the water and a strike-rate machine fashioned from an old wind-up darkroom clock. Did I know what he meant by strike rate? he asked kindly. I said I did, lying a little.

'Ooh,' he said, and made himself laugh. 'I sounded rather like Chris Tarrant then. People always say "Ooooooh!" when he phones them. I love *Millionaire.* But I have no hankering to go on it at all. I think I would fail at the very first question.' Certainly, sports questions would baffle him. He had never heard of the England cricket or rugby captains and of the England football captain, David Beckham, he admitted: 'I have absolutely no idea what he looks like.' I explained he could be spotted by the three lines he has shaved into his eyebrows. 'Golly,' said Lord Snowdon, while not really approving of such adornment. 'How tiresome,' he added.

The same could not be said of his pre-Boat Race exertions. They were far from tiring in any way. Largely, he smoked Gauloise. 'We stayed at the RAC Club in Epsom for about a month as our final preparation for the race. Everyone was in strict training except for me. I was allowed to smoke about eighty cigarettes a day so as not to eat. We were only allowed out once – to Eastbourne. There we are,' he said pointing to a black-and-white photograph of the crew on the steps of the Town Hall with the mayor. A card is pasted into the scrapbook which allows the bearer, by order of the County Borough of Eastbourne, free admission to the pier and promenade.

Clearly there was not a lot to do during the build-up to the big day. 'The only thing we were allowed to do was watch the frogs make love in the RAC Club pond.' I venture that this cannot have been terribly thrilling. But I am contradicted. 'Well, it was then,' he said. 'All the crew got terribly excited about it.' And so, reluctantly tearing themselves away from amorous amphibians, the momentous day arrived. Cambridge were slight favourites. A south-wester was blowing, the waves slapped and chopped at the flotilla on the water. A vast crowd congregated and speculated. The Cambridge cox was summoned for a pre-race interview. He thinks with John Snagge. He was thrumming with nerves. 'Oh, terrified, yes.'

The race began. And Armstrong-Jones, whose most arduous public appearance before this had been as Cobweb in *A Midsummer Night's Dream* aged six, began shouting. 'It was extremely *malvenu* to have a megaphone. They were absolutely not done. Americans had megaphones.' His tone implied he need say no more. 'Your voice was meant to be able to carry. Believe it or not, my voice is still quite loud. I was rather pleased the other day because I got a taxi going down the Gloucester Road. You could only just see him going past the mews for about one second, and he stopped. Then I apologised because I think it's awfully rude to shout.'

But in the grip of competitive fury, his manners deserted him. He unerringly urged the boat to the best water, his rival cox, R.J. Hinchcliffe (it said in the cuttings), followed suit. There was a mutual exchange of 'cross words' and, for the first time in the history of the Boat Race, oars clashed. The onlookers were agog, the next day's headlines huge. 'Coxswains Duel Nearly Ended in a Foul', they exclaimed and there, underneath, a shameless quote from the offending sportsman. 'The Cambridge cox, Armstrong-Jones, speaking of the incident near the Chiswick Steps when the boats nearly collided said, "I was a bit far out and Oxford came into my water. I moved to shove him over a bit. I uttered a word which wouldn't bear repetition in a newspaper. But strong language is quite common between coxes".' Fair enough, said Lord Snowdon, fifty-two years later.

But, one was forced to reprove him, it seems he was at the early helm of a decline in sporting standards that has reached its apotheosis in binge-drinking footballers under arrest. 'Oh dear,' he said, apologetically. 'How awful.' Anyway, Cambridge won. By three and a half lengths. And the victorious team swept off (after nearly demolishing his uncle's house) to the Empress Club for the Boat Race Gala Dinner (menu enclosed in scrapbook). 'Thank God we won,' said Lord Snowdon. 'Nothing worse than losing the Boat Race. I can't imagine anything more awful.'

There began and ended his sporting career. With one notable exception. Before his divorce from Princess Margaret in 1978, he often took dangerous part in a horse race on the Thursday morning at Royal Ascot, one that was hidden to public gaze because it involved most of the members of the Royal Family riding full tilt along the famous course. 'I always came last,' he said predictably. As a result of the polio he had suffered as a child, his legs were not able to control a horse with various disastrous consequences. 'I could never stop. I had no control at all. One year I remember my horse making directly for The Queen who had already finished the race. All I could do was yell, "Look out, look out!" and frantically wave at her.' A collision was missed by inches.

Lord Snowdon's loss to sport is perhaps not very great. He was safer behind a camera. He smiled amiably. His bad mood was not very bad at all. 'But I am feeling rather emotional today because I'm having to sell my little cottage in the country. I've known it since I was three. I'm trying to learn to hate it.' His expression suggested he had not yet succeeded. But resurrecting memories of the Boat Race had cheered him up a little. 'I remember it so well. It's like a window opening and it all comes flooding back. Do you know, it rates very highly as one of the greatest times of my life? It was the bond we forged as a crew. I'm still friends with many of them. That sort of friendship is everlasting.' He paused. 'That sounds a bit fey. But it's true.'

Sporting Champion: Antony Armstrong-Jones – Boat Race (1950).

APRIL

RED RUM – GRAND NATIONAL

RELIEF OF RED RUM'S UNSEATED RIDER

Robert Philip, 5 April 1999

Red Rum won the Grand National three times and became a four-legged Anthea Turner: every time you switched on the telly there he was popping up on *This is Your Life*, BBC Sports Personality of the Year, *Blue Peter*, *The Generation Game* and *Record Breakers*. He even had his flanks stroked by the fragrant Sally James on *Tiswas*. Brian Fletcher won the Grand National three times, the only jockey this century to do so, and, as befitting a nation of animal lovers, was promptly forgotten.

By the time a Japanese restaurateur by the name of 'Rocky' Aoki tried to buy Red Rum for £500,000 in 1977 as a promotional gimmick (the same year Kenny Dalglish moved to Liverpool from Celtic for £440,000), Fletcher, then only twenty-eight, had been forced into retirement by a serious head injury and was trapped in a hellish twilight zone. 'In boxing terms I was punch drunk,' recalled Fletcher, now restored to rude health and rebuilding his life with the help and encouragement of the Injured Jockeys' Fund. 'After I was forced to quit in '76, I spent three or four years in and out of various hospitals all over the place. I suffered blinding headaches, blackouts and loss of memory.'

Having coaxed Red Alligator to Aintree triumph at the age of nineteen in 1968, Fletcher guided 'Rummy' to successive victories in 1973 and 1974, but Fletcher's role in the Grand National legend has been blithely disregarded. Whichever jockey and horse gallops past the winning post at Aintree nowadays, they will be watched by a statue of Red Rum; no such monument exists for Brian Fletcher. 'Red Rum was such a great steeplechaser he deserves to be remembered and written about long after I'm dead and gone,' said Fletcher, with affection and nary a trace of resentment. 'But, yes, a lot of people do seem to think the horse goes round Aintree on his own and the riders are soon forgotten. However, there is a statue of both of us – at Ayr, where we won the Scottish Grand National in '74, just ten days after we'd won at Aintree.'

Twenty-five years after his second National victory on Red Rum, Fletcher, who now breeds Welsh cobs in an idyllic retreat on the slopes of the Cambrian Mountains, turns the pages of the scrapbook in his mind with a warm glow of nostalgia. 'Actually, I should have won the Grand National four times. I was third on Red Alligator in '67, the year of the great pile-up. He tried to jump the fence three times – we couldn't see where we were going because of all the loose horses and jockeys wandering around – and when we finally got over at the third attempt I was thrown off and had to remount. By the time we got going again, Foinavon was miles in front. We did win the following year – and won it easily – but Red Alligator had been a far better horse in '67, which is why I know for a fact that we'd have strolled it but for the mêlée.'

Fletcher's association with Red Rum began with a victory in a 3½-mile chase at Ayr in 1973; before he had even jumped down from the saddle, he told trainer Ginger McCain they were in the company of a future Grand National winner. He said: 'I was stunned by his alertness and intelligence. He was a lovely, lovely horse to sit on. You could have ridden him round Brands Hatch with all the racing cars whizzing about him and he wouldn't have batted an eyelid. A lot of steeplechasers go at each fence hell for leather, Red Rum had something upstairs. He was thinking all the way round. He was a very cute horse.'

Fletcher's admiration was not shared by the public at large in 1973 when, in arguably the greatest Grand National of them all, they snatched victory on the line from the noble Crisp and Richard Pitman. 'Aye, we were the villains all right,' said Fletcher, eyes a-twinkle. Crisp, a huge Australian chaser with a heart to match his prodigious jumping ability, had built up a seemingly unassailable twenty-five-length advantage, soaring over Becher's Brook and The Chair as though they were bundles of hay. But crossing the Melling Road two fences from home and still twenty lengths adrift, Fletcher spotted Crisp's tail begin to 'wave'. Like a drunk, Crisp suddenly began weaving all over the course as Red Rum's hoofbeats thudded ever closer. 'Crisp was almost standing still and I knew if the post didn't come too soon we'd catch him. And luckily, by God's judgment, we did catch him.' Both winner and gallant loser smashed the existing course record set by Golden Miller thirty-nine years earlier by almost nineteen seconds.

Twelve months later and now carrying the same onerous 12-stone top-weight, which had been Crisp's downfall, Red Rum and Fletcher fairly cantered to victory ahead of the dual Cheltenham Gold Cup winner L'Escargot. 'It was so easy I couldn't believe it. I was so jubilant during the run-in from the Elbow that when I heard the roar of the crowds I did something really stupid. Thirty yards from the post, I was so overcome by the occasion that I stood up in the stirrups and saluted everyone. Looking back, I can't help but wonder how I'd have felt if Rummy had ducked to one side and I'd fallen off. But strangely, I think his greatest performance came a week and a half later when we won the Scottish National at Ayr.' To this day, Red Rum and Brian Fletcher are the only horse and jockey to have achieved the double.

In 1975, Rummy was beaten into second place at Aintree by

L'Escargot on soft ground – 'he could never handle it when the ground was like treacle, it was his only weakness' – following which Fletcher was unceremoniously sacked. 'I loved Red Rum, I really loved him. We'd become great friends over the years and I felt he was getting past his prime. He'd lost a little bit of zip and zest, I don't think he was enjoying it as much. He still had the jumping ability and stamina needed for Aintree, but over shorter distances he'd begun to struggle. In a 3-mile chase at Newcastle one day we finished a well-beaten third and when I came into the unsaddling enclosure McCain asked me why I hadn't used the whip so we'd have been second. And all I said to him, "I'm sorry, Mr McCain, but I'm not going to abuse Red Rum. He's done too much for me to be knocking the spots off him just to win a few pounds' place money". And, of course, a few weeks later McCain phoned me say he was taking me off the horse because he didn't feel I was getting the most out of Red Rum.'

Red Rum did triumph again at Aintree in 1977 when ridden by Tommy Stack, himself just recovering from serious illness, by which time Fletcher was lying in a hospital bed. 'The trouble had begun in '71 when I fractured my skull in a fall. I was semi-conscious for a fortnight and it took me ten months to get my licence back. Safety standards have become far stricter over the years and if I had the same accident today I wouldn't be allowed to ride again, it's as simple as that. By 1976, when I was third on Eyecatcher at Aintree [behind his beloved Red Rum and winner Rag Trade], whenever I took a fall I'd suffer severe head pains. My reflexes were shot to pieces and one day after I'd been in a bad fall at Uttoxeter, I almost blacked out in the car driving back up the M6. I managed to pull over on to the hard shoulder, but I was scared, really scared. I sought medical advice and after what seemed like a hundred tests, the doctor told me the next fall could leave me paralysed or even kill me. I was only a young man so I was broken-hearted, but I knew if I didn't pack it in I could end up dead.'

Twenty-five years after his third Aintree triumph, Fletcher can finally cope without the aid of drugs and still enjoys a canter in the Welsh hills. When he watches the Grand National, he admits: 'Yes, there's a tear in my eye. Red Rum and I had such great times together it's impossible to watch the race and not see the old fella clattering up the run-in, ears pricked. Time moves on, but I'll never stop loving Red Rum.'

Sporting Champion: Red Rum – 3 Grand Nationals (1973, 1974, 1977); 1 Scottish Grand National (1974).

BOB CHAMPION – GRAND NATIONAL

CHAMPION AND THE WONDER HORSE

Jim White, 16 March 2010

Few people gave Bob Champion a chance when he was diagnosed with testicular cancer in 1979. Back then, it was largely considered to be a death sentence, with three months the standard gap between diagnosis and the end. But Champion the wonder horseman not only pulled through, he won the Grand National two years later, a recovery so astonishing it remains the most inspirational return in sporting history, lauded in a book and on the big screen. And it happened, he recalls, because he had a pretty straightforward attitude to the disease. 'I didn't want to die,' he says. 'Simple as that. And I wanted to ride again. I couldn't think of anything else I wanted to do. So that was the next goal. I think that aim, that goal, got me through. I'm a great believer in positive thought. Though I admit the drugs helped.'

Champion was thirty-one when he was told he had the condition. He had ridden a winner the day before, and felt not a twinge of illness, no pain, not so much as a moment's ache. But a suspicious swelling took him to the doctor and he was found to have a tumour. Eighteen months earlier and that would have been that. But new chemotherapy techniques were being pioneered and he was offered the chance to be a guinea pig. 'Nobody thought I'd pull through, never mind get back on a horse,' he recalls. 'But the professor who introduced me to the course of chemo told me if I were offered a 6–4 chance in a novice chase, I'd give it a ride wouldn't I? He was right, I would. And he got the odds about right.' The professor should have been a bookmaker. Though the drugs he gave Champion to fight the invasive tumour took their toll. Their toxicity stripped his lungs of their lining and, he is convinced, led to a heart attack in 2005. 'They haven't proved the link,' he says. 'But a lot of us who took those drugs have had heart attacks. Not that I'm complaining. They saved my life.'

Three decades on, Champion is still very much alive. And far from moaning about the attendant health complications, he has become one of the country's leading charity fundraisers, collecting over the years more than £12 million to fund research at the Bob Champion Cancer Trust at the Royal Marsden Hospital in Fulham. 'When I got testicular cancer, the doctors only gave me a forty per cent chance of living,' he says. 'Now, thanks to work in our unit and elsewhere, it's ninety-five per cent curable, provided it's caught early enough. So we've shifted a lot of our research emphasis to prostate cancer. One in fourteen men will get prostate cancer. It's still the secret killer. Trouble is, men are all the same. They're like me: when you've got a cold you're dying, but anything more serious and you pretend it's not happening.'

Looking back, movie scriptwriters could not make up

Champion's tale, which is why it was adapted for the big screen in the 1983 hit film *Champions*. 'It was frightening seeing myself up there on screen,' he recalls. 'I had a preview in a cinema in London, just me and Lord Grade who was the producer. And yes, it was emotional. Very. The music, terrific, that really brought it home for me. And I think John Hurt got me pretty well. It was how I was.' And the odd thing was, never for a moment did Champion think his personal screenplay would end any other way. He and Aldaniti, the mount he always refers to as 'the old horse' and who was making his own comeback from debilitating injury, seemed to share a sense of destiny when they memorably won the Grand National at Aintree in 1981. 'I suppose you can call it that, but I was certain I'd win that year,' he says. 'There was never a moment's doubt in my mind. I couldn't see us being beaten. On the way there, I said to Josh [Gifford, the horse's trainer], "I'm a certainty". He couldn't believe it. But that's how I felt. And I'd never known the old horse so relaxed as when I sat on him that morning. He'd normally pull like a train, but not that day. He knew all right. And it was clearly something about that day, because the next year we fell at the first.'

Champion, a quiet, unassuming Yorkshireman, found his life changed the moment he crossed the finishing line. Suddenly everyone wanted a piece of his life story, the return against the odds became a national story. 'I think it did change my life, definitely,' he says. 'From then on I was public property. I wasn't very good at that. I'm terribly shy. It didn't hit me immediately after the race. I had another race an hour later, and in all the madness and the interviews and the telly people round me all I could think was, "I mustn't forget to weigh in for the next race". I had a glass of Champagne in my hand at one point, but a photographer took it off me and never gave it me back. The first drink I had was a can of Coke on the motorway home.' And that was a journey which reminds him to this day how fortunate he was. 'I had dinner with John Thorne on the way home from Aintree,' he recalls. 'He'd finished second. He was the first person to come up and congratulate me after I crossed the line, the first person who confirmed it wasn't just in my imagination. What a leveller it is; John was a fantastic man and he was killed in a point-to-point the following season.'

Champion continued to race for a couple more years after his triumph, but he never repeated it. He had always struggled with his weight and the fight with cancer made the endless round of saunas and steam rooms even less palatable. These days he is rarely atop a horse. But that moment at Aintree remains constantly playing in his mental cinema. 'No, of course it's not irritating to be remembered for it,' he says. 'I was interviewed on television when I was seven at a race meeting at Redcar. The interviewer asked me what I wanted to do. I said I wanted to be a jockey and ride in the Grand National. There was nothing more I wanted in my life. I never dreamt of doing anything else. And I did it. I won. You can't ask for more than that.'

Sporting Champion: Bob Champion – 1 Grand National (1981).

TIGER WOODS – THE MASTERS

HOW TIGER BECAME 'THE CHOSEN ONE'

James Mossop, 20 April 1997

As the world drank to the phenomenon of a young black man winning the sixty-first US Masters in a Deep South state called Prejudice, it was time to consider the making of a twenty-one-year-old who almost lapped the field. If Hollywood had invented Mr and Mrs Earl Woods and their little boy Eldrick and told the story of their lives together, Augusta National would have read 'Fantasy Island'.

These days, of course, there are agents and coaches and million-dollar deals, but when Tiger was growing up it was his father, Earl Woods, who began the boy's journey to his karma when he was two days old. He put on a jazz record, the baby smiled and that, said Earl, meant they could march forward together. Then there were days when Earl's military training as a Green Beret in Vietnam, where discipline and mental toughness were paramount, was used to make sure the boy had those strengths. They worked together on the golf course, the man and the slender schoolboy, and Earl can now say: 'With Tiger there was never any guesswork. I knew him and how much he could take. So I pulled every dirty, nasty, rumbustious trick on my son week after week. I dropped a bag of clubs at the impact of his swing. I imitated a crow's voice while he was stroking a putt. When he was ready to hit a shot I would toss a ball right in front of his and it would cross his line of vision. I made sure that I stood in his line of sight and would move just as he was about to execute a shot. I would cough as he was taking the club back. I played with his mind and, don't forget, he was not permitted to say a word. Sometimes he got angry with me and he would stop his club inches before impact and grit his teeth and roll his eyes. He was exposed to every devious, diabolical, insidious trick that any future opponent might pull on him. He learnt. He became mentally tough.'

The results include three successive USGA Junior titles, three straight US Amateur championships, records at every point of the compass, and the US Masters. The pedigree of this young maestro with a snow-white smile and a future beyond legends is fascinating. What, everyone wonders, makes Tiger tick so perfectly? Is there a secret to his upbringing? It was certainly different. The influences were strong. There is the Buddhism of his Thai mother, Tida. There are the memories and experiences his father brought home from the killing fields where he was a lieutenant-colonel. Serenity married strength and the happy couple became joint authors of their baby's destiny.

From his first gulp of air when they called him Eldrick, he was known as Tiger after Earl's combat partner, Nguyen Phong. They had dodged sniper fire together and the soldier Tiger saved Earl's life when he killed a viper that was only inches from a strike. The stern codes of the Green Berets runs through Tiger's upbringing. The calmness and mothering of Tida created a blend of togetherness for the Woods and their only child. A return to a view of old calendars might help to understand the making of The Chosen One. Take his father, a man with a small measure of Chinese, some Cherokee and plenty of African-American blood in his veins. Somewhere, says Tida, there is a trace of European between them and that led to her saying in her quiet, Thai way: 'Tiger is the Universal Child. He can hold everyone together.' She made that statement after taking Tiger's astrological chart to Buddhist monks in Los Angeles and Bangkok. They told her that her son had wondrous powers and that if he ever went into politics he would become a president or a prime minister. In the military he would be a general. The ancient game, if not the current generation of players chasing major titles, should be grateful that he chose golf.

Earl believes that everything that happened to him was for a purpose. The military service was to prepare him with the resolve he would need to pass on to Tiger. The posting to public relations in New York was to provide the grounding for Tiger's dealings with an avaricious media. Perhaps his recent heart trouble was a Divine hint that the time had come for Tiger to stand alone. Only in 1996

Earl was telling guests at a dinner honouring his son that Tiger would transcend the game, bring to the world a humanitarianism it had never known before and that God Himself had decided that Earl was the man to nurture this treasure. Someone asked him, did he mean that Tiger would have more impact than Nelson Mandela, Ghandi or Buddha? 'Yes,' he replied, 'because he is playing a sport that is international. Because he is qualified through his ethnicity to accomplish miracles. He is the bridge between East and West. There is no limit because he has the guidance. I don't know exactly what form it will take. But he is The Chosen One. He will have the power to impact nations. Not people. Nations. The world is just getting a taste of his power.'

Earl and Tida have devoted all their waking hours to their only son. At six months old Tiger could stand perfectly erect on his father's palm as he walked around the room. At eleven months he was swinging a miniature club perfectly. At four he was spending eight hours a day on the golf course, winning money from players ten and twenty years older. His mother would drop him off at nine and collect him at five. And, yes, there were boys who called him 'nigger' and threw stones at him after tying him to a tree. He told no one for several days. In 1995 he was asked to leave a driving range because a nearby resident complained that some black teenager was trying to bombard her house with golf balls. In fact he was hitting them powerfully into a net. Earl took the young Tiger to the US Navy Club near their home in Cypress, California. They banned Tiger, saying he was too young. Earl took him back and made a deal with the professional: Give the kid, aged three, a shot a hole over nine holes and if he wins, return his playing certificate. Tiger won by two strokes, the professional reinstated him but the old fogeys went over his head and the boy was out again.

All the time Earl and Tida were preparing their son for a life they felt would change the world. Earl looked after the golf, Tida the education. Earl barked out military terms such as SOP (Standard Operating Procedure) which Tiger had to adopt as a set-up routine. 'You could never be laid more bare than I was with Tiger during some of our golf outings,' Earl reported. 'He was eighteen months old, couldn't count to five but he intuitively knew a par-five from a par-four and a par-three. He'd say, "Daddy, you got a double-bogey". Now that was six strokes and he couldn't count to five.' Stern lessons in course management (getting the ball round wisely) and mental toughness came later. All the time Tida was soothing father and son. Now the family is swollen by the money men.

Sporting Champion: Tiger Woods – 4 Masters (1997, 2001, 2002, 2005); 3 The Open Championships (2000, 2005, 2006); 3 US Opens (2000, 2002, 2008); 4 USPGA Championships (1999, 2000, 2006, 2007).

PAULA RADCLIFFE – LONDON MARATHON

RADCLIFFE SHOWS NO MERCY TO
THE RECORD BOOKS

Tom Knight, 14 April 2003

With a world record that marked a quantum leap in women's distance running, Paula Radcliffe graced the London Marathon with a performance that had even her biggest fans shaking their heads in disbelief. Radcliffe crossed the finish line in the Mall in two hours fifteen minutes twenty-five seconds. It was an astonishing display of running. Her time slashed one minute fifty-three seconds off the world record she set in Chicago in October 2002 and brought her home four and a half minutes ahead of Kenya's Catherine Ndereba in second place.

It was the biggest winning margin in this race since Ingrid Kristiansen won the last of her four London Marathon titles in 1988. That, though, was the least of Radcliffe's achievements on a day when not even the superlatives could keep pace with the twenty-nine year old from Bedford. The greatest marathon performance by a woman earned her £164,500 in prize money and time bonuses – but that was only the published figure. Add in the amount she was paid to start the race, performance bonuses from her kit sponsor, Nike, and from the event itself and Radcliffe will leave London more than £600,000 richer. It is the most any female athlete has earned in a day and means that since she won this race in 2002, a runner who used to be considered one of Britain's plucky losers will have amassed an estimated £2.5 million in prize money, bonuses and commercial sponsorship. Her commercial clout was not lost on Carey Pinkowski, the race director of the Chicago Marathon. 'She's turned everyone else into also-rans,' he said. 'I'd have to offer her a million dollars just to start a race now.'

Deena Drossin's two hours twenty-one minutes sixteen seconds in third place was an American record, slicing six seconds off the mark set by Joan Benoit in 1985. Those were the days when two hours twenty minutes was considered a magical barrier, but in three marathons over twelve months Radcliffe has exploded the myths surrounding what women are capable of achieving. Gerard Hartmann, the Limerick-based physical therapist whose care for Radcliffe has included up to four hours of treatment and massage every day since January, said she was 'one in a million' and added: 'This was a quantum leap in women's marathon running which made even the men's world record look soft.' It was Hartmann who put Radcliffe back together following her accident in March, when she clashed with a young cyclist during one of her long training runs in Albuquerque.

Contrary to what she wanted people to believe before the race, Radcliffe set about attacking her world record from the start on Blackheath. Tucking in behind Samson Loywapet and Christopher Kandie, two of the ten male pace-makers controversially brought in by the race organisers, she raced away from one of the best women's fields assembled in London. With Ndereba, Drossin, Susan Chepkemei and Ludmila Petrova left to settle into a pace that best suited their more conservative race plans, Radcliffe charged through the opening miles. Wearing sunglasses and white gloves to complement the flesh-coloured, knee-length socks which have become her trademark, Radcliffe was clocked at five minutes ten seconds for the first mile and five minutes eight seconds for the second. She already had a substantial lead and if members of the Radcliffe camp were worrying about her enthusiasm, they were beginning to get concerned when her third mile was timed at four minutes fifty-seven seconds.

Alec Stanton, the Bedford Athletic Club stalwart who has coached her since she was a youngster, admitted he was 'a little surprised', but there were also genuine fears from seasoned marathon-watchers that Radcliffe was overdoing things. It later transpired that she thought the same. She said: 'I was running with the pace-makers until I saw that the third mile was too fast so I backed off.' There followed the slightest of adjustments, but Radcliffe was still travelling at a two-hour fourteen-minute pace and by the fifth mile had a twenty-second lead. The race was over. It was a case of just how fast she could cover the distance.

She passed 13.1 miles in one hour eight minutes two seconds, quicker than any woman managed in a half-marathon during 2002, and still found the energy to run faster still. Only when she clocked five minutes three seconds for the twenty-fourth mile did her grimaces and head-bobbing reveal the extent of her pain. But she ran the second half of the race in one hour seven minutes twenty-three seconds and, with one final effort, the last 385 yards in fifty-nine seconds. Her finishing sprint into the Mall was the equivalent of a sixty-eight-second final lap in a track race and fifteen seconds quicker than she managed in Chicago. Across the line, she bent double and then wobbled as if to faint before grabbing a water bottle and remembering to pose for the photographers on the finish gantry. The perfect end to a perfect day for Radcliffe came when Carlos Cardoso, the Portuguese official sent by the International Association of Athletics Federations to monitor London's pace-making experiment, professed himself satisfied. The record will be ratified.

Sporting Champion: Paula Radcliffe – 3 London Marathons (2002, 2003, 2005); 3 New York Marathons (2004, 2007, 2008); 1 Chicago Marathon (2002); 1 World Championship (2005); 1 Commonwealth Games (2002); 1 European Championship (2002).

STEVE DAVIS – WORLD SNOOKER CHAMPIONSHIP

SATIRISTS' 'BORING' LABEL LED TO AN UPTURN IN PUBLIC SUPPORT

Robert Philip, 13 November 1995

From the instant his *Spitting Image* puppet cast an envious eye at Alex 'Hurricane' Higgins and Jimmy 'Whirlwind' White and demanded a suitably dashing nickname of his own, he has been known to us as Steve 'Interesting' Davis; while the Hurricane collected hangovers and the Whirlwind collected betting slips, 'Interesting' was depicted as the proud owner of the world's largest bus ticket collection. In person, Davis really is interesting (no, honestly, he is), but labours under no illusions when called upon to see himself as others might see him. 'I play chess for my local club here in Essex, I've talked about snooker and little else for twenty years, and although I don't collect bus tickets, I do collect 1960s soul-music records. So I fit the bill as a bit of an anorak, don't I? How do you picture a person who plays snooker, who enjoys a game of chess and who has a load of old forty-fives? You're not going to find him down there at Annabel's among the beautiful people, are you?'

Yet gradually, our image of the man has subtly altered. When he first strode across our screens as an unknown but imperious twenty-two-year-old to demolish that nice Terry Griffiths (the title holder) in the first round of the 1980 World Championship, we didn't quite like the cut of his jib, did we? But how could we when he appeared so smug in victory, so peevish in defeat? Oh, how the nation cheered when Dennis Taylor beat him in that most thrilling frame of all in 1985, briefly interrupting a decade of dominance during which Davis won six world titles. We could open our hearts to Higgins because of his frailties, we could delight in White because of his Artful Dodger vulnerability, but Steve Davis was too bloody good to be likeable.

Then along came *Spitting Image*, a new waist-coated Great One in the callow shape of Stephen Hendry, swiftly followed by a trail of pimple-chinned school-leavers possessing masters degrees in break-building to whom Steve Davis was as much a part of ancient history as Joe and Fred. We may admire a champion, but we reserve our deep affection for a loser. And so, since he has not won the world title since 1989, and now languishes at number eight in the provisional rankings, we have finally come to love him. In the bad old, good old days, spectators were known to boo Davis when he sank a crucial ball (albeit in suitably hushed tones); now they tend to commiserate with a sympathetic 'aaaaah' whenever he misses.

'I'm not sure I like that,' he muses, laughing at his misplaced sense of resentment. 'No, it is nice to be popular at last. Maybe because I was too good when I was younger, the public saw me as some kind of threat to Alex, Terry, Ray [Reardon], Cliff [Thorburn] and their other favourites. But I'm not so successful now and I'm older so I've become easier to like. Actually, I've always valued older people's opinion more than folk my own age because the younger generation is much more fickle. I think older snooker fans have always quite liked me, but as I've grown older myself so people my own age have warmed to me. But during the 1980s the crowds could be quite aggressive. Did I want to be liked? God, I can't remember. It's such a long time ago now. But I'm sure I wasn't bothered otherwise I'd have tried harder. All I did was try to be polite and not to come over as a smarmy, smart aleck. But you can't control your facial expressions and people accused me of being aloof and arrogant because that's the way you seem when you play. The only time you get to be human is during the after-match interviews. And even then you're still only talking about snooker so people think that's all you can, or want, to talk about.'

Though Davis began to display an altogether different side to his personality – mischievous, wryly amusing and possessed of an engaging ability to poke fun at himself – via his appearances on *A Question of Sport* and a hilarious cameo on the last *Morecambe and Wise Christmas Special*, the metamorphosis from tombstone-faced automaton to national treasure was brought about almost entirely by his alter-ego in latex. '*Spitting Image* was a godsend, an absolute godsend. That was the start of me being accepted by the public. As soon as you get tagged "boring" then you're no longer a threat to the bloke who thinks he must be more interesting than you. "Look at that Steve Davis", they'll say, "all that money and he's a boring bastard". That was the serious side of it, but I also got a lot of laughs out of it personally.'

So he was human after all. (At this point I should probably explain we are enjoying a beer in the snooker room of his father's home where, to my childish glee, Davis Junior has just potted the cue ball straight from the break.) He was soon starring in every second advertisement on television – from Wotta Lotta Bottle for the Milk Marketing Board to baked beans and garden peas – while earning his *Blue Peter* badge for 'potting' an entire pack of Brownies tumbling head-over-heels on a giant table. But for television, of course, Steve Davis would never have been deemed worthy of *Spitting Image's* mockery in the first place. Until the BBC began transmitting in colour in 1969, snooker was perceived as being the preserve of working men's clubs and seedy halls where hustlers lurked in every smoke-filled alcove to feed off those with more money than ability. 'What would I have been doing today . . .?' his voice tails off as he tries to imagine life in monochrome images. 'Working in a bank, or a record shop, maybe. I wasn't artistic and I wasn't exactly motivated at school, even though I got my O levels. I didn't have too much drive, so I'd probably have got a job which would have paid enough to let me enjoy my hobby – snooker. Even if snooker had never become as big as it has on TV it would still have been popular at grass-roots level. If I'd never become a professional I'd still be playing for my social club in league matches . . . and having just as much fun at a different level. Take my father, who's absolute crap at snooker ['Sorry, Dad,' he adds quickly as Davis Senior persuades a long red into the bottom corner pocket from an improbable angle]; he likes the game better than I do.'

Having claimed seventy titles during the 1980s, Davis has won but a handful of tournaments in the past five seasons and breezily admits a seventh world championship may now be beyond his powers – 'I haven't a clue whether I can win another one, I'd like to think so . . .' – but his love of spending hour upon hour in a darkened room is undiminished. Fear not, however, for his abundant talent should not be regarded as evidence of a misspent youth. Like his boyhood hero Just William, the youthful Steve Davis spent as much time building rafts, breaking windows, scoring goals, chasing rivals and running through streams with the wind in his hair and the rain in his face as he did bent double over his dad's 6-foot Joe Davis table in the family's kitchen.

'I didn't take snooker very seriously until I was about sixteen or seventeen, so I enjoyed a normal childhood. I do worry about kids today who are brilliant players at twelve but who might never see daylight. The only thing I missed out on was what you might call "pulling". I reckon I was twenty-one before I discovered real girls don't have a staple in their stomach. I think it helps being an ugly bastard if you want to be a good sportsman. Then when you're eighteen and your mates say, "Are you coming down the disco?" you can reply, "Nah, I've got to do eight hours' practice". Not because you want to do eight hours' practice, you understand, but because you know if you go down the disco all you'll get is a series of knock-backs.'

Now married to the lovely Judy and father of Greg, four and a half, and Jack, two and a half, Davis has an entirely different set of excuses for living a less than jet-set life in rural splendour on the outskirts of Romford. Seeing him in the role of soppy dad, it is difficult to remember him as the flint-eyed assassin who sat cradling his cue like a rifle while Thorburn cleared the table. 'Ah, fatherhood. A living, breathing, hilarious nightmare. But the thing about trophies is they don't really mean anything after you've got them. I mean holding the World Championship trophy doesn't compare with holding your newly born son, does it? I get no satisfaction from what I've achieved in the game. That's the curse. People say, "You've done everything, what's left?" It's not like that. I haven't "done everything" because nothing was important in the first place. The six world titles that have gone have no importance . . . the seventh one does, though. In fifty years' time I am certainly not going to be phoning up *Yellow Pages* trying to find a copy of my version of J.R. Hartley's *Fly Fishing.'*

So returning to Judy and the boys at night reduces the pain of defeat then? 'I can honestly say,' he testifies to accompanying chortles, 'it does not make a blind bit of difference. I'm sorry. It would be a very nice thing to say, "It softens the blow", but that's crap. Losing's horrible. I have two separate lives. Snooker player and husband and dad.' So now the secrets are coming out, does he ever leave his anorak at the door and sashay on to the dance floor at Annabel's? 'Dunno. I think I might have been there. I only seem to go up to London when I get drunk. And then I never know where I've been.' Interesting? I'll leave you to decide . . .

Sporting Champion: Steve Davis – 6 World Championships (1981, 1983, 1984, 1987, 1988, 1989); 6 UK Championships (1980, 1981, 1984, 1985, 1986, 1987); 3 Masters (1982, 1988, 1997).

STEPHEN HENDRY – WORLD SNOOKER CHAMPIONSHIP

GOODBYE TO THE ICE-VEINED TECHNOCRAT

Jim White, 3 May 2012

Stephen Hendry once said that if you're not winning then there's really no point in being involved in sport. And the great cue-man has now taken his own advice. After losing in the quarter-finals of snooker's World Championship, a tournament he once regarded as his own fiefdom, Hendry declared that was it. At forty-three he was retiring from the game, to spend more time with his burgeoning business interests in China.

So we bid farewell to undoubtedly the greatest player who has ever addressed the pink. Or at least that is what the statistics insist. A seven-time world champion, nine years at world number one, with 775 career centuries and thirty-six major titles, no one comes close to matching the contents of the Hendry trophy cabinet. This is the man who redefined his sport, who relentlessly accumulated records, who raised the standard across the game with his steely professionalism. And yet there was barely a damp eye in the house at his announcement. Had this been Ronnie O'Sullivan or Jimmy White walking away from the table, the eulogies would have run thick and fast. We would have been telling ourselves how the sport would never be the same again, replays of their finest breaks would have played on an endless YouTube loop. But with Hendry, the response to his departure was not much more than a respectful nod, a grudging acknowledgement of achievement with barely a hint that he will be missed.

Which is a reaction that will not have surprised him one jot. When I interviewed him, among an array of wry stories which belied his wider reputation for humourlessness, he told an anecdote about playing White in Glasgow. On Hendry home turf, you might have expected the support for a national sporting hero to be unequivocal. Yet he recalled all the locals cheering his opponent to the rafters. 'That's because we don't like winners in this country,' he said. 'We prefer characters. Jimmy is great to watch, but what did he ever win?' Well, certainly not the world title: to much public disappointment Hendry beat White four times in the Crucible final in the 1990s. Those finals were the matches that cemented the Scotsman's wider reputation: the ice-veined technocrat, utterly unswervable in pursuit of victory.

John Higgins suggests therein lies the great difference between the two most successful players of all time. Steve Davis, Higgins reckons, played because he loved the game. Hendry played because he loved to win. Davis's son Greg has barely seen his father win a major tournament – and he is twenty-two. Yet Davis – ten years Hendry's senior – still cheerfully puts himself through the World Championship qualification process because he likes nothing better in life than to have a cue in his hand. Hendry, who found being obliged to qualify for the first time since 1988 an uncomfortable process, shares no such romantic attachment to the baize. For him, losing is no way to earn a living.

Actually, it was a bit more than victory he sought. At his peak he challenged our sense of what a sportsman should be when he made a frank admission of a sadistic impulse. 'It's nice when you're beating an opponent and kicking him when he's down,' he said. 'That is what sport is all about, the only reason for playing.' You can see why Hendry cited Tiger Woods as his greatest inspiration. Dominant from an early age, intimidating in his single-minded pursuit of victory, apparently emotion-free at the critical point of competition: the parallels are pretty clear. Yet it may be another golfer who Hendry more closely resembles. In the wider suspicion of his pitiless thirst for success, he became to British tastes the

Nick Faldo of the extended cue. Faldo, too, never received the recognition his achievements merited largely because, while the public admired him, they did not love him. We can only hope that Hendry, in retirement, does not follow the Faldo career path too closely and attempt to reinvent himself as a chortling punster.

Hendry shares something else with Faldo: a disconcertingly unageing appearance. Watching him score a 147 break in the first round at the Crucible it was hard to believe he was forty-three. Fresh-faced and unencumbered by either grey hair or wrinkle, the only explanation for his looks is that he has a snooker table in his attic at home gradually warping, cracking and ageing in his stead. When he completed what was only the tenth maximum in the history of the competition (and he has three of them) his sheepish grin was identical to the one he wore when winning the title for the first time as a twenty-year-old. That youthful flush of his was a weapon he happily used in his early days: opponents could simply not believe someone as innocent looking as this was so cruel in his thirst for victory. It took the rest of the snooker world a long time to overcome their assumptions. Through the 1990s he was indomitable, unbeatable, his very name on the bill enough to drain the resolve from the rest of the field.

In the past decade, though, he has been largely overtaken. Younger players, brought up to emulate his gimlet-eyed approach, have gradually surpassed him. Now they better him constantly.

He has called those ten years a slippery slope to pointlessness. And he did not want to go any further. Sure, there will be exhibitions and greatest hits tours. But never again will he bring his icy certainty to a competitive table. Never again will he pursue the world title. And those of us who love the game should prepare as a result for a lesser sporting landscape. It is only now he is gone that we can finally appreciate this truth about Stephen Hendry: we will never see anyone as good at winning snooker matches again.

Sporting Champion: Stephen Hendry – 7 World Championships (1990, 1992, 1993, 1994, 1995, 1996, 1999); 5 UK Championships (1989, 1990, 1994, 1995, 1996); 6 Masters (1989, 1990, 1991, 1992, 1993, 1996).

WIGAN – RUGBY LEAGUE CHALLENGE CUP

WEST MAINTAINS GLORY YEARS IN STYLE AT WIGAN

John Whalley, 1 May 1995

For all the achievements of his acclaimed predecessors over the last eight years, Graeme West is on the verge of taking Wigan to new heights in his first full season as coach by winning every competition his side have entered. That is the inescapable conclusion after the champions outclassed Leeds, their nearest rivals, by five tries to one, thirty points to ten, in the Silk Cut Challenge Cup final at Wembley to win the competition for an unprecedented eighth year. In doing so they showed that the gap between Wigan and the rest is widening again.

This was the game which should have presented problems. The chance for Leeds to make a point that the domestic game will be dominated by two sides, not one, when the Super League era begins in 1996. As usual, Wigan made nonsense of all those optimistic noises about a serious challenge to their overwhelming superiority. Admittedly Leeds were disappointing, especially in the marking around play-the-balls, which directly led to two of Wigan's tries and is one reason the final was never going to be as close as 1994, when Wigan defeated the same opposition 26–16. The main factor for Wigan's success, however, was outstanding defence. Too often, Leeds were forced sideways in a final which failed to reach high expectations because it was so one-sided.

'Look at the scoreboard,' was the summing up of Ellery Hanley, the Leeds captain, afterwards.

A perfect day would have been completed for Wigan had Leeds, as looked likely for nearly all the match, been prevented from crossing their line. But James Lowes, following a quick tap penalty two minutes from time, forced his way over, much to the annoyance of this ultra-professional club whose standards continue to rise. Substitute Andrew Farrell, along with Denis Betts, Shaun Edwards and Phil Clarke, rivalled Jason Robinson for the man-of-the-match award which ultimately went to the winger for his two tries scored at crucial times. The first, after eighteen minutes, saw Robinson cut inside Francis Cummins from 40 metres, while the second, five minutes after the interval, came after the winger was presented with a huge gap 35 metres out. In between Robinson's tries, Henry Paul, Martin Hall and Va'aiga Tuigamala crossed, enabling Frano Botica to kick five goals from seven attempts.

So the cherry-and-white bandwagon continues apace. West has turned potential turmoil after the departure of John Dorahy into unending triumph by taking the Premiership, World Club Challenge, Regal Trophy, Championship and Challenge Cup in under twelve months.

Sporting Champions: Wigan – 19 Challenge Cup wins (1923–24, 1928–29, 1947–48, 1950–51, 1957–58, 1958–59, 1964–65, 1984–85, 1987–88, 1988–89, 1989–90, 1990–91, 1991–92, 1992–93, 1993–94, 1994–95, 2002, 2011, 2013).

ELLEN MacARTHUR – ROUND THE WORLD SAILING

SAILING'S FIRST LADY WILL KEEP CHASING DREAMS

Sue Mott, 30 April 2005

For once The Queen didn't have to reach up. This ennobling business is usually a pain in the neck for our monarch, blessed with strapping great rugby players and rowers to decorate somewhere two feet above her head, but when Ellen MacArthur (5 feet 2 inches in wet socks) received her damehood they were happily within the same range. Height is not the limit of their similarities either. Lone, stubborn, steely, dutiful, blue-eyed and remarkable, they dominate their respective environments, royalty and round-the-world sailing, with quietly adamant personalities.

Only Ellen has to make her own tea. Not much of it stays in the cup. 'D'you know, for only two days out of two and a half months could I drink a mug of tea without a lid on. It would have gone everywhere,' she said, in memory of her most recent seafaring adventure, the circumnavigation in seventy-one days, fourteen hours, eighteen minutes and thirty-three seconds that broke the world record and cemented her image in this country as a cross between Joan of Arc and Admiral Lord Nelson.

Last seen, she was on the dockside in Falmouth, waving to an ecstatic crowd and looking remarkably well for someone tormented by sleep deprivation, waves, wind, wet and whales for seventy-one days, fourteen hours and eighteen minutes longer than most sane humans would contemplate. And some of us would balk at the thirty-three seconds. Then she stepped away. To Scotland, as it happens, to plant trees, see friends and sail her first seagoing love, *Iduna*, back to sanity and health. Now she returns to action, in earnest record-attempt combat on board *B&Q*, the prosaically entitled and very orange 75-foot trimaran that carried her round the world, this time in the short, sharp 280-mile SNSM race off the coast of Brittany. Perhaps, by now, her previous voyage, for all its harrowing moments, has been recast in a romantic, golden glow. You must be joking. 'No, it's not romantic. It never will be,' she said emphatically, sitting, slightly restively, at the Team Ellen offices on the Isle of Wight, her nominal home but not quite the seascape she is used to. Ankle-deep waves and an off-course bicycle sticking upside down out of the water. 'There were some amazing moments and sailing the boat was fantastic. She was amazing. It wasn't her fault it was so hard.'

Ah, here it comes. A MacArthur whinge, immortalised by *Dead Ringers* and characterised by a stream of complaints delivered *en voyage* to camera about weather, water and what was falling off where on the boat, including the metal fitting on the mast that clonked her on the head leaving a small white scar. This, you have to say here and now, is terribly unfair. If we, as a race, have the temerity to moan about the roads, the railways, television, the French and the price of stamps, may not she, our greatest living sportswoman, have a go at 60-foot waves, Biblical hailstorms, equatorial overheating, pitiful exhaustion and her wheat allergy. A resounding 'yes' seems to be in order. 'Trying to control such a big, fast boat for so long when you're so on the edge, chasing down a record, with all that stress the whole time,' she said. 'It's so hard to describe. It's like – you know when you were a school kid and you woke up in the morning knowing you'd got an exam. You don't want any breakfast. You know that feeling? It's like that all day, every day. You can't relax. You can't chill out. You're firing this boat along and you can't get off. No matter how hard it gets.

'I had two really bad times. One in the Southern Ocean going towards Cape Horn. We were blasted by hail that sounded like gunfire and for three days and nights the wind blew with such force we were in danger of going over. The wind was up and down like a heart-rate monitor. I think I got twenty minutes' sleep in two days. The only things that kept me going were adrenalin and belief, I suppose. And then the second time was when we had just rounded Cape Horn. It's like the throat of the Southern Ocean as all this sea is squeezed between the Cape and the tip of Antarctica. Everything is accelerated through there. The conditions were horrendous. Huge seas. I had to haul the mainsail down. It was a nightmare to get it back up again. I had to do fourteen sail changes. I was just a wreck. I was exhausted. But there was no option.'

You do find yourself wondering whether lunacy or bravery play a predominant role in the life of MacArthur. Clearly both are in living operation. But she is the last person to ask. She can't see the courage at all. 'I'm not brave. I just choose to do things that push me very hard. That's not bravery, that's a choice. You think, "This is going to be really hard, so I'll go and do it". Now where's the logic in that? Now, real bravery is in the kids I go sailing with four weekends a year. Kids with cancer and leukaemia. When you see what they deal with every day, with big smiles and such energy, it's such a lesson. So humbling. It's taught me a lot. It really has. All that round-the-world sailing has taught me is that I must be crazy.'

Yes, but crazy in such a practical way. Something went wrong. It always does. This time it was the generators, crucial to keep the batteries charged. The first one was eating too much oil, then the back-up began overheating. Huge problem. Most of us would call in a heating engineer, but since that option was not available she took a heater apart and conducted cold air into the generator from outside the boat through an old engine exhaust. Now who would have thought of that? 'A lot of it's common sense,' she said airily. 'You've just got to understand engines. I spent a long time just kicking round the garage with my dad, building lawn mowers. I love practical things. I love working with my hands. There's a huge buzz when you fix something.'

You realise she had the perfect childhood in terms of preparation for the life she has chosen to live. That intense little schoolchild, obsessively hoarding her money to buy her first boat, content with mash and gravy day after day, fiddling with carburettors with ferocious fascination, spending hours at a time building lone dens in the woods. It is distinctly possible to see her as hermit-in-waiting. 'No, no,' she disagreed. 'I was always happy on my own. Even as a kid I'd be on the floor in the kitchen building something, talking to myself. I was never desperate to be with friends all the time. But people do get the wrong idea. This is more of a team sport than I could ever explain. I'm not escaping. That is so not the case.'

Indeed, for all that this twenty-eight-year-old woman is positively frightening in her scale of accomplishment, she is actually rather a sweetie. She has looked into the abyss on our behalf and returned. I'm expecting the harrowing gaze of the Ancient Mariner. I get a rolled-up map (autographed) for the children and a lift to the ferry terminal. But never underestimate the unnerving quality of her experience. It is the one question that threw her, glazing her eyes, if not with tears then a veil. We were talking innocently enough about the sheer physical toll of the voyage. 'It's brutal. It's brutal,' she was saying. 'You're never sleeping properly. You're not eating properly. You take supplements but some of those I couldn't take on this trip because I was saving oil for the broken generator. I ran it, in the end, on olive oil and rapeseed oil which I'd taken for my own use.

'It's physically and mentally exhausting. My leg was absolutely black with bruises because you end up jamming it between the mast and the sail when you go up the mast to stop yourself breaking a bone in your arm or your leg. The mast is huge, absolutely huge, and the movement at the top, a hundred feet up, is very violent. Trying to hold on to the sail a hundred feet up the mast – you just get beaten to bits. I mean, it's not swaying, it's punching. Once when I went up there the team doctor was really concerned. I drank three litres of isotonic sports drink but I was still hugely dehydrated from the heat, the effort and the protective clothing you have to wear up there. That night I was losing it completely.' What did she mean, losing it completely? That was the question that confounded her. 'I'm not great discussing it,' she said eventually, hunched as though all four points of her compass had been pulled protectively inward. 'It's not something that's particularly easy to go back to. You're not just distressed and screaming. You're absolutely empty. You have nothing left inside.

'Well, sleep deprivation is used in torture, isn't it? It does things to you that even you don't understand yourself. It was so much more intense a level than anything I had experienced on the Vendée Globe, my first round-the-world race alone. The mental stress was massive. You'd think that four years on and with two hundred thousand miles' experience on the sea, it would be all right, but you put your body and mind through so much more at that high speed. The motion of the boat was so aggressive. It was like driving a car off-road, extremely fast over rough terrain, hanging on to the steering wheel while being thrown around, only outside it's pitch black and you've got no windscreen, no wipers and no headlights.'

Put like that, most of us would rather go shopping. That may explain the almost mythical hold Dame Ellen exerts on her admirers in Britain and France. She is boldly going where few would dare to follow, in the best traditions of Columbus and Captain Kirk. She is seen not simply as an athlete, but a heroine, a buster of records and breaker of gender taboos. David Beckham, no less, phoned her when she landed home safely to say he had been following her progress and well done. 'He's very sweet,' she said. But she regards her sporting canonisation with suspicion.

Good for business, bad for the brain. 'You let a lot of that go over your head. I don't think it's healthy. It's amazingly touching but I don't know how to deal with it. I really don't want to change. Anonymity is a very precious thing.'

And gone forever. She knows that. 'I came back from the Vendée Globe four years ago to a very different life.' It was the price she paid for chasing down the dream that stalked her throughout her childhood and teens – that of sailing alone around the world. But though she was now open to the gaze of the world, at least she was curiously released to enjoy life a little more. 'I became more of an eighteen year old after the Vendée Globe than I had ever been in my teens. I chilled out. I became less intense. I even got drunk. To the point of throwing up. But not much.' She was still Ellen, all set to chase down other dreams.

Sporting Champion: Ellen MacArthur – Single-handed non-stop circumnavigation world record (2005).

MARTIN PIPE – NATIONAL HUNT TRAINERS' CHAMPIONSHIP

MOULD-BREAKER PIPE HANDS OVER THE REINS

Brough Scott, 30 April 2006

It began with a horse called Hit Parade. For a while, though, Martin Pipe was anything but top of the charts. To understand the mould-breaking drive behind the record-busting career you have to appreciate how unsuccessful and uncertain Pipe was at the start. He talks of his 'humble beginnings', but that gives a false picture. He was the son of the genial and cunning West

Country bookie Dave Pipe, began work clerking in one of his father's string of shops and was set up with a blue Rolls-Royce registered MCP 1 when his training operation was only just out of the joke stage.

This may sound absurd about someone awarded the CBE for his unprecedented fifteen training titles, thirty-five Cheltenham victories, 4,000 winners, but part of Martin Pipe's dynamic was an inferiority complex in comparison to his father. Another was an almost 'chippy' wish to find things out for himself rather than pursue the old-school follow-the-leader education normally deemed fit for the racehorse trainer. This meant that the operation he founded in Somerset at Nicolashayne was entirely self-taught and built at first on his own mistakes. In the wash of tributes to the great sea of Pipe success most have forgotten that when he began training in 1974 (after a singularly unsuccessful one-winner riding career) it took him until 1979 to get into double figures for a season, and until 1983 to get out of the twenties.

'Look,' he said in 1990 after logging the fourth of his fifteen titles, 'I'd never got on a horse until I was eighteen and then I promptly fell off the other side. When we started with point-to-pointers I didn't know anything except for bookmaking. I'd never even worked in another yard. So I just read books, tried to analyse and carried on from there. We are only just beginning. There are so many things that we don't know about the working of a horse.' By then he had already evolved the basis of his system and, like all mould-breakers, it was founded on a mistrust of the status quo, on having to accept the two most common of jockey excuses that 'there was no pace' (if the race was slow) or that the horse 'blew up' (if the pace was fast). Not being inculcated with the traditional 'long canter-long gallop' method, he installed a wide four-furlong (there wasn't room for further) uphill all-weather gallop on which his horses breezed up three abreast, hacked back down and did it again. Pipe had brought interval training to the jumping game.

The results began to become sensational. In the 1986–87 season he first became champion trainer with 106 winners. Two seasons later he saddled 243 and many of his fellow trainers were seething with resentment as the shape of jump racing and jump horses was transformed in front of their eyes. How could these greyhound-lean horses blaze off in front and keep finding extra? Unable to admit someone like this little limping bookie's son, with his former table tennis-playing side-kick Chester Barnes, could have reinvented the training manual, they resorted to the oldest of jealous refrains. Martin must be 'giving them something'. People who should have known better insisted that Martin was red-cell blood doping in the style of Lasse Viren despite the fact that this was anatomically impossible as a horse, unlike a human, already has a thirty per cent extra red-cell count in their spleen. Embittered rivals even fuelled an ITV *Cook Report* programme from which Pipe emerged correctly unscathed. I remember writing a piece entitled 'When will the losers learn?' in which stable jockey Peter Scudamore said: 'The reason his horses win more races is that they are fitter.'

Anyone visiting a leading jump trainer's yard nowadays will see how prophetic Scudamore was. All of them, especially the new champion Paul Nicholls, have developed their own short uphill training work benches, which have been the Pipe legacy along with the records that include every big race, bar the Cheltenham Gold Cup. It has been an awesome career, if not one in which his relations with his public were entirely comfortable. Even the nature of his leaving, a direct call to Channel 4's *The Morning Line* programme on the day his long-term rival Nicholls was at last to be crowned champion, could even be taken as a touch attention-seeking as well as an understandable wish to hand over to his son David with a significant flourish.

Pipe was a man on the edge and he found his perfect foil in the equally obsessive Tony McCoy with whom he shared so many triumphs. McCoy, a guest on *The Morning Line*, was as shocked as everybody, but then led the tributes. 'I would just like to thank Martin for everything he has done for me,' said the eleven-times champion jockey. 'I have learnt so much from working with him. He was a brilliant boss and racing will be the worse off without him.' But while Pipe hasn't been in the most robust of health he is still likely to play a major if less-stressful role under the banner of the son in whom he and his wife Carol have such justifiable pride. After more than thirty relentless years, he may even allow us to see more of his softer side. Maybe he, and we, deserve it.

Sporting Champion: Martin Pipe – 15 National Hunt Trainers' Championships (1988–89, 1989–90, 1990–91, 1991–92, 1992–93, 1995–96, 1996–97, 1997–98, 1998–99, 1999–2000, 2000–01, 2001–02, 2002–03, 2003–04, 2004–05).

MAY

AYRTON SENNA – SAN MARINO GRAND PRIX

FREE SPIRIT WHO BECAME A SLAVE TO HIS OBSESSION

Michael Calvin, 3 May 1994

To value life, to understand the fatal attraction of Formula One, you flaunt your track pass and take a narrow, dusty path, lined with pine trees. It leads to the end of the straight preceding the Tamburello curve, which will forever be associated with the death of Ayrton Senna. Isolated from the crowds, you stand behind a waist-high concrete barrier and a wire fence, with a fire-suited marshal for company. Your senses are somehow sharpened. The noise of unseen cars, accelerating from the start line on the Imola circuit, initially intrigues you. It excites you as it increases in intensity. Eventually, despite the precaution of earplugs, it consumes you. The drivers are pin-pricks, blurs of crash-helmeted colour. It is difficult to swivel your head sufficiently fast to follow their progress. The danger is tangible, the margin for error infinitesimal. As the cars disappear around the bend, the air is suddenly thick with the syrupy smell of fuel, the incense of motorsport.

There is a thrilling intimacy about the moment. It surpasses being ringside at a heavyweight title fight, where being showered with sweat and specks of blood is an occupational hazard. It is a privilege far greater than admission to the winners' dressing room on FA Cup final day. It evokes awe, though not in the sense of that generated by Nick Faldo's pursuit of perfection, or Steffi Graf's domination of her sport. It is a primeval form of admiration, torn from the heart. It helps to explain why Senna was my favourite sportsman, the most intriguing of the thousands I have interviewed. For all his faults and foibles, he had a depth of character, a breadth of vision and a freedom of spirit without equal. He was easy to misunderstand, impossible to *really* know. He was a mass of compelling contradictions.

He was unpopular, unnervingly self-righteous. He was insensitive, inordinately aware of his financial muscle. Yet he was universally admired, unfailingly polite to those he respected. He had an intuitive grasp of his audience, and insisted his charitable work go unpublicised. He was a mystical character who periodically portrayed himself as a martyr. He did not really belong to a sporting world, populated by mediocrities. His pursuit of truth, of self-knowledge, was more suited to the seminary than the racetrack.

I often studied him on the grid in the final minutes before a race. He would sit in the cockpit, his hands clasped as if in prayer, exuding a Zen-like calm. His was not the aggressive concentration of a Linford Christie, but his dark, expressive eyes would stare beyond those hovering around him. He was impervious to attention. 'For me, the only way to be stronger is to concentrate deeply,' he once explained, tellingly. 'You must think of everything in this enormous turmoil at the start. It is wrong to recognise people, except your mechanics, perhaps. People always think that the start of the race is something terrible, that your heart beats like mad, that your brain is about to explode. But it is a totally unreal moment; it is like a dream, like entering another world. Your spirit goes and the body sets itself free.' The words capture the man. Intelligent, intense. Thoughtful to the point of being spiritual. Little wonder his grasp of mortality, highlighted by references to his religious beliefs, became a matter of acrimonious debate.

Alain Prost articulated the case for the opposition when he made the observation that: 'Ayrton has a small problem. He thinks he can't kill himself because he believes in God and I think that's dangerous for other drivers.' I still consider that to be a simplistic judgment, clouded by the unworthy emotions of a personal rivalry so poisonous that Senna desecrated the traditions of their sport by deliberately running into his erstwhile team-mate in the 1990 Japanese Grand Prix.

The Brazilian was a devout Christian – he preferred to worship on his own because 'only then can I find peace' – and devoured books on theology. He was unafraid of statements of faith, saying: 'If you have God on your side, everything becomes clear. White becomes white again and black becomes black. You realise what is really important in life.' But, above all, he had an uncanny ability to define his own limits. He was intrigued by the sublime moments, when he would be driving so flawlessly it was as if his job required no conscious thought. He would feel as if the car was on railway tracks, at speeds surpassing 200mph. His subconscious might have suggested he was invulnerable, but he forced himself to respond to an instinctive sense of danger. He would slow down because he realised he was 'over the level I considered reasonable'.

When he raced, he thought in his native Portuguese. But when he tested his cars, he thought in English, the language of his pit crew. When he held court, switching between seven different languages, he was the epitome of self-containment. Of course, there was a price to be paid. He wept when reminded of the friends he had ignored, in his single-minded assault on his sport. He was often lonely, a slave to his obsession. Dennis Rushen, who owned the Formula One team for whom Senna raced in 1982, feared the worst. 'I want to see him quit before he kills himself,' he admitted at the height of the Brazilian's fame. 'That's always a fear I have. You can want it too much on just that one lap. He wants it more than anyone else, doesn't he? You never know in this business. Your luck runs out one day.'

Sporting Champion: Ayrton Senna – 3 Formula One World Championships (1988, 1990, 1991).

ROGER BANNISTER – OXFORD UNIVERSITY v AAA

THE RECORD-BREAKERS' RECORD-BREAKER

Andrew Baker, 6 May 2004

Half a century after Roger Bannister ran the first sub-four-minute mile, he sat down in the drawing room of his Oxford home with Sebastian Coe, who himself held the world record for the mile three times. Although separated by a generation and more – Coe first held the mile record twenty-five years after Bannister set his celebrated mark – the two former athletes have a great deal in common. Both applied a cerebral approach to middle-distance running, Bannister drawing on his background as a medical student and Coe employing unusual training methods and ground-breaking physiological analysis. Both have gone on to successful careers beyond the track, Bannister as an eminent neurologist and Master of Pembroke College, Oxford, Coe as a politician and sports administrator.

As they chatted and pored over ancient training schedules, however, surrounded by the mementoes of Bannister's two successful careers, a stronger bond was apparent: shared membership of the brotherhood of the middle-distance runner, an exclusive society whose members know more than most, more than they would perhaps wish to know, of the agonies which are involved in trying to run a mile faster than it has been run before. Their discussion covered the strengths and weaknesses of their rivals, training techniques, physiology and the athletic capabilities of our distant ancestors. And it started with the surprising notion that the four-minute mile might not have been Bannister's greatest run.

Sebastian Coe: Everybody talks about the four-minute mile, but I've been going through your times and I think that your most impressive run was actually over three-quarters of a mile.

Roger Bannister: I agree.

SC: Which was two minutes fifty-two seconds.

RB: Two fifty-two nine.

SC: Two fifty-two nine would see a lot of people off today. That is still world-record schedule. It's probably heresy to say it in this town, but I think in terms of athletic achievement that is ahead of the sub-four. It tells me that you were naturally very talented, much more so than you have admitted, and that the quality of your training was way ahead of its time.

RB: Other times, other customs, that's the nub of it. No runner runs faster than he has to. The task is to set up a world record or to beat opponents, and the training is such as will enable the athlete to do that. So I was forced to run the four-minute mile as a preparation for having to race against John Landy [of Australia]. He'd done 4.02, 4.03 six times in the previous year, so I absolutely had to be able to run that. I was really aiming at the race with John Landy in Vancouver [at the Empire Games], that in my view was far more important than the four-minute mile.

SC: John has always said the same thing to me.

RB: I think he was the stronger runner, but he didn't break the record in Australia because he didn't have the pacing and the assistance. The challenge of your contemporaries drives the record down. You knew that you had to be pretty smart to beat

Steve Ovett, and you said that he was naturally probably the best ever runner in terms of style, physique, range of distance.

SC: I think he was. In terms of my own training, I didn't sense, when I was fifteen or sixteen, that I was doing anything dramatically different, although I clearly was. Because at that stage in my career I didn't have the intellectual breadth to recognise it. I knew that fellow athletes in my club were running sixty or seventy miles a week, while I was doing speed drills and hills. I realise now that what I was doing was in a way on a different planet from the orthodox thinking. How aware were you that some of the stuff which you were doing was twenty to thirty years ahead of what had even been contemplated before?

RB: I simply took what the Swedes had done. They were doing interval running, on soft surfaces, and they did not regard it as necessary to have a stopwatch. You could call it common sense. What you're doing is trying to liberate the total aerobic and anaerobic capacity of somebody in four minutes, or one-forty-something or whatever. If the person is healthy, and has led an active life, I can't see that quantity is really important. You can see from my schedule that I did absolutely nothing for five days [before the record attempt]. That was in order to increase the specialness of the event. To prepare me for something which was exceptional.

SC: I love the way your training schedules are on obstetrics forms.

RB: I was doing obstetrics at the time, and I wasn't interested in obstetrics. My attitude was that I wouldn't race unless I was going to race at my best. I wanted to feel special when the gun went and when the bell went. That was why I often did fast last laps which weren't necessary. I just thought, 'Keep it sharp'.

SC: There's too little experimentation in races. I used to use a county championship for crazy things: if my fastest first lap in an

800 metres was forty-nine seconds, I would try one year to find out what it felt like if I went through the first lap in forty-seven seconds. And at 600 metres, I found out.

RB: When I was training I was trying to run as hard as I could at speeds faster than I would ever have to run, in intervals. The effect of doing that was to impose my own mental drive, rather than having coaches with lists saying, 'Today we do this and this'. It was highly specialised, and if I had overdone it, and felt unable to do anything the next day, I would have to drop the schedule back a bit. I now know the physiology of sport, and it transpires that we [middle-distance runners] have an unusual mixture of fast and slow fibres. The basis of what you might call our gift is the genetic make-up of our muscles, more important than height or size. We have to give credit to our parents. It was only late in life that my father told me that he had won the mile at his school. And, perhaps more interesting, that each time he did it he collapsed.

SC: My father was not a runner, but a more than useful road cyclist. What's your resting pulse-rate?

RB: Not as low as yours. It's in the forties. Of course it goes up to 160, and that is the point where the collapse of any athlete occurs. But it is not just a cardiac collapse. I think you might agree, it is a total collapse of the integrated system – legs, heart, lungs. This is where science is way behind the athlete, because we've spent hundreds of thousands of years putting these things together, because the one who has got them together escapes from the tiger and catches the mammoth. Evolutionary survival. It's the brain, I suppose, that drives the whole system. But you don't have to think about any of these things. All you have to think about is the target: winning.

Sporting Champion: Roger Bannister – 1 British Empire & Commonwealth Games (1954); 1 European Championship (1954).

SIR ALEX FERGUSON – PREMIER LEAGUE

FIREBRAND WHO USED ADVERSITY TO
BUILD A DYNASTY

Paul Hayward, 9 May 2013

You can still see the boy in Sir Alex Ferguson, even now we have reached the end. The elder statesman who called a halt after twenty-seven years at Manchester United needs a hip replacement and feels he has won all his battles. But in his bursts of laughter, his lust for life, you can still pick out the young Glasgow firebrand who rose to become the greatest manager in British football. Some people have an essence, a spirit that survives the ravages of age. Ferguson's is not diminished, however scared he might be of retirement. It was there in his early phase of building flotsam teams in Scottish outposts and it shone when Eric Cantona, Roy Keane and Cristiano Ronaldo crossed the threshold at Old Trafford. Ferguson loved big personalities because he is one himself. His life has been a search for kindred spirits who could play from the soul and the imagination.

Unusually, though, United's great leader combines the non-conforming instincts of a trade union radical with the controlling urges of a factory owner or dictator. From his first day as a manager at East Stirlingshire in 1974, where players earned £60 a week, he learnt that football management was largely about control (a word he prefers to power). Either the players are in control or the manager is: a truth he applied with brutal force in clashes with Roy Keane and David Beckham. The caricature of Ferguson as a fulminating bully annoys his family because they know his career would have ended long before now had the 'hairdryer' been his only psychological tactic. In his last ten years he would be just as likely to ignore or 'cold-shoulder' a player who had been needlessly sent off or committed some other transgression. He used ice as much as fire to direct the thinking of his players in directions that would shape their futures positively. To span the ages from East Stirling and St Mirren to Ronaldo and Robin van Persie and two Champions League wins over thirty-nine years in management is a stunning confirmation of the link between the top and bottom of the game.

In his last ten years at United the challenge became one of managing constant and seismic change as United passed from plc to Glazer-owned debt mountain and multi-millionaire players became one-man corporations with immensely powerful entourages. By changing as the game changed, Ferguson honed his talent for working two steps ahead of his contemporaries. He saw a team in multiple dimensions: the XI he wrote on that day's team-sheet and the United side of twelve and twenty-four months hence. Only once in his twenty-seven years at Old Trafford did he deviate badly from his principle of constant building: in the relatively fallow years of 2004–06 before a second Champions League-winning side was built around Wayne Rooney and Ronaldo.

The breathtaking scope of his work starts with comparative failure as a player, and especially his nondescript spell at Rangers, the stage on which he hoped to make his name as a Scottish warrior forward to rank with his hero, Denis Law. 'The adversity gave me a sense of determination that has shaped my life,' he said. 'I made up my mind that I would never give in.' Plenty fail as players – in their own minds, at any rate – without going on to win forty-nine trophies, thirteen Premier League titles and two European Cups.

Scottish football alone might have immolated Ferguson's dream of becoming a great general of the game. His confrontational style and zero tolerance for half-heartedness might have earned him more enemies than any young hopeful manager could hope to deal with. But from the start there was cleverness to go with the truculence. A carousing striker told he would 'never play for the club again' would be left to dangle just long enough for him to return to the side desperate and grateful – and to reward Ferguson with a hat-trick. In the shipyards of Govan, the Glasgow pubs he ran and all the teams he managed, Ferguson accepted that conflict was unavoidable. His disputatious nature is partly an acknowledgement that consensus is seldom possible in an organisation of perhaps 500 people, in which results on the field of play shape countless families' lives. A believer in clans or tribes himself, he pulled United's wagons in tight. Those inside the circle could expect to be defended. Those outside were hostile forces unless they could prove otherwise, which they almost never could.

Aberdeen were Ferguson's transition to Britain, to Europe, to the big tests of football, which he negotiated with Jock Stein's wisdom filed away in his brain. Stein taught Ferguson how not to handle players, how to see the world through their eyes. He also regaled him with countless funny stories about Jimmy Johnstone – 'Wee Jinky' – the Celtic winger who would cause Stein to stare at his phone on a Friday evening in expectation of a phone call from the police. Ferguson is never happier than when reciting anecdotes from those early days. His comic sense may have kept him sane. He is drawn not to automatons but funny and cheeky people. His staff are not terrified of him, except when he enters one of his thunderous moods for the specific purpose of putting something right. They still tease him about 'Ralphy Milne', by consent the least successful purchase of his Manchester United career, because it is more fun than constantly praising him for picking out Ronaldo.

But even Ferguson's energy and appetite for a fight was

never going to defy the laws of time. The physical toll exerted
by Manchester City's dramatic late win in the 2011–12 Premier
League title race was unusually severe. More galling than City's
first championship win for forty-four years was the knowledge that
United had tossed away a commanding lead. With the loss of power
in Manchester itself came an even more painful disappointment:
a failure of strength on the run-in, which has been a hallmark
of Ferguson's teams since his first Premier League triumph in
1993. So the summer of 2012 was one of angst and self-reproach
which offered Ferguson a choice: abandon ship straight away or
go in one more time to avenge City's impertinent late surge. He
chose the second, more difficult course, but with an internal voice
doubtless warning that these challenges could not be faced down
indefinitely. To knock City back down into a subservient role in
the metropolis would complete the set of uprisings quelled. 'I've
still got a wee bit of anger in me, thinking of how we threw the
league away,' Ferguson told the Harvard Business School, who
were sufficiently intrigued by his mastery of management to
commission a study of his record and methods. 'My motivation
to the players will be that we can't let City beat us twice in a row.'

The precise arc of his trophy-winning years started with the
Scottish First Division with St Mirren in 1976–77 and ended
with United's twentieth English championship in May 2013. In
between he broke the duopoly of Rangers and Celtic in Scotland
with Aberdeen and found United in arguably the perfect state to
forge his reputation in world football. Imagine Ferguson taking
over a smoothly run, teetotal, talent-packed United back in 1986.
To remake the faded home of Best, Law and Charlton in his own
image he had to first smash what it had become. For United to
put its drink down and cut its hair the club had to become an
extension of Ferguson's own fierce and restless personality. This
was the glory of the opportunity he was given, and he survived the

early turmoil to construct a majestic team around Mark Hughes, Bryan Robson, Cantona, Paul Ince and Andrei Kanchelskis.

Liverpool were the first to be brought down. Ferguson knew the Anfield aura well from his visits with Aberdeen. To him, Liverpool were a bastion where surrendering possession of the ball would bring long periods of spectating. English football's dominant club were synonymous with strong men (Shankly, Paisley, Dalglish) and billboard-topping talents: Souness, Rush, Beardsley, Barnes. Ferguson arrived in Manchester as the bright young star of Scottish management with what could be described as an inferiority complex in relation to Liverpool. He has no recollection of saying he would 'knock them off their perch' but the sentiment was there, and acted upon. By the time United began their run of thirteen League titles and two Champions League crowns Liverpool were already in shadow. New forces were arrayed against him: Arsène Wenger's jazzed-up Arsenal, then the Chelsea of Roman Abramovich and finally City, who seemed intent on claiming the very soul of Manchester with their vast Etihad Campus and local emphasis.

To endure all this, Ferguson has relied on a cast of allies: a republican guard led by Ryan Giggs, Paul Scholes and Gary Neville, who speak truth to power and spread the kind of values Ferguson built his final decade on. Youth development, self-improvement, loyalty and progression through science. So thorough and driven has Ferguson become in the athletic sphere that Wayne Rooney's occasional lapses into chubbiness offend the very spirit of the manager's work, as he demonstrated by leaving 'Wazza' on the bench. Mourinho's Chelsea caught United at a time when they were lulled into buying players off the peg (Kleberson, Eric Djemba-Djemba), before Ferguson redirected the emphasis into finding pearls that could be polished at Carrington. Phil Jones is perhaps the best recent example of a player spotted young at another club (Blackburn Rovers) and seized by United with decisive speed. Rooney and Ronaldo are earlier examples. The internationalisation of United's scouting network was another example of Ferguson extending the range of his work to take account of changes in the industry.

Twelve years after retirement first entered his head (the U-turn of 2002 stopped Sven-Göran Eriksson becoming United manager), United fans can look back on a decade in which Ferguson's teams won a Champions League final against Chelsea in Moscow, home town of Abramovich, and in which the lull of 2004–06 was followed by three consecutive Premier League titles from 2007–09, the last year ending with the first of two Champions League final defeats by Barcelona, Ferguson's nemesis on the biggest stage. In those years a potentially crushing assortment of challenges came and went with Ferguson still on top. Keane, who began acting like the *de facto* United manager, berating the squad's young players on MUTV and arguing with the manager and his staff when he found things not to his liking, was purged, at great emotional cost to Ferguson himself, who nevertheless knew he had won one of the biggest political struggles of his career. Beckham's burgeoning fame presented another kind of dilemma. Unlike Giggs, Scholes, Nicky Butt and the Neville brothers, Beckham looked beyond the United fence for affirmation and Ferguson began to feel the distractions in his life were undermining the footballer who had been arguably the most enthusiastic of anyone in what became known as the 'Class of '92'. The pattern was repeated: friction, crossroads, exit stage left, the player. The same was true, for other reasons, with Ruud van Nistelrooy. Contrast this with José Mourinho's difficulties at Real Madrid, where his authority was broken for the first time. Over twenty-seven years Ferguson built up such a credit-line of success that no player or cabal could have any hope of defeating him. Rooney successfully engineered a huge pay rise but it was no guarantee of a starting place when his performances dipped.

Throughout every reconstruction, and in all his individual dealings, Ferguson was able to employ a vast store of wisdom, experience and natural managerial talent to keep the whole organisation moving forward. With his team quizzes on trains and at meal times, his enthusiastic renditions of classic songs and his love of mischief, Ferguson might have come across to the younger players like a slightly eccentric uncle. His world is still populated by friends from Govan he has known for sixty years. When management became too consuming, and his life felt too narrow, he turned to horse racing, wine collecting and intense reading on subjects such as the Kennedy assassination and the American civil war. A developing obsession with the Turf led to the biggest crisis of his reign: a dispute with the so-called 'Coolmore mafia', who also owned shares in United, over breeding rights to the prolific Rock of Gibraltar.

His professional life conformed to the Japanese masks-of-life template. Around friends and family he is gregarious and quick to joke or sing. But the journey from home to Carrington or Old Trafford brought another mask from his bag: that of intense concentration. His ability to think on several levels at once and across ten or twelve problems simultaneously is rare in management. Without his intelligence, his passion and strength of character might not have taken him this far.

As a football romantic whose love of attacking football was fanned by the great Real Madrid sides of the 1960s, Ferguson has featured heavily in that great Spanish tradition, and not just through United's many tussles with the club of Puskas and Di Stéfano. Surely his greatest association with world-class talent – Giggs and Beckham aside – was to invest his faith in the seventeen-year-old Ronaldo when many in English football were dismissing him as a 'show pony'. In Madeira, via Lisbon, Ferguson found the player of his dreams, steering him away from theatricality and unlocking the physical courage inside. To make one of the great footballers from such raw material from another culture was Ferguson's finest individual achievement. To sell him to Real Madrid for £80 million confirmed that transformation. Somehow, too, the sale went through with United appearing broken and bereft: a mark of the club's strength, their ability to recover from setbacks. Deep in his psyche, Ferguson welcomed these chances to display his gift for recovery.

He also relished confrontations with match officials and journalists, both of whom he often suspected of working against United's interests, if only by being unfit (in the case of referees). With the media, he ceased to be comfortable with reporters when he could no longer control the discussion, or recognise more than twenty per cent of the faces staring at him in a press conference room. The life of a director, ambassador, public speaker, raconteur and grandfather now beckons. Even Ferguson himself would not pretend that it will be comfortable for him to walk away from the daily bonfire of managing United. One day soon, the camera will train itself on the United dugout and we will search in vain for the bespectacled, gum-chewing, dark-overcoat-and-zip-up-wearing autocrat who made the club an extension of his own character, and who lit up our days and nights with his brilliance and his energy. Letting go is not going to be easy, for him or us.

Sporting Champion: Sir Alex Ferguson – (selected, all Manchester United unless stated) 13 Premier Leagues (1992–93, 1993–94, 1995–96, 1996–97, 1998–99, 1999–2000, 2000–01, 2002–03, 2006–07, 2007–08, 2008–09, 2010–11, 2012–13); 5 FA Cups (1989–90, 1993–94, 1995–96, 1998–99, 2003–04); 4 League Cups (1991–92, 2005–06, 2008–09, 2009–10); 2 UEFA Champions Leagues (1998–99, 2007–08);

2 European Cup-Winners' Cups (1982–93 with Aberdeen, 1990–91);
3 Scottish Premier Divisions (1979–80, 1983–84, 1984–85 all with
Aberdeen); 4 Scottish FA Cups (1981–82, 1982–83, 1983–84, 1985–86
all with Aberdeen).

RYAN GIGGS – PREMIER LEAGUE

GIGGS TAKES CENTRE STAGE

Roy Collins, 13 May 2007

You just knew that Ryan Giggs would not turn out to be one
of those footballers who keeps his medals in a neat line on
the mantelpiece with instructions to the cleaner to run a duster
over them once a week. Players who accumulate trophies at such
a prolific rate tend not to have time for such nonsense. Sure
enough, Giggs reveals that all his medals are actually gathering
dust in the Manchester United Museum. A footballing dinosaur
at thirty-three, some thought he would have been in there
himself long ago, stuffed and mounted like a favourite pet. Giggs,
however, has cheated football's four horsemen of the apocalypse
by reinventing himself as a midfield creator, where speed of
thought is more important than speed of foot. Fans may still sing
about him running down the wing but only because 'Ryan Giggs,
Ryan Giggs, jogging just behind the two main strikers' doesn't
really scan. Mainly, however, that is where he plays these days, with
occasional memory lapses which see him firing in crosses from
the flanks.

He said: 'Playing there has extended my career because
you're not running up and down the wing all day and waiting for
someone to give you the ball. Even when I play on the wing, I'm

not playing like I did ten years ago. You use your experience and positional sense and just try to be clever, really, just to get in the right positions defensively and in attack. At seventeen, eighteen, as soon as you get the ball you're looking for the full-back because you want to beat him, but as you get older you look to add other things and I was always keen to develop my game. I looked at John Barnes, who I always admired, and the way he developed his game. You've got to develop your game because you're not going to be as quick at thirty-three as you were at eighteen, though you're probably a bit quicker in the brain.'

Giggs's brain is a blur of memories of big occasions, flashes of goals scored, chances missed, passes made. When he steps out at the new Wembley in his seventh FA Cup final, his video tape of a mind will inevitably rewind to his first final, also against Chelsea, in 1994. He said: 'That was one of the few times I enjoyed playing at Wembley because it was always sticky and dry, the grass was always long and lush and for someone who likes to dribble, it was tough. But in '94 it rained, which was a help to me. Chelsea were the best team in the first half and John Spencer hit the crossbar, but we ended up winning 4–0.'

It is not just a change of position that has acted like collagen on Giggs's career. The injection of youth into the dressing room in the form of Wayne Rooney and Cristiano Ronaldo, bringing their own sense of fashion, music and mischief, has cranked up the atmosphere and the sheer sense of fun. 'It's constant wind-ups,' said Giggs. 'Every day you walk into training, if you are wearing something dodgy, it gets hung up right in the middle of the dressing room so when you come back in, you find that everyone is taking the mickey out of a top you thought was half-decent. We have so many different characters from different backgrounds. You have the likes of Cristiano and Wayne and you've even got Nev [Gary Neville] in his own little way, walking around moaning about everything – that gives everyone a lift. I think there are certain players who have given me a new lease of life. You get a buzz from watching them play and in the past few days, I've got a real buzz from seeing the faces of Cristiano, Wayne, Darren [Fletcher] after winning their first title. I remember when I won my first championship, it's the best feeling in the world and to get that buzz from seeing their faces has definitely been a factor in enjoying my football a little more now.'

Victory at Wembley would give Giggs and his manager Sir Alex Ferguson their fourth League and Cup double, once considered an impossible feat. And even the Champions League semi-final defeat by AC Milan cannot take the gloss off that achievement, although constant failures in Europe are a blight on both men. Giggs said: 'Maybe when I'm on holiday in the summer and reflecting on the season, the Milan defeat might seem a disappointment. But we set out this season to win the Premiership and we've done that. The title was a big thing for me because I'd never gone three years without winning it before and so you do worry that you might not get another.'

With such a head full of past glories, Giggs says that he has no need to watch tapes of United's winning FA Cup finals in 1994, 1996, 1999 and 2004, although he admits to almost wearing out the tape of his wonder semi-final winner against Arsenal in 1999, which he gets out when he is feeling low or not playing well. As for all those other triumphs, nothing matters to Giggs as much as the next one. Although he could be about to equal Phil Neal's record of sixteen domestic winners' medals, he said: 'All these records don't mean a lot to me while I am playing. That's why my medals are in the museum, where they are safe. I wouldn't know what to do with them.'

Sporting Champion: Ryan Giggs – 13 Premier Leagues (1992–93,

1993–94, 1995–96, 1996–97, 1998–99, 1999–2000, 2000–01, 2002–03, 2006–07, 2007–08, 2008–09, 2010–11, 2012–13); 4 FA Cups (1993–94, 1995–96, 1998–99, 2003–04); 4 Football League Cups (1991–92, 2005–06, 2008–09, 2009–10); 2 UEFA Champions Leagues (1998–99, 2007–08).

PIPPA FUNNELL – BADMINTON HORSE TRIALS

STAYING A JUMP AHEAD

Sue Mott, 7 June 2003

Pippa Funnell turns negatives into positives. It makes her sound like some kind of ionising device in a science laboratory. In fact, she spent years being all too human on horseback in a field. On Derby Day it is not inappropriate to celebrate that other form of equine-inspired madness – three-day eventing – when Britain has turned up yet another superhuman performer in the discipline. 'Oh!' she gasps, neat and trim as a pin with a small pearl in either ear like a precious punctuation mark. 'I'm not in the same league as Lucinda Green or Ginny Leng or Mark Todd. They're up there on a pedestal.' She is not on a pedestal in her own mind. She's sitting at the kitchen table in a farm near Dorking. It does not make the comparison untrue, however. Funnell has ridden, literally and metaphorically, through a period of public neurosis and private trauma to become apparently invincible.

Small girls in jodhpurs squeak at the sight of their thirty-four-year-old heroine aboard one of her four-star horses, Jurassic Rising, who is not quite up there with Supreme Rock ('Rocky' she calls him in unconscious tribute to the qualities he shares with Sylvester Stallone) but still impressive enough to make the

Pony Club swoon. And so they should. As role models go, there can be few finer than the great Mrs Funnell, even though she once couldn't see a tricky fence at Badminton without imagining all the ways she might mishandle it. And then it came true. She stopped, she stalled, she fell off. There was a barely a man-made pond she hadn't sat in.

'It all went belly up. Pear-shaped,' she said. 'I was definitely affected by nerves. I found it very hard. Because my dressage was so strong I was always in the lead or up with the leaders going into the cross-country and so everyone noticed where I was failing. It just seemed to happen over and over again. I'd think, "Yes, I'm up there but it won't be long before I make a mistake". And it wasn't. It started to wreak havoc with my confidence. And this went on for five or six years. I was so demoralised. To a degree I was just obsessed by it. What depressed me most was the thought that I was letting everyone down. So much so that at one stage I thought, "Do I want to do this anymore?" I thought maybe I'm just cut out for producing the horses and leave the riding to someone else. But in the end I was just too selfish. I thought I'm not going to chuck away years of work.' She fought back, against the trickiest enemy in the world: herself.

This is classic Funnell strategy. Her life story is full of it. Basically, it distils down to iron will. It may come in petite and feminine packing, but no one wins Badminton twice in a row (2002 and 2003) without the quality of determination that hauled Sir Steve Redgrave to the finish line at the Sydney Olympics or A.P. McCoy to the winning post at any given National Hunt meeting. Witness: her father did not want her to leave Wadhurst College at sixteen and go to ride horses with the trainer, Ruth McMullan, in Norfolk. They argued like mad but look who won. Miss Nolan, as she was then, went to Norfolk. 'I rode up to ten horses a day, every day. Everything from thoroughbred race horses to tiny show ponies. I was constantly being bucked off because I was the mug who didn't mind breaking the horses in.'

It was an important experience. It began the process that makes her one of the most formidable dressage exponents in the world. A particularly rigorous world where she pays attention to the tiniest sponge of finger, the merest squeeze of leg or the imperceptible straightening of shoulders to make her mounts as hoof-step perfect as Fred Astaire. It is her forté. And, of course, for a while, her bane, as it made everyone take notice. It was McMullan who introduced her to Sir Barnaby, an inspired piece of matchmaking. He was small and she was a teenager, but what they lacked in size and age between them was vastly compensated for by mutual courage, intelligence and heart. In 1987 they won the European Young Riders Championship in Poland. Three years later they were fifth at Badminton. When you see the old footage of a young girl crossing the finish line, throwing her arms round her horse's neck, sobbing into his mane for pure joy and falling off all at the same time, the measure of her passion is tangible.

They were a wonderful combination and the package was merely enhanced when Miss Nolan married the international showjumper, William Funnell, at the age of twenty-five. 'William helped enormously,' she said time and again. They moved in together to farm, mutually supportive but separately competitive. William helped with her training, particularly over jumps and he tried to reawaken her ailing confidence. 'He was brilliant. He kept telling me over and over again how well I had done and how well I could do again, but you know what it's like when people close to you tell you that. You don't really believe them. I was getting quite a bit of stick from people.' One of them was Mark Phillips, who thought she needed to go back to basics to reinvent her style when Sir Barnaby retired. 'People looked at me and said, "Gosh, she's not going to make it as a World Championship rider after all".'

Into this desperate mix came a sports psychologist, Nicky Heath, one of a breed not entirely trusted in the wider sporting world. To hell with it, thought Funnell, I'll be a guinea pig, what do I have to lose? 'I didn't lie on a couch or anything. I sat at her kitchen table actually, drinking tea and just having a chat. What came to light was that I was thinking too much. I'd walk the course – say at Badminton or Burghley – four times and just before the competition I'd have a sleepless night convinced that taking the water jump would be like flinging myself off Beachy Head. Now, apart from the time I am actually walking the course when I am completely focused, I don't let myself dwell on it at all. If I find myself sliding into those thoughts, I play games on my mobile phone. The snake game – I'm up to the highest level and the fastest speed. People may say it's crazy, but it works. In other words, I've dealt with the nerves by putting a system in my head.'

The transformation was little less than astonishing. She was a silver medallist at the Sydney Olympics and was 'gutted' not to win a team gold. She won the European Championships on 'Rocky' the following year. In 2002 she competed in fourteen events, won four (including Badminton), came second four times, third twice and received a bronze medal at the World Equestrian Games in Spain. In 2003 she has already won two legs of a potential four-star triple crown, triumphant in Lexington and Badminton. If she wins Burghley she will earn £160,000, a Rolex and a place in equine posterity. 'It would be nice,' she said, dreamily. 'It would be lovely.'

It would. And it would be all the more remarkable because for a spell in 2001, William left her for the wife of a French international showjumper. The affair is all over and she is as straight on the subject as she has been on any one of her lifetime ambitions. 'We've always got on incredibly well,' she said in temperate retrospect. 'And then we had this little blip. But then I think realistically that

I don't know of one single marriage where there hasn't been one little blip at some stage. I stayed strong because you either did or you didn't. There wasn't an option. You either let yourself be beaten or you stay strong. You have to, don't you?' Yes you do, but who does? Funnell did. 'I didn't hate Willie. No, no, no, never.' He returned, he was forgiven and now they are thinking very seriously about having children. 'Here's my husband,' she said, as he walked into the kitchen, properly dishevelled and mud-streaked from a hard morning's work over jumps. 'We definitely are keen to have children, aren't we?' asked his wife. He was. 'We'll get ruthless about it at some point,' she said. He is not discomfited by this conversation at all, even when Funnell confides that we had been talking about their 'blip'. 'That's history,' he said politely and we quickly moved on.

For an illustrious couple, survivors of controversy and resplendent in success, they are not the least fraction showy. We are not in Beckham territory. There is no trace of sequinned bustiers and when she presents a prize on Ladies' Day at Royal Ascot (as she has been asked to do) she will be decorously encased in duck-egg blue rather than a small lampshade and 6-inch stilettos. Life with horses tends to pull you back to earth. Funnell returned victorious from a trip to France where she won an event in Saumur on another of her up-and-coming horses, Walk On Star. If she felt rather pleased with herself, that was soon countermanded by the discovery that the breeches she had piled into a bin bag for washing had been carted away by the dustmen.

'I don't feel any different,' she says on the subject of fame and, more to the point, popularity. She is truly admired and revered. You can see why. She broke into tears at Badminton this year but it had nothing to do with herself. Someone had just told her that her beloved Supreme Rock could be considered an all-time great with back-to-back wins at both Badminton and the European

Championships. 'That set me off. It made me think, "God, what an honour". It wasn't for me I was crying. And then I was gutted that he'll be too old to ride in the next World Championships which are three years away. He deserves a world championship but he'll be eighteen by then.' Will he hold it against her? She laughs. 'He won't know at all, will he? He's not human after all.' She is and has lived to tell a remarkable, far-from-over tale.

Sporting Champion: Pippa Funnell – 3 Badminton Horse Trials (2002, 2003, 2005); 1 Burghley Horse Trials (2003); 5 European Championships (1999 – 2, 2001 – 2, 2003).

STANLEY MATTHEWS – FA CUP

MATTHEWS LAUGHS AT AGE AND SELECTORS

Frank Coles, 4 May 1953

Coronation year Cup final will be remembered for all time as the match Stanley Matthews won, and in doing so gave the answer to the England selectors, who omitted him from the team against Scotland a fortnight ago and from the party about to leave for South America. On the second issue there is time for amends to be made. The too-old-at-thirty-eight cry was stifled for all time by Matthews himself in the grandstand finish he staged against Bolton. If, as I understand, Matthews is invited to make the tour, all the football world will be delighted.

I have watched his climb to the heights since the day he started twenty-two years ago. One of the fittest men in football, he should in five years' time still be selling his dummies and laughing at age. Quite apart from the Matthews masterpiece, there has never been a Wembley final to match this one. It began with the drama of Lofthouse's first-minute goal and ended with Perry's last-minute match winner for Blackpool, 4–3 victors. Then there was the tragedy of Farm's two goalkeeping blunders and the sight of hopping [injured] Bell, heading a hero's goal. Just one of these incidents would have been enough to feature in the story of any normal big match. On this never-to-be-forgotten afternoon there were half-a-dozen other thrills and in nearly all of them Matthews drew the 100,000-strong crowd to him like a magnet. Matthews the maestro. Matthews the Wizard of the Dribble. Old Man Matthews thrown into the discard by the selectors – the captions have been used over and over again. Now it was Matthews, the complete footballer in the flesh who inspired the greatest rally Wembley has known in thirty years.

When, ten minutes after the interval, Bell headed home Holden's ideal cross from the right wing to put Bolton 3–1 up, Blackpool's stock stood at zero and it was as plain as anything could be that Garrett, Robinson (playing his first Cup-tie) and Perry, the whole of the team's left flank, were rapidly losing touch. None but a player of genius could have saved this critical situation. Matthews saw his opportunity, seized it with both feet and without any exaggeration played Bolton out of the match in the gripping climax.

Blackpool's rally, which was to end in glorious triumph, began with twenty-three minutes to go: Matthews, in full cry, placed the ball from the right away over towards the far post where goalkeeper Hanson seemed to have it covered. But a scramble and a scuffle developed and the next thing we saw was Mortensen and the ball in the net. Bolton were shaken and about to be shattered. The handicap of having their left-half Bell, who pulled a leg muscle early in the game, a passenger at outside left, was doubled when Banks, the left-back, was also injured and Blackpool at once took full strategic advantage of their luck. Pulling Perry across from the left wing, they attacked mercilessly down the right flank with Tom Thumb Taylor forever drawing the defence before sending Matthews away to torment his pursuers. Matthews has never had a better service, and in this final phase he played the game of his life, with the fascinated crowd swaying this way and that in harmony with his bewildering body swerves and pattern weaving.

Something simply had to give way, but the harassed Bolton defence held out until less than three minutes from time when Blackpool were awarded a free-kick a couple of yards outside the penalty area. As Bolton packed their goal it looked impossible for a loophole to be found in the human wall, but Mortensen saw one and a terrific shot whistled into the roof of the net before the goalkeeper could move. The day was saved for Blackpool, and their excited players did everything but tear Mortensen's shirt off his back. 'Come on, Stanley!' yelled the crowd – and the magnificent Matthews did not let his audience down. Only one minute was left and again he flashed along the right wing. Poor Banks was left standing, and Matthews made the way easy for a scoring chance as I have so often seen him do. Instead of passing square he dribbled the ball along the line almost to the goalpost. Then ever so gently he touched it back to the onrushing Perry and into the net it flashed. Matthews (and Blackpool) had won the Cup at the third time of asking in circumstances as dramatic as any final has produced. Matthews and his captain Harry Johnston were carried off shoulder high. Bolton, bitterly disappointed though they must have been, took the defeat like men.

When Farm presented them with a goal in the first minute of the match by allowing a 25-yard drifting shot by Lofthouse to bounce over his right shoulder, the odds were heavily on Bolton, and they were desperately unlucky not to be two up when another

Lofthouse drive beat Farm and hit the post. The fates were also kind to Blackpool when the scores were levelled at the thirty-sixth minute. Hassall, who strove gallantly at left-half after Bell's injury, was racing back to cut off a break-through when Mortensen's shot struck his leg and the ball was diverted into the net. Before half-time, however, the faltering Farm had landed Blackpool back into trouble. Langton swung across a high ball from almost the same spot that led to Bolton's first fluke goal, and once more Farm misjudged the flight as Moir challenged him. The ball went into the net off Moir's head. Bell's goal which made it 3–1 for Bolton came ten minutes after the interval as the prelude to the Matthews rescue act with two goals in the last three minutes.

The Queen presented the Cup to Johnston, Blackpool's captain, and medals to all the players. Before the match both teams were presented to the Duke of Edinburgh. The gate receipts, £49,900, set up a British record.

Sporting Champion: Stanley Matthews – 1 FA Cup (1953); 2 Football League Division Two championships (1932–33, 1962–63 – both with Stoke).

DIDIER DROGBA – FA CUP

DROGBA'S STAR ROLE ON HIS FAVOURITE STAGE

Henry Winter, 6 May 2012

Everyone has been asking questions of Didier Drogba this season, even Graham Norton, but he keeps finding answers. Oft-criticised, oft-written off, the Chelsea striker is now the first player to score in four FA Cup finals, the man who has struck eight goals in eight competitive games at Wembley, yet he is still expected to leave Chelsea. The club need to answer a question from their fans. Why? Why let Drogba go? The talisman with the occasional tantrum in him always has a goal in him. The player who always seems to have the final word in finals does not have the final word in his Chelsea career. At thirty-four, Drogba wants a two-year contract at the Bridge, which the club are loath to offer as they seek to rejuvenate the squad. But he is still a force, still a goal-scoring threat, and still apparently booked on a slow boat or fast plane to China and the riches of Shanghai Shenhua.

The way he kissed a post and touched the Wembley turf amid Chelsea's post-match celebrations looked like a man saying his farewells to a favourite venue. Maybe Chelsea should keep him just for Wembley. In the 2007 final, Drogba played a one-two with Frank Lampard and scored the only goal to beat Manchester United. Two years later, Drogba struck the equaliser in the 2–1 win over Everton (settled by Lampard). His free-kick finished off Portsmouth in 2010. Drogba drove in another fine goal here which proved the winner against Liverpool. No wonder he views Wembley as his 'lucky stadium'. Ever since watching pictures of Eric Cantona score against Liverpool in the 1996 FA Cup final, Drogba has been obsessed by the place.

His thoughts now turn away from Wembley. Drogba still has more to look forward to in the blue of Chelsea, a point made constantly by their fans with their chant of '*qué será, será*, whatever will be, will be, we're going to Germany'. Munich beckons. Drogba could be off with the greatest club prize of all, a winner's medal from the Champions League final at the Allianz Arena. After his frustration in the 2008 showdown with Manchester United, sent off in Moscow, Drogba will crave redemption. Drogba takes on a Bayern Munich defence shorn through suspension of that excellent centre-half, Holger Badstuber, and Gustavo, the defensive midfielder. Drogba is a force against full-strength defences let alone weakened ones.

At Wembley, Drogba was up against an experienced, in-form centre-half in Martin Skrtel. Drogba's face adorned the £10 Cup final programme, facing up to Skrtel, a duel that soon broke out here. Within twenty-eight seconds, Drogba was dropping off Skrtel, latching on to Lampard's knock-down and trying his luck, sending a shot spinning over. Liverpool could not take their eyes off Chelsea's number eleven. Skrtel, probably Liverpool's player of the season with Luis Suárez, had to be on his toes. When Drogba strode through early on, Skrtel calmly read the danger and nicked the ball. Drogba was so obsessing Liverpool's centre-halves, drawing Skrtel and Daniel Agger, that space opened up for Ramires to pour through for Chelsea's eleventh-minute opener. Even without direct involvement, Drogba had contributed. His work-rate was superb, his stamina exceptional.

Drogba feels so fit, smiling that he has 'a few kilometres left' in him. He certainly put in the hard yards here, even chasing back to hound Craig Bellamy. Moments later, he was back upfront, linking with Juan Mata, then spreading play wide to Ramires. Drogba kept imposing himself on all Liverpool defenders, inspecting the backline like a particularly demanding Regimental Sergeant Major. First Glen Johnson was worked over. Then Drogba moved across to trouble Agger. He then tested José Enrique. Drogba has looked so sharp and hungry in recent semi-final weeks, bullying an array of centre-halves from Carles Puyol of Barcelona to William Gallas of Spurs. A decision to analyse the way Alan Shearer played during his Newcastle days, muscling into centre-halves, giving them no respite, paid off. A beacon up front, Drogba also proved a great 'out' ball, controlling a clearance from John Obi Mikel. If Chelsea decide against keeping him, they also will miss the Ivorian's presence at defending corners. Just before half-time, following a Bellamy delivery, Drogba rose far more determinedly to clear the ball ahead of Skrtel. He has that strength, that determination.

Up close, he is remarkably different from the battle-scarred heavyweight of popular perception. Drogba is lithe, slightly angular with an athlete's frame rather than a boxer's. And deadly in front of goal. Seven minutes into the second half, Lampard released Drogba and he placed a low, firm shot between Skrtel's legs and past Pepe Reina. Wembley was treated to a trademark Drogba celebration, sliding across the turf towards the Chelsea fans, arms outstretched. If the attention then turned to the compelling Andy Carroll–John Terry duel down the other end, Drogba proved once again the man for the great stage of Wembley, the man who has the answers.

Sporting Champion: Didier Drogba – 4 FA Cups (2006–07, 2008–09, 2009–10, 2011–12); 3 Premier Leagues (2004–05, 2005–06, 2009–10); 2 Football League Cups (2004–05, 2006–07), 1 UEFA Champions League (2011–12).

CARL FOGARTY – WORLD SUPERBIKES CHAMPIONSHIP

WINNING IS THE THING THAT DRIVES FOGARTY

Sue Mott, 1 May 1999

Warning. You are about to enter an area of unbridled male fantasy. To paraphrase Bill Shankly: this isn't a matter of a pneumatic blonde or playing lead guitar with the Rolling Stones, it's much more important than that. It is about donning black leather for the reason God intended – that of going at 190mph on a motorbike. Just why grown men whimper with envy and admiration at the mere mention of Carl Fogarty's name becomes instantaneously clear. It is not that he is the three times World Superbike champion, with a beautiful wife and daughters and a football net in his back garden. It is that his wife lets him park his motorbike in the hall.

The decorator let us in and there it was. A great hulking brute of a machine, gleaming with menace, about the size and shape of a white rhino, perched on a mirror-backed platform, under spotlights. The Fogie replica Ducati of which there are only 200 in the world. This was number two into creation. Number one is in an Italian museum. So I was not looking at a souvenir. I was standing before a sacred relic. 'I'll go and get him,' said the decorator. 'He's in here somewhere,' he added, as though the champion was a gerbil gone coyly missing in his cage and he'd have to lure him out with a carrot. The waiting was awful. Anyone who knows anything about Superbikes (huge, powerful, but you or I could drive them down the street should we choose to be sufficiently insane) knows that Fogarty is a lone wolf with a pale-eyed stare and that animal's instinct for raw aggression and getting to the prey – or the finish line – first. I was expecting a creature as cruel, cold and steel-ribbed as his machine.

'Hello,' he said. What was this? A scaled-down hologram? But it was him. Tiny by comparison to the Robocop of my imagination, wiry, winsome, charming, funny, as down to the rich Lancashire earth beneath his feet as a world-renowned superstar on the same kind of boot deal as David Beckham could possibly be. He was totally unapologetic about his bike as an *objet d'art*. 'It might be odd for some people, but not for me. It's what I do.' At the Donington Park round of the Superbikes Championship, if there was room to accommodate them, a crowd twice the size of

Manchester United's would be there to watch and worship. As it is, he'll pull 60,000. 'It's scary and daunting,' he said, two words you wouldn't expect to escape his lips, decorated either side by small pale moustache and goatee-ish beard. But he was talking about the attention he commands, not the obvious and literally breakneck dangers of his sport. 'It's a lot for one person. I'm on television all the time. Sky, Eurosport. I don't go out round here in Blackburn. Wouldn't even dream of it. No way. I'd get mobbed and hassled all night. Can't go to Preston either. I feel like I've got something sticking out me 'ead, you know. Everybody's staring. I might go out with my wife and mates on a Saturday night. Few of us for a meal and a nightclub. I get left alone in nightclubs because I'm up in the VIP lounge out of the way. And, anyway, everybody's too busy looking at the women in bikinis. That's what they wear now. Bikinis with a jacket over. I can't believe it . . . Not that I've noticed. So I'm told.'

But it's not really the pressing attentions of semi-naked women to which he is most prone. It is the adoring moist-eyed male who is most impressed by Fogarty, the one who never quite found the courage to trade his childhood scooter for a motorised one. Unusually for a male sports star, he is a fantasy figure for the guys. 'I know,' he said, ruefully. 'And I'm a bit worried about it.' He isn't. One thing and one thing only dominates the life and worries of Carl Fogarty. Winning. Since his dad, a TT racer in his prime, gave him a little Honda 50 on which to fly around the local fields and frighten the chickens as a boy, he has loved the competition. And beating it. 'I'm just a bad loser. I don't like losing anything,' he said. His earring is a gold number one. 'When I lost as a kid, I sulked. Cried a lot. Never liked losing. I don't think it's a bad thing. I always wanted to win. People say to me, "You must love riding bikes". I don't love riding. I love winning. The only time I actually enjoy riding is when a few of us go off-roading on Enduro bikes. Across the rough terrain. Over hills. Through a few rivers and streams. I'm going up to the Lakes this week.' That must be nice for the ramblers, I mention casually. Red rag to a bull. 'Big problem,' he said. 'They don't like it because they get guys flying past them covering them in stones. We don't do that,' he added. 'We always slow right down.' But there his generosity ends. 'They can cause problems, too. They think they own everything. If they want a walk, why don't they have a nice walk down the shops and leave the lovely moors and things for us to go biking on?' I couldn't bank on the fact he was joking. 'That's when I enjoy riding my bike. Racing's different. You can't enjoy something that's your job, your life, that puts you under so much pressure. The only time I enjoy it is when I cross the finish line first on a Sunday afternoon.'

The foregoing is typical Fogartyism, as heedless of tact or dissenting views, in its own way, as McCarthyism. (Although McCarthy would surely have balked at the red leather.) There cannot be many people in or out of sport who take such a tough line on cricket, for example. 'I think it's the worst sport in the world. I absolutely hate it. I can't stand it. It's so slow, it's so complicated. Not like our sport. You go round twenty-five times and the first one back wins.' Or shopping. 'I don't like going in shops. Seeing that horrible smiling guy behind the counter. Footballers don't mind because most of them are thick.' (We had been talking about footballers' propensity to consume: Armani, Versace, Mercedes and, as he informed me, Fogie Replicas. Les Ferdinand's got one apparently. And so has Dougie Hall, the Newcastle director. I'm saying nothing.) The result of the Fogarty shopping phobia is that he possesses only one suit, a black one with no distinguishing features so that he can wear it time and time again and no one will say: 'Seen you in that before.' He only bought his Porsche because he got a deal on it. In fact, he only bought his lawnmower because he got a deal on it.

But someone's been shopping. The house the decorator is doing up is turning into a Roman villa on the Lancashire moors. The pale stone tiles on the floor could have been Caesar's. The walls are reddish gold. The swimming pool is heated. A Blackburn footballer lives next door. A plinth holds one of his enormous trophies ('1E Prijs, Assen, 8th September 1996'). And just before you get any ideas, the Alsatians are called Diesel and Tara. His dad was a self-made man – in warehousing and haulage – and now the son is a self-made emperor. He does not flinch when the £600,000-a-year Beckham boot deal is mentioned. 'Yeah?' he said, as in 'So?'

He is very old for thirty-two. Richer, wiser, more experienced than most people in their early thirties would have any right to be. The wisdom is thanks to his sport. He learnt nothing at school. 'It was all wrong for me.' But thanks to racing he had to force his way through his overwhelming shyness and acquire a working knowledge of geography (getting on the right plane), maths (getting on the right wages), languages (getting on with the right people) and physics (not falling off). The last wasn't easy. 'Win a few, crash a few' marked his progress in the early years on his Yamaha 250. He broke his femur in 1986 and spent eight weeks in traction in Blackburn hospital. He was testing at Oulton Park when it happened, lost the rear end and broke the bone so badly it was sticking out through his skin. 'That set me back a bit,' he said. 'Because I broke it again the year after.'

It was a testing apprenticeship that forged a champion. He thinks footballers have it way too easy. 'If you had all that money so young you'd go off your 'ead, wouldn't you?' he said in acute and succinct appraisal of our national game. Some would say he is more demonstrably off his 'ead than any footballer, racing round

Brands Hatch or Hockenheim at approaching 200mph without the comforting padding of a car frame around him, merely the width of his lavishly sponsored leathers. This argument he has heard approximately 7,000 times (once a day for his twenty years on a bike) and dismisses it accordingly. 'I don't think about getting injured. I think about not winning. That's a bigger disaster to me. It gets harder to motivate myself but the will to win is still there. There's more and more pressure on me. I get less and less sleep. But as long as I enjoy winning I won't retire.'

The police have retired him from driving a couple of times. He has served two bans. 'But just from the totting-up process,' he said, declaring minor infractions like driving at 100mph on the motorway. It's easily done, I sympathise, in a SL320 silver convertible Merc, registration plate: FOG1E. 'I don't ever speed round here,' he pointed out, on the twisty, turning, single-tracked country lanes where he lives. That's because you'd know the people you were running over, I suggested. 'Well yeah,' he said.

He is a mystery. How can such a sweet, honest, self-deprecating man making us a cup of tea in his kitchen turn into a beast as mean as his machine at the mere touch of a set of handlebars? 'When I'm relaxing at home I'm one thing. But when I'm at the track, I'm working very, very hard. People say hello to me, and I don't even see them. I put my helmet on and I don't care what I do or what I say. I don't care. I just want to win. Keep winning. I've always said there are two Carl Fogartys.' And they're both allowed to park their bike in the hall.

Sporting Champion: Carl Fogarty – 4 World Superbikes Championships (1994, 1995, 1998, 1999).

GEORGE BEST – EUROPEAN CUP

MY FRIEND HAD NO REGRETS

Michael Parkinson, 25 November 2005

Matt Busby loved talking about George Best. He never worked him out, but he loved him. One day, just before Matt died, he said to me: 'I keep having this terrible thought that one day George will end it all. That he'll commit suicide.' He was right. It just took him longer than either of us thought.

George knew what was happening. Ten years ago he confided: 'A doctor friend once told me that one day I'd wake up and either switch on life or switch it off.' And that is what he did. Why? The easy explanation is he was a chronic alcoholic. That's what killed him, but why did he drink so much? In all the time I knew him and all the hours we talked he never said. He would sidestep the question with a joke. But drinking didn't make him happy. So why? I used to think it was because he was bored. He was the supremely gifted athlete who found playing football a simple matter. So was finding a mate. Women offered themselves and he took them. Simple as that. No sweat.

He had a sharp intelligence, but strangely, little confidence in displaying it in the early years. In his maturity, even when the booze had taken hold, it was possible to glimpse what might have been. I last saw him a couple of months ago when I persuaded him to attend a reunion of the players who were at Old Trafford with him. He sat all evening without a drink and reminisced. He said to me later it was one of the most enjoyable occasions he could remember. I said: 'That's because you were sober.' He said: 'Whatever, I was certainly very happy.' And I thought, not for the first time, maybe, just maybe, we'd got him back. A week later he was drinking again and the final spiral of his life had begun.

When I sat down to write his obituary it occurred I had been doing so for the past fifteen years or so, in the sense that everything I wrote about him in that time seemed like a valediction. What I decided is to reprint, with slight amendments, an article I wrote for this paper in 1999. I think it captures at least some of him and gives a sense of a remarkable man. George Best was sometimes a difficult man to defend in the aftermath of a drunken episode. What was never a problem was to talk of his genius as a player and to love him as a friend. That was easy.

When Manchester United played Benfica in the final of the European Cup in 1968, I was bored stiff for most of the game. United were lucky it went to extra time because Eusebio should have scored with three minutes left. Alex Stepney's reflex save was astonishing, but a player of Eusebio's calibre should have buried the chance. In the opening minutes of extra time, Stepney cleared the ball downfield, Brian Kidd flicked it on and George Best stuck it through the centre-half's legs. Now he was one on one with the goalkeeper. A foregone conclusion. George dummied, the goalkeeper fell for it, and United were ahead. From that moment on, Benfica crumbled and Matt Busby fulfilled his final ambition.

George Best remembered the game but little else. There was a reception, a banquet and a trip to a nightclub, but he had no recollection of the celebrations. His friends told him he had the meal but afterwards nipped off to spend the night with a girlfriend. Looking back, he thought it might have been the moment when his life went into freefall, when Bacchus replaced Busby.

It is difficult explaining to people who didn't see him play how different George Best was. It is near impossible to convince young people who have only known the portly and frayed impostor of recent years that this was once not only a great footballer but also a man as glamorous as any film star. I would have given anything to see Best playing in the Premier League. It would have been the perfect theatre for him to cast his spell. Beckham on the right, Best on the left – now that would be something to make even cynics drool.

When considering the qualities of players like Best, who operated at the sharp end, you have to remember the 1960s was the time when forwards were not a protected species. In fact, it was open season for defenders, who were given *carte blanche* to kick opponents. British football in those days was no place for players of a nervous disposition. The fainthearted had nowhere to hide. At Highbury, Peter Storey awaited; at Chelsea, 'Chopper' Harris clattered all comers; Tommy Smith bossed Anfield; and at Elland Road, if Norman Hunter didn't get you then there was a fair chance Billy Bremner would. And there was always Jack Charlton on hand to mop up.

Best had his card marked in his very first game. It was against West Bromwich Albion at Old Trafford and he was opposed by a feisty full-back called Graham Williams, who spent most of the first half trying to persuade George he was in the wrong job. Best in those days had the physique of a knitting needle but he took Williams on, even daring to nutmeg him, which was the equivalent of signing his own death warrant. In the second half, Busby switched Best to the other wing, thus ensuring that his career lasted one more game. Ever after, when Williams met Best, he would ask him to stand still so he could study his face. 'I want to know what you look like because all I've ever seen of you is your arse disappearing down the touchline,' he said.

Best survived, prospered and triumphed because he was supremely gifted to overcome any challenge, physical, mental or tactical. Like all great players, the foundation of his talent was his balance. His low-slung way of running allowed him to ride the roughest passage as if equipped with stabilisers. His speed often took him away from trouble before it could hinder him, and his stamina ensured that he was still operating flat-out when the opposition became heavy-legged. Those qualities were God-given, but what he built on that foundation is an example today's players might take to heart. He made himself into a two-footed player, not in the sense he was marvellous with one and adequate with the other, but to the point where he had forgotten which was his natural foot. This gave him all the options when it came to beating an opponent, but particularly in the box, where Best was one of the most certain finishers I ever saw.

Bobby Charlton was another who was completely two-footed. Few of the current crop of forwards are. You might think that with upwards of £50,000 a week coming in, they would bother to learn. After all, they have nothing else to do. Best was the complete player. The most naturally gifted Busby ever saw. When he was at his most sublime, he was unstoppable and irresistible. After a virtuoso performance against Chelsea at Stamford Bridge, the crowd stood and applauded him off the field. His love of showboating often led to frustration among team members who would spend the afternoon running into support positions, only to watch Best being indulgent. In training, he kept the ball for so long they introduced two-touch football. Two touches and you gave the ball away. Best took one touch, then played the ball against the shins of an opponent, taking the return and setting himself up for another two. So they introduced one-touch football. Again, he played the first touch against the team-mate's legs, took the rebound and, like a pinball wizard, cannoned his way through defence to goal.

When he bought his first house, he invited a gang of friends to see Manchester United play Newcastle before going on to the house-warming party. The game was a fairly dull affair, with

George keeping out of trouble until he received a throw from the goalkeeper and ran to the touchline below his guests. He gave us a wave and then stood, foot on ball, awaiting the arrival of the Newcastle defence. Three of them approached and, just when it seemed they had him cornered, he flicked three wall passes off their legs, chipped over their heads, collected the ball, turned and gave us a bow. He was a man in love with his virtuosity, certain of his ability because he had taken nothing for granted.

George Best did not arrive on Earth the complete player. He made himself into a truly exceptional footballer by working hard and intelligently at the game. Which made his downfall even more of a mystery. I don't know why he chose to drink himself into oblivion. Nor, I suspect, did he. It is for sure he could have been better looked after when he arrived at Manchester United, particularly when it became obvious he was as much a pop star as a footballer. He was the first player to step into showbiz. That was the problem. The present crop take their lifestyles and their acclaim for granted. They are represented (more often than not, misrepresented) by agents, managers and protected by bodyguards. Best lived in digs with Mrs Fullaway, parked his Jaguar outside and had ten sacks of unanswered fan letters in his bedroom. No one bothered because no one knew what was happening, and by the time they cottoned on it was too late.

At first, he was having a lovely time. The football was magical, and the 1960s a perfect time to be single, good-looking and horny. Sometimes, when he wanted to escape, he would come and stay. He spent most of his time in the garden playing football with my sons. One of them was asked by their teacher to tell the class what he had done over the weekend. 'Please, Miss,' he said, 'yesterday I played football with George Best.' She gave him a dressing down for telling fibs. One night, he went out to a nightclub and next morning at breakfast asked if I could take him to London. Mary was making herself a cup of coffee when down the stairs from George's bedroom walked a pretty young woman wearing evening dress and smoking a Balkan Sobranie. George had brought her home from his night out but had omitted to inform us. She was a nice girl and offered to do the washing-up. Mary thought she might ruin her dress so the girl, determined to impress, started tottering around the house on high heels doing the Hoovering.

I was a friend of George Best for more than forty years and it was never dull. On the other hand, I suspect that his friends – or most of them I know – had a better time than George did. There was within him a profound melancholy, not altogether attributable to Celtic gloom. If Best had no regrets then it would be presumptuous of those lucky enough to have watched him and known him to have felt cheated. Yet the fact remains he left the game aged twenty-seven, before he reached his prime. We don't know what might have been. The ultimate affliction of George Best was, neither did he.

Sporting Champion: George Best – 1 European Cup (1967–68); 2 Division One championships (1964–65, 1966–67).

LIVERPOOL – UEFA CHAMPIONS LEAGUE

GERRARD LEADS GLORIOUS FIGHTBACK

Henry Winter, 26 May 2005

Steven Gerrard planted a delicate kiss on the European Cup, acting like a bashful boy on a first date, before seizing it passionately with both hands and raising it to the heavens. Liverpool's love affair with this trophy has never ebbed. Its twenty-one-year absence from Anfield's embrace has simply made this wonderful club's heart beat stronger for it. And few hearts beat more strongly than Gerrard's. One of the many banners waved by the magnificent Kop on tour in Istanbul paid tribute to their gladiator leader, declaring: 'And You Will Know My Name is Gerrard, And I Will Lay My Vengeance Upon You.'

It was Gerrard's guts and lust for glory, his refusal to countenance defeat even when its dark hand fell across Liverpool like the coldest of shadows as Milan strolled into a three-goal lead, that kept his team's dream alive. Liverpool's captain was immense, deservedly voted man of the match, for single-handedly dragging his team back from the brink of utter humiliation. Making light of those early goals from Paolo Maldini and a brace from Hernan Crespo, Gerrard tore into the Italians from the first whistle of the second half, scoring, creating the space for Vladimir Smicer to strike and then winning the penalty from which Xabi Alonso eventually drove Liverpool level. After the first-half torture, parity felt like paradise. Gerrard then dropped into defence throughout extra time, joining the outstanding Jamie Carragher in repelling Milan on ground and in the air. And when Liverpool's foreigners wrapped up the penalty shoot-out, Gerrard led the wild celebrations. He kept running towards the huge banks of red-clad humanity, such stirring testament to the extraordinary depths of loyalty Liverpool arouse. Gerrard punched the air and screamed his delight. Behind him, Liverpool's kitman was ripping open a box of T-shirts emblazoned with the words 'Champions League Winners'. There is nothing like packing everything you might need on trips abroad. And Liverpool fans, having unsportingly whistled during Milan's penalties, made amends by saluting Maldini and his forlorn colleagues when they walked reluctantly up to collect their losers' medals.

Liverpool's players followed, their stride far jauntier, their faces awash with smiles. Last came their warrior-leader, Gerrard, advancing to collect the silvery spoils of war, the European Cup. The moment he lifted Liverpool's fifth European Cup, it felt like the pages of history were being illuminated by the thousands of flashbulbs. This sweet, astonishing victory brought back memories of Liverpool's past four European Cups, of Kevin Keegan leading Borussia Mönchengladbach's Berti Vogts a merry dance in Rome in 1977, of Graeme Souness slipping Kenny Dalglish through to defeat Bruges at Wembley a year later, of Alan Kennedy's heroics in 1981 and 1984.

'Rafa's Red Armada', as one banner lauded them, deserve the right to defend the European Cup, to embark on what yet another flag described as 'The Famous Kopites on Another European Tour to Glory'. European football needs Liverpool, particularly after such a resilient display as this. Their resolve was tested to the limit here. Milan had dominated the first half, scoring through Maldini's firm header, before the brilliant Brazilian, Kaká, helped construct two poacher's goals for Crespo before half-time. Humiliation was engulfing Liverpool. Here was a time for them to show their character, to respond to Benítez's dressing-room exhortations, to remember their club's proud traditions and take the game to Milan and their hordes of mocking fans.

Running into the *Fossa dei Leoni*, the Lions' Den, Liverpool delivered one of the most famous fifteen-minute spells of football imaginable. This was football from the gods, bringing the faithful hordes to their feet, songs flowing ceaselessly from Liverpool lips. Gerrard, inevitably, led the charge, meeting John Arne Riise's cross with a strong and well-directed header that flew past Dida. Liverpool's captain was unmarked but he still had to rise high to meet the ball, still needed to twist his body to inject the requisite power. Dida stood no chance. Not with Gerrard in this mood, the adrenalin pumping.

Liverpool's resistance movement was up and running. Smicer let fly from range: 3–2. As the Kop's celebrated anthem swirled around the ground, their idols in red were more than walking on with hope in their hearts. They were running, chasing every loose ball, every lost cause. Gerrard was everywhere, sprinting into the box on the hour mark, until brought down by Gennaro Gattuso, allowing Alonso to convert the penalty. Extra-time came and went, leading to more penalties. When Serginho fired wildly over, Liverpool had the initiative, particularly when Hamann stroked his spot-kick home. Then came Andrea Pirlo, whistles ringing around the Ataturk Stadium, the Liverpool jeers turning to cheers when Jerzy Dudek saved. The noise doubled when Djibril Cissé slotted home. Jon Dahl Tomasson converted his for Milan, and when Riise saw his effort saved by Dida, Kaká made it 2–2. Up stepped Smicer, ramming his penalty past Dida, placing real pressure on Andrei Shevchenko, who was denied by the superb Dudek. Gerrard then lifted the European Cup, victory sealed with a kiss.

Sporting Champions: Liverpool – 5 European Cups/UEFA Champions League (1977, 1978, 1981, 1984, 2005); 3 UEFA Cups (1973, 1976, 2001).

JUNE

RICKY HATTON – WORLD LIGHT-WELTERWEIGHT CHAMPIONSHIP

LOCAL HERO HATTON HITS THE BIG-TIME
Paul Hayward, 6 June 2005

Around three in the morning in the corner of a boxing ring in Manchester, Ricky Hatton's trainer asked his man a question. It was Billy Graham's moment to make a speech that only prize-fighters can really understand: 'We need this last round to be sure of winning. Can you do it? Have you got it in you?' Hatton was on his stool waiting for the twelfth and final bell in the fight of his life. 'F****** right I've got it in me,' he answered. As he lowered his head over a bucket to receive a cooling splash of water, he heard Graham's voice again, this time saying: 'He's not come out. He's not come out!' In the opposite corner, Johnny Lewis was calling time on Kostya Tszyu's distinguished career. This simple act of compassion recalled Eddie Futch's famous injunction to Joe Frazier at the end of the fourteenth round of the 'Thriller in Manila' with Muhammad Ali: 'Sit down, son. It's all over. But no one will ever forget what you did here today.'

Tszyu, the world light-welterweight champion and odds-on favourite, was a broken fighter, pinned to his stool. As Hatton's corner levitated, the Tszyu camp tightened into a low protective huddle. Hatton rose, Tszyu fell. Boxing elevates while it destroys. The eruption of noise inside the MEN Arena must have stirred the dead in the city's graveyards. At 3.10 a.m. on a night of ferocious violence, Hatton was officially crowned the new king of the 10-stone division.

'To beat someone who's recognised as the world number one is end-of-the-rainbow stuff,' he reflected, as Tszyu was being taken to hospital for precautionary checks and American television executives were predicting global stardom for the victorious hometown gladiator. 'The sky's the limit. He's entered the world stage and he's entered it with a marching band,' enthused Jay Larkin of the Showtime network, who were already visualising huge pay-days against Diego Corrales, the number one lightweight (9 stone 9 lb), and Miguel Cotto, the formidable Puerto Rican light-welterweight, unbeaten in twenty-three bouts.

These two can wait, together with Arturo Gatti and Vivian Harris – two other stellar light-welterweights – because Hatton's most pressing obligation was the bad shirt contest at the New Inn pub near his home in Hyde, a district of Manchester that drags the grim baggage of the Moors Murders and the foul deeds of Harold Shipman. 'I've missed my two friends, Mr Guinness and Mr Dom Pérignon,' he joked as he finally departed the arena with the International Boxing Federation's belt, leaving more than 20,000 acolytes to stagger into the thin grey light of dawn. 'I'm a Mancunian born and bred, and I really feel I'm no different to the man in the crowd,' he told us later. 'I think that's why I get the respect I do. I have an exciting style, sure, but I just think people say, "Oh, Ricky, he's one of the lads". It's nice to reward them like this. Even when the big fights fell through, there were still 15,000 cheering me on. The crowd here deserved it as much as I do.'

The greats of British boxing have been joined by a twenty-six-year-old, unbeaten threshing machine who combines ring savvy, spirit, humour and skill. Larkin said that only two experts he spoke to forecast a Hatton victory. One was Sugar Ray Leonard, the other Mike Tyson, who predicted that Hatton's all-action style would 'frustrate Tszyu'. No one who witnessed his elevation from cult hero to global gladiator will surrender the memory of Hatton standing motionless against the ropes before the maelstrom began, absorbing the will of the crowd: their passion, their venom. A small nod of his head to the mob seemed to say: 'Everything is right. I'm ready. It's coming.' The heart was fully engaged, for sure, but the mind played the decisive part. Hatton's victory was a tactical triumph, assisted by a retaliatory low blow in the ninth round that seemed to suck the belligerence from Tszyu ('It's not a tickling contest, is it?' said Hatton, by way of a justification). By the time Tszyu's corner invoked the spirit of Eddie Futch, Hatton was ahead on all three scorecards, and Lewis was calculating: 'We needed a knockout to win, and Kostya just didn't have a knockout in him.'

Hatton explained the plan: 'I thought he would be at his sharpest and most destructive in the first four or five rounds, but right from the start I seemed to be timing his right hand well. I was slipping it and moving in on him to close the gap. When Kostya fought Sharmba Mitchell and Zab Judah, his power, his leverage, was at the end of the punch. So giving ground to him is what he wants you to do. I timed his right hand and then moved in close. If I'd backed off he would have just nailed me. I knew I'd take a few shots, and expected Kostya to have his nose in front after four or five rounds. But my plan was to take it out of him in the first half of the fight: lean on him, smother him, push him back, sap his strength – and then come on again in the later rounds. In the last four or five I really came on like a Trojan. I had it between my teeth for the last round. I was really up for those last three minutes. And maybe Mr Lewis and Kostya sensed I was going to come on to him. They did the right thing to stop it. I felt he was weakening, tiring. It was a physical fight – pushing and shoving and mauling, and that's right up my street.'

An Australian reporter wondered whether Tszyu's nemesis was 'disappointed' that the outgoing champion stayed on his stool at the end of the eleventh: a capitulation that was at once sensible and sad. 'Disappointed? Was I b*******. I just wanted to win,' was Hatton's response. Nothing will ever quite beat Roberto Duran's surrender to Sugar Ray Leonard in the eighth round of their rematch: '*No mas, no mas.*' No more, no more. But through the throng of bodies extending sympathy to Tszyu, Hatton could see the scale of his conquest, and the brutality of his trade.

Sporting Champion: Ricky Hatton – World Light-Welterweight Championship (2005–09).

SHERGAR – THE DERBY

SWINBURN'S BOND WITH SHERGAR
STILL STRONG

Robert Philip, 4 June 2001

For a few brief months they were the most celebrated six-legged duo since Roy Rogers and Trigger; Walter Swinburn and Shergar did not merely win the 1981 Derby, they flew across the Epsom Downs to pass the finishing post a stupendous ten lengths in front of the cream of Europe's thoroughbreds. It was the very stuff of Flat racing legend; the tale of a nineteen-year-old novice jockey being plucked from anonymity to ride a priceless horse owned by the Aga Khan and whom many turf experts regarded as the greatest equine athlete of all time. Together they raced to victory on four occasions, all with such ridiculous ease, however, that they won the hearts of millions. Even those who had never visited a racecourse or stepped inside a bookies' shop, knew of Shergar the wonder horse and his teenage companion.

What happened next, of course, served only to increase the mystique. In February 1983, Shergar was kidnapped from his stable at Ballymany Stud in County Kildare – most probably by an IRA splinter group – and vanished, never to be seen again despite more rumoured sightings than Elvis Presley and Lord Lucan combined. Over the years, 'Shergar' has been spotted pulling a gypsy caravan down a country lane or grazing contentedly in countless fields the length and breadth of Ireland. Less savoury were the images that he had ended up in a tin of dog food. An IRA informer later revealed that Shergar had been stolen by a gang from County Kerry and shot because they were unable to control the horse in hiding.

Now Swinburn can only look back on their great adventure with tangible affection and regret. 'Because of all the hullabaloo surrounding Shergar, the excitement started to build weeks and weeks beforehand. Everyone knew there was no way Shergar would be beaten provided I could stay in the saddle. All anyone wanted to talk about was by how far he was winning his races despite having this inexperienced boy on board. In fact, the Derby was our easiest and eeriest race; I'd heard all the stories from my father [former top jockey, Wally Senior] about how rough it could be, how the start was crucial and how you could get knocked about. Yet all through the race I saw only two horses in front of me so I followed them all the way round before Shergar took it upon himself to hit the front coming down the hill. When you were galloping, he was the sort of horse you didn't realise exactly how fast you were going because he had this really short, daisy-cutting action. He never wasted any time in the air and stayed really low. When he pulled me to the front I remember thinking, "Whooah", but he was gone, he was on his way.'

Although Frankie Dettori describes Swinburn as 'the most naturally talented jockey of his generation', the engagingly modest Irishman is at pains to minimalise his contribution to the famous partnership. 'Anyone could have ridden Shergar, it's true, honestly. He was such a great, great horse. The greatest? It's impossible to compare him with Sea Bird II, say. All I can say is that he was far and away the greatest horse I ever rode and that is no insult to my two other Derby winners, Shahrastani and Lammtarra. That's why my overwhelming emotion when I entered the unsaddling enclosure was one of relief. I kept repeating, "Thank God, I didn't mess it up for him". I think I only fully appreciated what could have gone wrong five years later when Greville Starkey was blamed for Dancing Brave's failure. It just about finished poor Greville and, who knows, if I'd done something similar it might have been the end of me. Don't forget, I had no idea how far we were in front – in fact, I still get embarrassed every time I see the film – so I actually picked up my whip a furlong out when I was ten lengths clear because I heard a voice on the other side of the rails shouting, "Go on, Lester". I thought it was Lester Piggott on Shotgun coming to haunt me. It was undoubtedly a housewife who mistook me for Lester thinking only the great man would be given a horse as good as Shergar to ride.'

Piggott was given the opportunity to ride Shergar when, with Swinburn suspended, they cruised to victory in the 1981 Irish Derby, but the teenage tyro was back in the saddle for the King George VI Stakes and the St Leger when the 'invincibles' were finally beaten. 'He was over the top by then; for all his brilliance, he was a particularly hard horse to get fit, plus the fact he had me on top of him winning by ten, twenty lengths or whatever. Whereas I'm sure that if he'd had Lester on board he'd have been winning by three or four lengths and saving a bit.' Is that a criticism of yourself at such a tender age? 'Yes and no; whenever I mention that to people, they say, "Well, if he hadn't been winning by those margins, we wouldn't still be talking about him twenty years later". But I do know he was a tired horse by the time of the St Leger that September.

'I don't know what really occurred during Shergar's last days – and it's probably just as well I don't – but he didn't deserve what happened to him. He was a smashing fellow. Our family home is still littered with pictures of him, not in racing colours, but relaxing on the stud where he was like a family pet. The Aga Khan was heartbroken, as was trainer Michael Stoute, and it still saddens us all even after all these years.'

Sporting Champion: Shergar – 1 The Derby (1981); 1 Irish Derby (1981); 1 King George VI & Queen Elizabeth Stakes (1981).

JOEY DUNLOP – ISLE OF MAN TT RACES

PUBLICITY-SHY ULSTER PUBLICAN CONTINUES TO LIVE DANGEROUSLY

Sarah Edworthy, 5 June 1996

After a record haul of twenty Isle of Man TT wins – six more than Mike 'The Bike' Hailwood – Joey Dunlop is revered as Master of the Mountain, King of the Roads. But the long-haired elfin Ulsterman is not one to hold court among the mass of leather-clad young pretenders who roar off the IoM Steam Packet Company ferries. In road-racing annals, William Joseph Dunlop OBE MBE leads the field. Off the road, he is a reluctant leader of the pack, a publican in his hometown of Ballymoney, County Antrim, who longs for more time for mercy mission trips to Bosnia,

Albania and Romania, and whose hobbies include playing darts and pool in local leagues. Why should the doyen of Formula One, 250cc and 125cc revel in adulation when he returns, as he has for twenty-one years now, simply as a competitor who wants to win the most gruelling road race in the world?

'Come on, Joey,' anguished reporters have harangued him down the years. 'Why are you so special here?'
'I enjoy it.'
'But what do you find each year to motivate you?'
'It's just something I look forward to. I enjoy doing the work on the bikes as much as I do riding them. That's the difference.'

Like traffic on the anachronistic 37¾-mile circuit, conversation with Dunlop during practice week is one-way, more stop than start, with certain avenues closed off and unexpected patches of fog. He is so famously reticent, so content to be seen in terms of that great motorcycling cliché of a man articulate only at 180mph, that anyone securing a minute of dialogue with him in public is practically showered in Champagne. Many question the sanity of competitors who race knowing that on average two riders are killed annually (four to date this year, increasing the total to 168) on a circuit whose pit-lane is overshadowed by the island's hillside cemetery, their overpowered bikes winding through roads lined with pavements, telegraph poles, telephone boxes and stone walls. But Dunlop's self-containment emphasises the private compulsions that fuel the madness. 'You don't bounce here,' say the locals chillingly, but critics who see a gladiatorial spectacle face the argument about personal liberty: that it is presumptuous to tell others how they should live. 'It's very dangerous, especially in wet conditions,' admitted Dunlop, whose family are too immersed in the sport to be anything but a support. 'You just have to slow up if you don't think you can take the chance. I never push it in practice.'

Dunlop's twentieth victory came a week after the death during practice of rival Mick Lofthouse. Dunlop had so feared Lofthouse's challenge in the 125cc race that he had taken the extraordinary step of swapping his lucky number three for eighteen in order to distance himself in the ten-second staggered starts from Lofthouse at number four. It is a measure of Dunlop's inner will that this shy family man, spending his favourite two weeks in a self-catering chalet with his wife Linda and five children, Julie (twenty-one), Donna (fifteen), Garry (twelve), Richard (nine) and Joanne (six), went on to race so defiantly. His disappointing seventh in the Formula One TT occurred largely because his pit crew were not ready when he came in to change from wet tyres to slicks after the first lap.

The mythology that has grown up around the TT Races since they started in 1907, prompted by restrictions on road-racing on the mainland, is matched by Dunlop's personal cache of stories. Press cuttings chronicle his string of wins in deadpan reportage. 'Dunlop won his nth title,' they read, 'despite being drenched in fuel from a leaking petrol cap', 'despite being shipwrecked en route', 'despite a mystery virus', 'despite his brother Robert's horrific accident', 'despite the pouring rain . . .'

'I think the time the boat went down was the worst,' Dunlop recalled. 'But I've been coming here that long, every year there seems to be something different. The thing that's changed is the pressure. People don't expect anything from me anymore. They just want to see me ride. It doesn't matter whether I come first or fifteenth and that's the way I like it.' Dunlop used to make the hop across the Irish Sea in 'wee fishing boats'. The one of legend sunk with thirteen men, five bikes, spares and fuel, five minutes after foundering on the rocks at the entrance of Strangford Lough in the early hours of Sunday, 26 May 1985. The boat had left without someone who had missed the departure time. Early into the trip, the radio crackled with a message: the latecomer had duly turned up. Dunlop and his friends generously turned back, picked him up and set off again. Unfortunately, they missed the tide and the boat was whipped against rocks in heaving seas. Everyone survived thanks to Dunlop, who emptied the fuel tanks and strung them together as a makeshift giant float. His own bikes had been taken across by Honda and later that week he went on to complete the first of his two hat-tricks, a feat also claimed only by Hailwood and Steve Hislop.

Dunlop was never tempted to direct his talent towards grand prix racing, a glossy image, fancy set of leathers and a large bank balance. 'During the 1980s, I won as many circuit races as road races, but I prefer the roads,' he said, talking about riches in terms of the opportunities for travel his sport and charity work have given him. On the Isle of Man, he is the superstar member of the Honda Britain team, fondly regarded as an eccentric. He prefers to prepare his bikes himself, tinkering away in a private workshop in Mann Auto Services, 500 yards from the official mechanics' base. Back in Ballymoney, the staff prepare for the pilgrimage of German bikers whose second lifetime ambition, after doing the Isle of Man circuit on Mad Sunday, is to have a drink in Joey's pub. The former Railway Inn was recently renamed Joey's Bar to ease their visit. That is about as showy as Dunlop gets.

Sporting Champion: Joey Dunlop – 26 Isle of Man race wins; 5 TT Formula One World Championships (1982, 1983, 1984, 1985, 1986).

STEFFI GRAF – FRENCH OPEN

GRAF SETTLES INTO EASY LIFE AFTER
TURMOIL OF THE CIRCUIT

Sebastian Coe, 18 December 2000

Steffi Graf is, for the first time in her life, a woman of leisure. At least enough leisure time to have recently spent ten days walking in Peru, the highlight a five-hour trek to the Inca ruins at Machu Picchu. 'It was just something I could never have done when I was on the circuit,' she says. 'Tennis was eleven months of the year and even my month off was spent preparing for the Australian Open.' It was preparation well spent. She won the title four times, which included three consecutive victories from 1988 to 1990.

Her career, which began in 1982 and ended in 1999 after a two-year battle with injury, witnessed a domination of her sport rarely seen in any other arena this century. Twenty-two Grand Slam titles, seven of them at Wimbledon, five at the US Open and six at Roland Garros in the French Open, 107 titles in total including Olympic gold in Seoul in 1988. Only Martina Navratilova and Chris Evert, who Graf is quite happy to place on the pedestal of the 'greats', are ahead of her in overall ranking. But for sheer consistency and dominance – she occupied the number one slot for a total of 377 weeks – it is surely not unreasonable to consider her the greatest woman player of all time.

Graf began playing tennis at the age of four. Her parents, Heidi and Peter, were regular club players, and her father would become her first coach and later her manager. 'I certainly didn't have a vision or dream to be a great tennis player and actually enjoyed other sports more,' she says. It didn't take too long, however, for her renowned focus to develop. At the age of thirteen, after her first professional tournament win at the Porsche Grand Prix at Filderstadt, she shocked television viewers and the German tennis fraternity in equal measure by the candour of her ambition to become the world's number one. Five years later she achieved it, and for the next 186 weeks stayed there, a feat unsurpassed by any tennis player, male or female. She looks back on the early years as just simply being a 'natural transition'. 'I kept progressing through the leagues,' she says. 'I didn't really find it that hard and I kept winning things which excited me. But more than the winning it was the physical side of the game that always motivated me. I wanted to improve all aspects of my game every year and, for most of my career, I did. If I was in good physical shape, then I was mentally confident and if they came together, I won.'

It is when she describes her love of 'working out' that she is barely able to disguise her acute sadness at her relatively sedentary existence now. It is the price she has paid for the physical demands of modern sport. Injury to her left knee and subsequent major surgery, damage exacerbated by a fall on a visit to a Japanese shrine a year ago, have left her unable to play tennis or do anything of a twisting or load-bearing nature. Now thirty-one, she can jog only with pain, and occasionally she rides a bike. 'I find it very difficult and depressing not being physically able. I can't even hit golf balls.' Her battle with injury towards the end of her career was, she admits, her low point, although she is able to compartmentalise this as only a small part of a glittering playing career. 'I kept getting injured and then returning. Unfortunately so did the injuries. For two years I couldn't train properly. My body just wouldn't respond, no matter what I did. For the first time in my career I got nervous before matches – not about my opponent but simply about my physical condition, which in the past had always been my strength.'

At the height of that 'strength' she won all four Grand Slam tournaments, which was a prelude to what she considers to be one of the highlights of her career. She left New York after winning the US Open 'exhausted' for a three-day journey to the Seoul Olympic Games via Frankfurt, where she joined other German Olympians. 'I had gone to LA four years earlier, at the age of fifteen, when tennis was only an exhibition sport and realised that this was something special, so I had to take the opportunity to compete in the real thing in Seoul. Although I was so tired that, at the time, I needed a break, I thought of it only as another tournament. It was only when I arrived in the Village and started watching other people training that I realised where I was. I have always loved track and field [she has run 800 metres in just outside two minutes] and on the first day in the Village I teamed up with the 400 metres hurdler Harold Schmidt, who I had met on the flight from Frankfurt. I went down to the track with him and his training partners and decided I would try and run with them, which meant that I was running as fast as I could. For three days afterwards, I had such muscle soreness I wasn't sure I was even going to be able to play. It was just so important to be part of it all.' She defeated Gabriela Sabatini in the final.

At the age of nineteen, and having won everything there was to win, and being well on course to become the highest-earning female athlete of all time, Graf's seemingly effortless ascent to stardom was derailed by the much publicised conviction and subsequent imprisonment of her father for tax evasion. Understandably, Graf is not prepared to be drawn on this painful episode. It was her love of the game and her obsession for physical performance that saw her through this turmoil. It was also her recognition that there was more to life than tennis, which has always provided her with a psychological cushion. 'Although tennis ran my day I never liked hanging around the tournament scene for very long after I had finished. Often I would pack my bags and be out of the hotel within hours of stepping off the court. I never liked sitting around hotel lobbies talking about the match. I enjoyed slipping away as soon as I could to spend time exploring a city or just walking around an art gallery.'

She has a keen interest in the arts, something she has in common with her boyfriend, Andre Agassi, another Wimbledon champion and Olympic gold medallist. Could she ever pursue her interest with anonymity? 'I was never constantly bothered. I think people thought I was a private person and for that reason gave me my space. With Andre, it's very different. They treat him with less reserve because they see him as being more open. It's very interesting to observe the difference, but he also values taking time away from the game.' Now that she follows Agassi, thirty, to the major tournaments, does she find it difficult to no longer be in the limelight? 'Not at all. I feel strange about it but I don't miss it at all. The transition has been extremely easy. I'm very lucky. I left the sport happy and fulfilled. Two years after knee surgery I won Paris and got to the Wimbledon final. Once there was nothing more to achieve and I'd done it all, my motivation went. That was it. I've never looked back. It's only since I've stopped playing that I realised that when playing at that level you are in a permanent emotional turmoil. I don't have any more doubts, I don't have to ask any more questions about myself.'

Sporting Champion: Steffi Graf – 6 French Opens (1987, 1988, 1993, 1995, 1996, 1999); 7 Wimbledons (1988, 1989, 1991, 1992, 1993, 1995, 1996); 5 US Opens (1988, 1989, 1993, 1995, 1996); 4 Australian Opens (1988, 1989, 1990, 1994); 2 Olympic Games (1984, 1988).

RAFAEL NADAL – FRENCH OPEN

KING OF CLAY RECLAIMS HIS THRONE IN STYLE

Simon Briggs, 10 June 2013

After powering one final forehand uppercut into the open court, Rafael Nadal performed the obligatory modern victory celebration – lying down on his back in the wet clay of Court Philippe Chatrier. It had been a strange day at Roland Garros. Drizzle fell steadily from a dove-grey Parisian sky. Protesters interrupted play and even startled Nadal briefly out of his usual meditative focus. David Ferrer, the sacrificial victim, was almost obsequious in his determination not to spoil the party. Ultimately, though, only one thing mattered. Nadal won his eighth French Open title and his twelfth Grand Slam in all, moving to equal third in the all-time standings alongside Roy Emerson. Only Pete Sampras and Roger Federer, the man Nadal has tormented for much of the past decade, remain ahead of him. However, with this triumph Nadal has become the first man since the First World War to win the same Grand Slam title eight times.

'I never like to compare years,' Nadal said after his 6–3, 6–2, 6–3 victory. 'But it's true that this year means something very special for me. Five months ago, nobody on my team dreamt about a comeback like this.' Did he ever doubt, during the seven months he was stuck at home in Majorca, that he would be able to compete at this level? 'People who don't have doubts is because they are so arrogant,' Nadal replied. 'I for sure have doubts, but I work as much as I can to be here. That's the only thing I can do.' The key to getting back on the court, said Nadal, was staying off it for large parts of his Majorca retreat. 'I don't feel fitter than before. I feel like I was fitter in other parts of my career. But that's normal because I didn't practise as much as in the past. In the past eight weeks, my practice has been my matches. I don't know how we did it to be back here. My movement when I came back was very bad, but after a few weeks I started to move well with the right intensity and the tennis was there.'

Realistically, there were only two men with a shot at winning this title: Nadal and Novak Djokovic. So, from the moment that they both landed in the same half of the draw, everyone guessed that the word 'final' would have a different meaning at Roland Garros in 2013. It would be the last match, yes, but not the decisive one. Arriving in a cold Paris in what seemed like autumn rather than springtime, Nadal was scratchy in his first few matches, dropping a set against world number fifty-nine Daniel Brands on the first Monday of the tournament. But then he began gradually to crank up his arsenal, like a video-gamer finding a new and improved weapon on each level. It was an echo of his entire season.

'In Vina del Mar, he was terrible,' said Toni Nadal, his coach and uncle, as he thought back to Rafael's first tournament of the year in Chile four months before. 'Then in São Paulo he was very, very down, because he had so much pain. Before playing the semi-final, I talked with him for half an hour because he was really sad then.' The pep-talk must have worked, because Nadal went out and struggled to a hard-fought victory against world number 111 Martin Alund. From that moment, the Spaniard has lost only once – to Djokovic in the final of the Monte Carlo Masters. The unfortunate Ferrer has crossed his path four times in 2013 and been dispatched on each occasion.

Here Nadal was superior in every single statistic, from his first-serve percentage to his break-point conversion rate. He would have finished a sudoku puzzle quicker than Ferrer, or named more members of Real Madrid's European Cup-winning side of 1960, had it come to that. He was just in that sort of mood. The first break of Ferrer's serve came up in the third game of the match and there would be seven more before the match was done. The drizzle kept up a steady patter on mackintoshes and umbrellas almost throughout, further dampening what was already a rather flat atmosphere. The only fireworks were the ones held by the protesters objecting to France's recent law legalising same-sex marriage. First play was stopped for a few moments while two people holding a banner were ejected from the upper tier. Then some bare-chested hothead in a mask lit a flare and jumped on to the side of the court, where he was rugby-tackled by a security guard. Nadal was momentarily alarmed, and went on to be broken in a loose game that featured a double-fault. But Ferrer immediately offered back two double-faults of his own to lose the second set.

'He served better, he played very aggressive with his forehand, he didn't make mistakes, he played more regular and consistent than me,' Ferrer said. 'Rafael, in important moments he's the best. I think he has the best mentality I've ever seen in my career. He has everything, no? He can play five sets two days ago and today he can play similar tennis.' This was perhaps the only concern for the Nadal camp: no one knew how his dodgy knees would hold up after his first five-set match of the year. But he said: 'I was able to compete with my one hundred per cent, so that's fantastic.'

Sporting Champion: Rafael Nadal – 9 French Opens (2005, 2006, 2007, 2008, 2010, 2011, 2012, 2013, 2014); 2 Wimbledons (2008, 2010); 2 US Opens (2010, 2013); 1 Australian Open (2009); 1 Olympic Games (2008); 4 Davis Cups (2004, 2008, 2009, 2011).

JUSTIN ROSE – US OPEN GOLF

INSPIRED BY DAD AND A FEAR OF FADING AWAY, A CHAMPION BLOOMED

Paul Hayward, 18 June 2013

From boy wonder to last man standing is a journey few complete. But Justin Rose has made it all the way from the precocity of Royal Birkdale fifteen years ago through collapse and recovery to become England's first US Open champion since Tony Jacklin in 1970. Hold the front page: life can be kind to those who deserve it. Displaying consummate grace under pressure on the eighteenth hole made famous by Ben Hogan in 1950, Rose, now thirty-two, delivered on the show-stopping promise of his fourth-place finish as a seventeen-year-old amateur in the 1998 Open at Royal Birkdale, where he chipped in at the eighteenth and strode gawkily on to the green to receive the love of the crowd. That day the television camera picked out his father Ken, whose death four years later was a touchstone in Rose's inspiring victory at Merion.

'At times it feels twenty-five years since Birkdale, and other times it feels like it was just yesterday. There's a lot of water under the bridge,' Rose said during a classically eloquent post-tournament debrief. 'I sort of announced myself on the golfing scene probably before I was ready to handle it. Golf can be a cruel game. And definitely I have had the ups and downs, but I think that ultimately it's made me stronger and able to handle situations like today.'

The 'downs' he was referring to were the multitude of missed cuts after he rushed into the professional ranks and dumped the young farmer look he had worn at Birkdale. Justin rose, then fell, was a popular interpretation at the time. 'When I was missing twenty-one cuts in a row, I mean I was just trying to not fade away, really,' he admitted as the US Open trophy sent sparkle-rays across Merion. 'I just didn't want to be known as a one-hit wonder, a flash in the pan. I believed in myself inherently. Deep down I always knew I had a talent to play the game. And I simply thought that if I put talent and hard work together, surely it will work out in the end, in the long run. I think the other thing that I was able to do during that period was not beat myself further and further into the ground. If I missed a cut by one [shot] one week, and I missed a cut by five one week and two the next week, I would kind of tell myself that I was getting better. I wouldn't kind of beat myself further into the ground. So I think that's how I worked my way out of it a little bit. But also there have been times in my career where I found it hard to finish tournaments, finish events, close out tournaments, and I think a lot of that goes back to that scar tissue of early in my career. I had a two-win season over here on the PGA Tour in 2010 and I felt like I was over the start to my pro career and I could kind of move on and believe in myself and be confident and trust myself under pressure.'

This is how it looked as Rose fought off Phil Mickelson (now a six-time US Open runner-up), Jason Day and Hunter Mahan in an event that has eluded English golfers for forty-three years. Both this season's majors have featured talented golfers wriggling free from the dead hand of bad experiences. Adam Scott won the Masters after blowing his chance in the 2012 Open and Rose, a close friend, affirmed the value of perseverance and faith for those who begin careers spectacularly but lose their way when youth's audacity expires. Rose said: 'It just takes time to heal. I've never really talked about it because you don't want to admit to that being the case, but I think when you've got past something you can talk openly about it. In a moment like this, I can talk about how I feel I've come full circle confidence-wise and game-development-wise. This is a journey. And it goes back twenty, thirty years for me of dreaming, of hoping, of practising, of calloused hands. This could be the most satisfying, because there's no one helping you along the way. You've had to do it the hard way. You've had to do it yourself.'

Born in Johannesburg to English parents who moved back to Hampshire when he was five, Rose played in the 1997 Walker Cup at seventeen and turned pro the day after Birkdale. Though he joined golf's Florida set in Orlando, he says England 'feels like home' and says: 'I do have a pride in representing England.' The 2002 Dunhill Championship was his breakthrough victory, but only in 2010 with his wins in the Memorial and AT&T tournaments did he establish himself as an American Tour heavyweight. 'I've been striving my whole life really to win a major championship,' he said. 'I've holed a putt to win a major championship hundreds of thousands of times on the putting green at home. Preparing for this tournament, I dreamt about the moment of having a putt to win. I'm pretty happy it was a two-incher on the last. And I'm just glad I was kind of the last man standing.'

Discussing Merion, a local caddie told him: 'The first six holes are drama, the second six holes are comedy, and the last six holes are tragedy.' His father's death entered that mix when Sean Foley, his coach, sent him a text on the eve of the final round. 'He said something along the lines of, "Just go out there and be the man that your dad taught you to be and be the man that your kids can look up to", sort of be a role model,' Rose said. 'I miss him [his father Ken] immensely. And I thought today was just a fitting time in which I could honour him by looking up. Even if Phil had finished birdie, birdie, I just felt like I'd done what I could out there. I felt like I sort of put into practice a lot of the lessons he's taught me, and I felt like I conducted myself in a way that he would be proud of, win or lose. That's what today was about for me in a lot of ways as well.

'I was twenty-one when he passed away and I always think that the time together we had was quality, not quantity. I would rather have had twenty-one fantastic years with my dad than forty years of a relationship that was, hey, you know, so-so. But I have very fond memories of the way I grew up. My dad and I were lucky enough to spend a lot of quality time together learning to play the game, after school on the driving range, so I can look back at our life together with a lot of fondness.' Rose said the primary pleasure is 'knowing you've answered the doubts in your own head, you've answered the questions, you've taken on the challenge and you've risen to it'. If a press conference could be better than a winning round of golf, this was close. 'I think my dad always believed I was capable of this,' he said. 'When he was close to passing away, he kind of told my mum, "Don't worry, Justin will be OK. He'll know what to do".'

Sporting Champion: Justin Rose – 1 US Open (2013).

YEATS – ROYAL ASCOT

YEATS EARNS TITLE OF 'THE GREATEST'

Hotspur (J.A. McGrath), 19 June 2009

The welcome custom of naming bars in the new Ascot grandstand after famous winners is certain to force change at The Queen's racecourse. For those who witnessed the magnificent stayer Yeats winning an historic fourth Gold Cup will surely demand a suitable sanctuary in which to celebrate. There have been many great days at Royal Ascot, but this must rank as one of the most special. I never had the pleasure of seeing Brown Jack win any of his seven races here, nor of watching the great Trelawny notching up his collection of fine staying victories. Surely, though, neither could have surpassed this achievement of winning four consecutive runnings of the feature race at the premier Flat meeting. Johnny Murtagh, who has come to love Ballydoyle's galloping flagship with a passion, described his feelings as something extraordinary. 'The brewing of the crowd for the last furlong carried the horse home. I've never experienced anything like it. It's probably the greatest day of my career,' he said.

If the Irishman felt any pressure, he never let it show at any stage of the 2½ mile test. He bounced Yeats out of the stalls to be prominent on the outside, close enough to keep tabs on Frankie Dettori, who had adopted an unusually wide position on Veracity, and far enough ahead of Geordieland to set his chief rival a task when required. Lack of a solid pace in the first half of the race always looked likely to set the race up for Yeats. It was a mystery why Shane Kelly sat four lengths adrift of the champion past the half-mile and never moved up before the home bend. At this point, Murtagh could wait no longer and, in two bounds, Yeats produced acceleration worthy of the Derby favourite he had been five years earlier.

There was a moment, just over a furlong out, when he looked vulnerable, when Patkai appeared likely to spoil the party. Yeats, with the determination of a prize-fighter knowing he is well ahead on points and needs only to stay on his feet in the final round, responded courageously and held on to win by three and a half lengths. Patkai ran his finest race to take second, with a fifteen-length gap to Geordieland in third. 'He's the greatest,' declared Murtagh. 'Yeats has shown here that he is the ultimate heavyweight champion. There was no doubt. He comes to life at Royal Ascot, and Aidan [O'Brien] always said after Navan [when the horse was well beaten] that he would be ready for

Ascot. Yeats is everything positive about racing,' he added.

Two decades ago, John Magnier and his wife Sue might have considered it unlikely that a great stayer, able to run extreme distances at the highest level would be the pin-up horse in their vast collection of thoroughbreds worldwide. Sadler's Wells, Yeats's sire, has been a gold mine at stud, while Galileo is in the same mould. But neither will have given more pleasure on the racecourse. Magnier, who owns the horse in partnership with his wife, as well as close friends, David and Diane Nagle, marvelled at how an isolated change of policy had led to racing history being created. 'We're all delighted and proud to be associated with him, but you can see the people genuinely like this horse, so we're lucky for once that we didn't send him off to stud when he was three or four,' he said. Before the race, Magnier had described Yeats as 'everybody's horse', and how right he was. In a way, everybody present at Ascot has a piece of the horse, who has become one of the Turf's immortals.

Sporting Champion: Yeats – 4 Ascot Gold Cups (2006, 2007, 2008, 2009).

BRAZIL – FOOTBALL WORLD CUP

FOUR MINUTES OF MAGIC SHATTER ITALIAN DREAMS
Donald Saunders, 22 June 1970

Brazil proved beyond all possible doubt that they are the greatest soccer nation in the world, sweeping to a handsome 4–1 victory over Italy, the European champions, at the Aztec Stadium in Mexico City. The gifted Latin-Americans experienced greater difficulty reaching the safety of the dressing room after winning their third World Cup final in twelve years than they had in wrecking the Italian defence during the second half of a memorable match. Within seconds of the final whistle, the Brazilian players were dragged to the turf by deliriously happy supporters and stripped of their green and yellow jerseys. Indeed, Rivelino was so badly mauled that he had to be carried on a stretcher from the pitch where he had helped to make history.

Yet, with more than an hour gone, nobody would have been prepared to bet on which of these teams was to earn the distinction of becoming the first outright holders of the Jules Rimet trophy. But the six greatest footballers in the world refused to be harnessed. Pelé, Jairzinho, Tostão, Rivelino, Gérson and Clodoaldo decided the Italian defence could be shattered. Midway through the second half they proved their point with four minutes of magic. Two goals in that crucial period left Italy without a hope of becoming the first European nation to win the World Cup on the western side of the Atlantic.

Then, as the stadium clock ticked to within four minutes of the final whistle, Carlos Alberto, Brazil's captain, raced upfield to score his first goal in the tournament. Half an hour later, Carlos Alberto led his merry men on a lap of honour, the gold cup gleaming in his hands. So ended what is certainly the greatest of the four World Cup competitions I have watched in the past dozen years. And nobody is likely to argue that the wrong country are taking home the trophy.

From their first match – against Czechoslovakia – I had doubted the ability of Pelé and his ballet dancers to 'carry' a vulnerable defence right through to final victory. Now I am happy to report that they succeeded. Even after Brazil had jumped ahead in the eighteenth minute, with Pelé heading home a perfectly placed cross from Rivelino, I still was uncertain of a Latin-American triumph. The doubts increased twenty minutes later when Brazil's defence committed the dreadful sort of error to which they have been so prone in Mexico, and were severely punished by their opponents. Piazza, Brito and Félix got themselves into an awful tangle, and Boninsegna was left to place the ball in the unguarded net.

With Mazzola matching Gérson in midfield and Riva causing problems upfront after the interval, one wondered whether a European triumph yet might be achieved. Such dreams ended between the sixty-seventh and seventy-first minutes. First, Jairzinho and Gérson brought off a brilliant scissors move that ended with Gérson thumping Jairzinho's pass into the net from the edge of the penalty box. The Italians were allowed no time to recover. Within four minutes Pelé headed on a cross from Gérson to Jairzinho, who ran the ball into the net.

Italy sent on Juliano for Bertinio, and near the end Rivera replaced Boninsegna, but their cause was lost. To underline that fact, Carlos Alberto sprinted on to a pass from Pelé and drove a fourth goal past the helpless Albertosi. So utter, conclusive victory went to the team who have shown us, throughout these three weeks, that they are the true masters of the art of soccer.

Sporting Champions: Brazil – 5 World Cups (1958, 1962, 1970, 1994, 2002).

SOUTH AFRICA – RUGBY WORLD CUP

SPRINGBOKS REACH THEIR CROCK OF GOLD

John Mason, 26 June 1995

On another famous day in the history of the new South Africa, the newly crowned world champions also unearthed another trim, eager number six to rival the potency of captain Francois Pienaar, albeit an old favourite in a new guise. President Mandela's supreme sense of public relations made his inspired decision to wear a replica Springbok number-six jersey in no way cosmetic or embarrassing. As he has done in other more fraught fields, the president pointed the way. Pienaar, the other number six wearing a South African shirt at Ellis Park, and his colleagues, required no second bidding in beating New Zealand. They were magnificent, against all odds and, in some respects, the better team. Few teams have ever defended so consistently well.

Here was a second occasion – day one of the tournament and the win over Australia being the other – in which the nationwide desire for success was as powerful as it was tangible. It was a force as real as the Boeing jumbo jet that twice thundered over the stadium at little more than grandstand height beforehand, the message 'Good Luck, Bokkies' painted in giant letters on the underside of the wings. The ramifications of victory in extra time over New Zealand, the favourites, will, said Pienaar, take an age to sink in. For the present, he and the squad wanted to enjoy at leisure what they had achieved in the past month. Many things made South Africa's winning of the World Cup possible: a fervent tide of national emotion personified by President Mandela, deep pride and sheer bloodymindedness in demonstrating to the rest of the world that being South African was nothing of which to be ashamed. Those aspects, though, were ingredients only. The driving force on the pitch was Pienaar. Off it, too, I suspect, though, shrewd person that he is, South Africa's captain insisted that the roles of management – coach Kitch Christie and manager Morné du Plessis – were essential planks of a winning campaign.

For a long time it appeared that South Africa might falter on the last agonising lap. Churlish as it will sound, New Zealand let the big one get away. They dug a succession of holes for themselves, a sequence of unforced errors severely curtailing the menace and rhythm of the attacking schemes that had so upset previous opponents. Fluency was always a fingertip away. Handling was suspect long before South Africa applied the defensive brakes, passing slap-dash. At times the besetting desire to get Jonah Lomu, the giant on the left, into the action was counter-productive. Flanker Josh Kronfeld battled well but was ultimately seen off by Kruger.

When the All Blacks suddenly appreciated that they had a match on their hands, the boys among the All Blacks looked vulnerable: Jeff Wilson, Glen Osborne, Andrew Mehrtens. Poor Mehrtens, brave as his penalty goal from 55 yards in the opening minutes of extra time was, his dropped goal miss from in front two minutes from full-time will haunt him for ever. New Zealand, the World Cup within tantalising reach half-a-dozen times in a spell-binding contest, were finally undone by Joel Stransky, the outside-half whom Robert Jones, the Wales and Swansea scrum-half who has played for Western Province, insisted a year before was the one player who possessed the key to sustained South African success.

The tone for a remarkable afternoon having been set by the president and another enterprising pageant to mark the closing day. New Zealand led 3–0, 6–3 and, in the second minute of extra time, 12–9. South Africa, having drawn level three times, got back to 12–12 in the twelfth of the twenty minutes' extra time necessary because it was 9–9 at full-time. The prospect that because of two dismissals against Canada in a pool match, South Africa would forfeit the trophy if the scores remained tied was too much to bear. Renewed pleas from Pienaar, plus superb policing of Lomu, did the trick. The defensive shutters were double-locked and barred. There was no way through. Silly obstruction, uncharacteristic risks and the English disease of kicking the ball away, abetted by running across, not straight, meant that the All Blacks were moving down a gear, not increasing the tempo of the contest.

Not a try in sight but for an exchange of penalty goals and dropped goals by the outside-halves, the match offered everything else, even the ugly fist of Richard Loe which he raised in idiotic anger within three minutes of arriving as replacement for Craig Dowd. Loe was lucky that he got a warning only from referee Ed Morrison. There were six minutes twenty-six seconds remaining when Stransky made an indelible entry in the record books: a dropped goal, to make it 15–12.

Sporting Champions: South Africa – 2 World Cups (1995, 2007).

SOME PICTURE – ENGLISH GREYHOUND DERBY

GREYHOUND RACING'S ANSWER TO
COE, PELÉ AND NIJINKSY

Giles Smith, 4 October 1997

I said to Steve Spiteri: 'Maybe we could meet for lunch,' and he said: 'That would be lush.' So we arranged to meet beside the dry-cleaners outside Cannon Street station in the City, just along the road from where Steve works. Steve is a trader on the London Metal Exchange. He spends his days moving copper and zinc around with a phone and a computer screen. This earns him money (quite a lot of money: he's currently trying to 'sort out a lake' for his house in Kent) which in turn buys him greyhounds for racing, one of which could prove itself to be the greatest dog the sport has seen, the all-time dog of dogs, king dog.

When Steve arrived at the dry-cleaners, he was wearing a dark suit, a light blue shirt and a quality silk tie with urns on it, its knot askew. Everyone in his office has a nickname, and Steve's is Spit. He is thirty-six and he has black hair, brushed back, which starts to get curly on its way down to his collar. He had his mobile pressed against his ear, so we had to sort of mime hello and then walk up the street a while until Steve's call was finished. Steve ends his phone calls with a rapid 'Bye-bye-bye'. As it turned out, this lunchtime Steve wasn't hungry. I didn't know whether to put this down to his mounting nerves ahead of the Irish Derby in Dublin, which has certainly made him a little jittery, a bit fired-up. He says he has already run the race in his head thousands of times – the hare whirring round, the traps flipping open, his dog Some Picture streaking away to the crucial first bend, legging it home from there.

Some Picture has already won the Scottish Derby and the English Derby (Steve posed for photos afterwards with Wimbledon football manager Joe Kinnear), so if he wins again, there's £50,000 prize money, plus a £100,000 Triple Crown bonus, courtesy of the sponsors. Not to mention a place in dog history. A single-season Triple Crown is unheard of in greyhound racing. The impossible leg of the impossible treble. Not even Mick the Miller pulled that off. The bookies don't even want to think about it.

But in any case, lunch – as the movie *Wall Street* pointed out – is for wimps. So Steve and I went to a pub instead – one with a selection of well-kept real ales, not that that particularly interested Steve, who asked for two bottles of Becks in a pint glass. Steve told me he once got barred from this pub by the landlady for putting his cigarette out on the carpet, but that was a while ago and now 'everything's sweet'. The bar was wedged tight so we went and stood out on the pavement in the warm autumn sun while the City went by on its lunch-hour.

Steve is not alone in his excitement about Some Picture. The *Racing Post* said recently: 'Athletics had Coe. Football had Pelé. Horse racing had Nijinsky. But for greyhound racing there has always been a blank space . . . until now.' The paper was referring to Some Picture – an implausibly consistent ball of energy in a notoriously capricious sport. The entire British Greyhound Racing Board, too, are hopping excitedly from one foot to the other, knowing what a phenomenon could do to speed the recovery of an ailing game. The board are lobbying for Some Picture as BBC Sports Personality of the Year. 'Some Picture has got more personality than most of the sports stars in this country put together,' a spokesman said. William Hill will currently offer you 20–1 about that. Steve does his bit for the bigger cause. 'Families go dog racing, you know,' he told me, through the smoke from a Marlboro Light. 'I've got photos of my son at Hackney dog track in a pushchair.' Steve has three children from his marriage; and now he's with a girlfriend, Michelle, who has three more. 'I say to the kids, "Do you want to come racing? We're going racing". And we go racing.' He grew up in Wapping in the East End of London and his mum would take him to holiday meetings at Catford. Soon he was skiving off school to go during the day. You got in for nothing if you were accompanied by an adult, so Steve and his mate would hang around outside until they found someone willing to take them in. Steve says he used his pocket money 'to bet a few dogs'. But even with no money, he would walk to Catford just to watch them run. 'It's fast,' he said, 'and, don't forget, it's flesh and blood out there.'

Steve came to the City at sixteen as a messenger, did a spell as a ring-dealer in the trading pit but got 'fed up shouting all the time' and worked his way up to an office job. One year he got a £350 bonus, borrowed another £50 and called up for a dog advertised in the *Sporting Life.* Face the Village won fifteen races out of twenty-nine. Steve bought some more dogs and began putting them through graded races, then open races, then classics. He took up with a gifted trainer, Charlie Lister from Nottingham, and eventually, as Steve puts it, 'we started to fall on fast dogs'. Steve couldn't really explain how he picked out his dogs (he presently has eight) but a lot of it seemed to come down to 'good feelings'. He had 'good feelings' about Spring Rose, who earned him £30,000 in prize money in 1996, and he had 'good feelings' about Some Picture, who Charlie Lister pointed him towards in August 1996. 'When Charlie got him out of the kennel, I knew he was special just by looking at him. He really looked the part. He's seventy-eight pounds, he's black, he's got great physique, he's got great balance, everything about him's class. I love him. He's a flying machine.' Steve paid £12,000 for him. Some Picture has so far earned £93,000 in prize money.

'Charlie knows I'm dog mad and he respects my opinion,' Steve said. 'And Charlie's been in the game a long time and I rate him as the best trainer in the country. He puts so much effort into the dogs. Each dog is given individual care. He feeds the best that can be fed to a dog. He's a great planner. With any athlete, it's all about form and it's all about peaking them at the right time. At the Scottish Derby, we didn't think the track would suit the dog because it was a short run to the bend, and we thought we'd have to turn at the back. But come the final, he exploded. He went round the bend third, but did the fastest run of the Scottish Derby right there.'

At some points in our conversation, Steve talked as if he himself would be running the race. 'I don't expect I'll sleep too well on Friday night,' he said. 'I'll get up early Saturday morning, get my papers, get everything together, get to the airport and go racing. If I don't win it,' he added, 'I will spend the rest of my life trying to win it. And I will win it.' At Shelbourne Park, Some Picture has been drawn in trap four. 'We just need a bit of luck round that first bend and this dog will run a big, big race.' Steve insists he is 'not really a big gambler, as such. But I backed him at 10–1 and I'll pick up a right few quid if he wins. And I won a right few quid at the English Derby, as well. I backed him at twenty-fives and I pressed him up again at elevens just before the first round.'

It will be Some Picture's last race before he is retired to stud. This thought saddens Steve. 'I've always managed to chuck the day of him retiring out of my mind,' he said. Before the English Derby final, a consortium of Australian dog breeders wanted to talk to Steve about buying Some Picture and, as Steve said, 'well, I was quite rude to them, actually. I was, like, "Leave me alone, this is my race dog. I don't want to talk about stud".' Steve seemed to become quite misty when he said all this, and I don't think it was just the second pint. 'You'll read I'm going to make a lot of money out of the dog going to stud,' Steve said, when he had recomposed himself. Indeed. One estimate says covering fees will be around £1,000 per time, maybe twice a week. 'But this is where I make my money,' Steve added, 'up in the City. Stud is not what I'm interested in.'

I asked Steve if he knew what he was going to wear in Dublin. He admitted he'd been thinking about it. Ideally, he said, he'd wear a replica England football shirt, a pair of jeans and some Doc Martens, but he couldn't see that going over very well at the presentation ceremony. So maybe it would be the beige suit he wore for the English Derby – 'without wanting to be superstitious about it'. Finally Steve told me: 'It would be nice to pick up Regal's hundred grand, don't get me wrong. I'd have it well spent: it wouldn't be in my pocket too long. But I would run Some Picture in Dublin for nothing.' And I believed him.

Sporting Champion: Some Picture – 1 English Greyhound Derby (1997); 1 Scottish Greyhound Derby (1997).

JULY

SPAIN – EUROPEAN FOOTBALL CHAMPIONSHIP

MATA SEALS TREBLE AS SPAIN CONJURE FINAL TO TREASURE

Henry Winter, 2 July 2012

Spain's 4–0 victory over Italy was so much more than a stunning scoreline conjured up by one of the most magical collections of footballers in history. This was a statement by Spain, a thrilling ninety-minute advertisement to the world about how the game should be played, with skill, movement, bursts of unstoppable pace, with pass after pass after pass. This was simplicity and beauty, golden football leading to silverware. This was history in the making, Spain recording an unprecedented three trophies in a row – European Championship, World Cup, European Championship.

Vicente del Bosque's side of all the talents were good from back to front. Iker Casillas made some important aerial interceptions. Jordi Alba was all shimmering class at left-back, Xavi and Andrés Iniesta controlled midfield as if they had been presented with the title deeds, while Cesc Fàbregas was immense in attack. David Silva and Alba got the party started with first-half goals before the Chelsea pair of Fernando Torres and Juan Mata put the Italians out of their misery late on. It was a joy to watch, a riposte to their critics, a compelling end to a fantastic Euros.

Boring? Make that beautiful. These sublime Spaniards had been derided as lacking a penetrative edge. Their style had been described as *passenachio, tiki-taka* or tippy-tapas, but they started with far greater tempo, pressing high in their usual fashion but really shifting the ball forward quicker than during their run to the final. Before Iniesta, Fàbregas and Silva combined so devastatingly after thirteen minutes, Italy enjoyed an early flourish, providing the ultimate in false dawns. Antonio Cassano began working the left, looking to muscle past Álvaro Arbeloa. Sergio Ramos climbed above Mario Balotelli to head clear, making sure the Italian was aware of his presence with a little nudge on the way down. Andrea Pirlo let fly. Spain then clicked into gear, gloriously so. Ramos headed over. A mesmerising move climaxed with Fàbregas, Spain's number ten with a 'false number nine' role, squared to Xavi, who shot over.

Building like a rising tide against a dam wall, Spain had to break through. The pressure was too much. Xavi, inevitably, was involved, finding Iniesta, inevitably. Xavi could find Iniesta in the Kalahari let alone in Kiev. Even by his standards of distribution, Iniesta's response was majestic. He guided a pass of elegance and malevolence behind Giorgio Chiellini, the ball almost winking mockingly at the full-back as it sped past. Fàbregas controlled the ball effortlessly with his first touch, his second cutting it back strongly but accurately towards Silva. The little gem that Manchester City fans call Merlin scored with an unstoppable header. It was as if Spain had been storing up this special display, the ball moved as quickly as an ice hockey puck, the determination to demonstrate their class palpable. Boring? No chance. Not with this sort of football, all neat touch and clever interchanging. Not with this sort of ambition.

Italy still had to scavenge for scraps. Balotelli tried to run through on goal, attempting to outpace Ramos but Casillas was out quickly to clear. Another swirling Pirlo corner produced a marvellous punched clearance from Casillas. For all these little moments of defiance, Pirlo, Daniele De Rossi and company were tackling Everest without oxygen. The Italians soon became breathless chasing the ball. They rallied during the middle of a compelling half, pressuring at corners. Yet the force was against them, their defence requiring rejigging when Chiellini hobbled off after twenty-one minutes with his hamstring damaged.

Spain were so good in so many departments. Affronted when Italy dared dwell in possession, Spain worked in gangs to win the ball back, like pickpockets swarming around their victim. Little Silva put in some big challenges. The crowd looked on, utterly absorbed, cries of 'Italia' mingling with the endless chants of '*olé*' from the more populated Spanish section. Sadly, the Olympic Stadium was not full, a reflection on the perfect storm of economic ravages, inflated ticket prices and long distances, although some Spaniards did drive. It was a cosmopolitan audience, reflected in the fans' flags hailing allegiance to Spain, Italy, Ukraine, Poland, Germany, Portsmouth, Chesterfield and Renfrewshire United. They had so much to watch. Gerard Piqué flew in on Cassano, and flew into Pedro Proença's book as much for the angle of his advance. The excellent Casillas punched away a Cassano shot. De Rossi was seeking to drive Italy forward, attempting to turn back the red tide. No chance. Spain just absorbed the pressure, hitting back in style.

Forget *tiki-taka*. Spain's second was turbo-taka. Alba, looking an absolute snip at the £14 million Barcelona paid Valencia, has experienced some serious challenges for left-back of the tournament, notably from Portugal's Fábio Coentrão, but he showed why he was the best here. Passing to Xavi, Alba took off like a sprinter, hurtling upfield, knowing that Xavi would return the compliment. Xavi did. Right into the full-back's path. Alba then finished expertly, sliding the ball past Gianluigi Buffon.

Italy looked rattled and Andrea Barzagli treated Iniesta to

some rugged old-school Italian defending. Half-time arrived, the DJ surely paying tribute to Spain's effect on opponents with 'Another One Bites the Dust' and then reminding everyone what Del Bosque's side were to the rest – 'one step beyond'. Watching from the sidelines, Italy's coach, Cesare Prandelli, must have felt like a fireman facing a towering inferno with a pipette of water. He removed Cassano, sent on Antonio Di Natale, who should have scored but headed over Ignazio Abate's cross.

Spain just flicked at the afterburners again. Fàbregas embarked on a wonderful dribble, gliding past Balzaretti and Leonardo Bonucci, before Italy managed to man the beleaguered barricades. Bonucci was then fortunate not to concede a penalty when handling. The additional assistant referee behind the goal saw nothing wrong, much to Spain's annoyance. Poor Italy. They really needed twelve men to live with Spain. Soon they were down to ten when Thiago Motta, who had come on for Riccardo Montolivo, was carried off on a stretcher. Reduced in numbers, Italy were further behind seven minutes from time. Spain's fans had been chanting '*campeones*' for some time when Xavi sent Torres through and he finished in style, stroking the ball past Buffon. The poacher then turned goalmaker, Torres inviting his Chelsea team-mate Mata to make it 4–0. Some statement.

Sporting Champions: Spain – 3 European Championships (1964, 2008, 2012); 1 World Cup (2010).

NIGEL MANSELL – BRITISH GRAND PRIX

PEOPLE'S CHAMPION WHO HAS
MOTOR RACING IN HIS BLOOD

Michael Parkinson, 2 October 1995

The first time Nigel Mansell had an accident he was still at school and driving a go-kart. He was coming down a hill on a fast track at Morecambe at 100mph when his steering snapped. The kart hit a kerb, somersaulted and he was knocked unconscious. When they picked him up he was haemorrhaging from the ears and nose. They took him to hospital, where he drifted in and out of consciousness. He awoke to find a priest at the end of the bed and realised he was being given the last rites. 'And what else can I do for you, my son?' asked the priest. 'Sod off,' said Nigel Mansell. Since then anyone standing between Mansell and his ambition to be the best racing driver in the world received a similar rebuke. Naked and brutal ambition did not make him the most popular figure in the Machiavellian court of Formula One, but it made him one of the most successful.

At present he is resting. He has not retired. He has taken some time off to concentrate on the beautiful golf course and country club he has bought at Woodbury Park in Devon. In the grounds he is supervising the completion of a leisure centre complete with pool, two championship-standard indoor tennis courts, gymnasium and squash courts. I asked him how much it was costing. 'Tens of millions,' he said. Did he have partners? 'My wife,' he said. In between times he sat down and finished his autobiography. *Mansell: The Autobiography* is as plain a title as you might expect from someone who is generally believed – wrongly, as it turns out – to have as much personality as a bag of sprouts. In fact, it is an absorbing account of a man's pursuit of a dream and leaves you wondering how anyone who has lived such a dramatic and fascinating life could end up with the reputation of being boring. Perhaps the reason is that not until now has Nigel Mansell found it necessary to explain himself or assess his life. He has been too obsessed with winning races to worry about trivial matters like beauty contests.

We met in his office at his golf course: large desk, deep leather chairs, comfortable but business-like. When I asked him what conclusions he had reached having journeyed back through his life for the book, he took me into another room. When he switched on the lights the place gleamed with gold and glittered with silver. On display behind glass were the hundreds of trophies he had won in a lifetime of racing. 'This is unique. Nothing like it in the world,' he said. Then you realise he has won thirty-one grands prix, making him the third best of all time in the world and the most successful British driver in history. He is the only person to win consecutive Formula One and IndyCar titles. He holds a record of nine grand prix wins in a season. He was once world champion. He is the only person to win the IndyCar title in his first season. He said: 'Sometimes I don't think I've done very much and then I come in here and have to change my mind.'

He was born in 1953 in Upton-on-Severn and christened Nigel Ernest James Mansell. His father was an engineer, his mother ran a tea shop. He followed in his father's footsteps but always wanted to be a racing driver. He told me: 'I can remember when I was seven or eight, driving vehicles on a farm and I'd race through long grass not able to see where I was going. It was like driving through rain. Very exciting.' He fell out with his father when he moved from carts into cars. He met his wife Rosanne when she was seventeen, married her when he was twenty-one. They are still together. She worked an eighty-hour week to fund his early ambitions. He left the engineering job and became a window cleaner. To finance his way into Formula Three they borrowed money and sold their house. They have been paupers and millionaires and, like most couples who have stood firm through good times and bad, they are two parts of the same whole. Neither is complete without the other. Mansell's ambition was so remorseless, his wife's support so total that they frightened away any close acquaintances. They were friendless as well as being penniless. An exciting evening out was taking the dog for a walk. They would sit for hours and plan for the day when Nigel Mansell would be a force to be reckoned with in grand prix racing. Looking back, Rosanne wonders what kept them going. 'He had such self-belief and I suppose I believed in him,' she said.

He was, he says, always an outsider in motorsport. He was told at the beginning of his career that he would never make it to Formula One with a name like Nigel Mansell. In those early days he became aware of a group of drivers he christened 'The Chosen Ones'. These were the men who received special attention from the media and had plentiful backing from sponsors or corporations. 'The word would go out, "Keep an eye on this boy, he's a future world champion",' said Mansell. He stood outside the magic circle. The first man to realise his potential was Colin Chapman. He declared Mansell would be world champion. 'He liked me because he liked a driver who would take one of his cars and wring its neck. A driver who always gave everything he had and more,' said Mansell. 'I compare driving a racing car to operating on a jagged edge. If you push too hard it can kill you and a lot of people have gone over the edge. Knowing how to operate on the edge is a talent in itself.'

One of the most fascinating passages in the book is where he describes what it is like to be inside a Formula One car. 'The body receives a terrible pummelling . . . from the thousands of shocks which travel up through the steering wheel, the foot rest and the seat as you fly along the ground at 200mph. Through the corners the G forces try to snap your head off. When you brake your insides are thrown forward with violence . . . when you accelerate your head is thrown back violently against the carbon-fibre wall at the back of the cockpit, which is the only thing separating you from a 200-litre bag of fuel . . . the cockpit is hotter than a sauna and you are wearing thick fireproof overalls and underwear.'

I asked him if he had anxiety dreams before a race. 'Everyone does. Private and horrific. They are not something I discuss,' he replies. I said he talked in the book of going wheel to wheel, lap after lap, with the likes of Ayrton Senna and the public not knowing what it was like. So what was it like? 'Sometimes pretty scary. If you didn't do it professionally you'd had it. Fortunately Ayrton and I had a lot of respect for one another. What seems to be lacking nowadays is that respect. When I first started in Formula One, drivers like Alan Jones and Niki Lauda would soon tick off any new driver who was not looking in his mirror or was getting in the way. There would be a terrible rumpus. Nowadays, if it happens the culprit is likely to tell you to piss off. Not much respect there.' I asked him if he thought Michael Schumacher and Damon Hill might do each other serious injury. 'I will defuse that question by saying Formula One is the pinnacle of motorsport and I like to think that a driver will always demonstrate the full range of his skills while being properly professional about it. Let us hope they bear that in mind and do a little better in future,' he said.

I wondered if taking time off from racing, spending time with his family, had dulled his competitive edge. Daft question. He reminded me that he had taken twenty quid off me that very morning playing golf around his course. We teed off in an early-morning mist that obscured the second shot to the green. This did not deter my opponent, who started with a birdie and was level par after seven holes. I had noticed him spending some time on his mobile phone between shots so I inquired politely if there was a problem. 'Not at all,' he said. 'As a matter of fact I keep phoning the greenkeeper to ask where the flag is on the greens we can't see.' And I thought he had X-ray eyes. When the sun burnt through and we could see the course in all its splendour he became more helpful. On one hole, a long par-four, he said: 'Hit it straight down the fairway.' I did as I was told. 'Good shot,' he said. 'I only hope it gets over the ditch.' 'What ditch?' I said. 'The ditch your ball has just gone into,' he said. He went round the course and only dropped three shots. Had he putted well it could have been even better. His swing is tailored to accommodate the fact that he has broken his back three times and his neck once during his career. He is a subscriber to the Brian Close theory that there is no such thing as pain. He says his career owes everything to his ability to blank out pain.

He saw a four-ball holding up a two-ball and drove across to keep the traffic moving. When the players recognised the marshal, they reacted as they would meeting an old friend. It was one of Mansell's greatest gifts that in a sport of private jets, presidential suites and limos with smoked-glass windows he managed to come across as an ordinary bloke doing an extraordinary job. No other driver has engaged the British fans as Mansell did. He might have lacked the glamour and polish of others but no one performed with more brio and courage. 'I think that sometimes the drivers of today forget the spectators. I always regarded myself as a driver and an entertainer. I've always had a marvellous relationship with the fans. The new breed of drivers coming through don't understand it and I think they miss a lot,' he said. I suggested that maybe it was because he had a life before becoming a racing driver. In other words Mansell, the world champion, was also Nigel the guy who used to clean their windows. And perhaps in his achievements they recognised their own dreams and aspirations. He thought for a moment and raised an eyebrow (his eyebrows, by the way, are the same size as his famous moustache): 'I like that. I think you have a valid point,' he said.

It is impossible not to feel pleased for Nigel Mansell as he gazes out on his 350 acres of sunlit Devon countryside. At forty-two he can look back with satisfaction at a job well done and forward with equanimity. But a devil stirs within him. He feels he should still be racing, that the last year or so spun out of control and what should have been a triumphant return to Formula One with the Williams team developed into low farce at McLaren. At McLaren he had difficulty fitting into the cockpit. There was a design fault. The critics said he couldn't fit in the car because of the size of his wallet. He said: 'This year I felt I should have been in a Williams car going for my second world championship.' Why wasn't he? 'Let us just say that some drivers are hired not because they are the best but because there are market forces at work. The driver sits on tens of millions of dollars. There is a lot of wheeling and dealing going on. A lot of . . .' he paused searching for a word. 'Skulduggery,' I suggested. 'Intrigue,' he said with a cold smile.

Would he let his two sons go into motor racing? 'No way. In any case it's predicted they will be well over six feet tall in manhood so the question doesn't arise,' he said. But why didn't he want to give them the chance of achieving what he had? 'I want them to be competitive. I want them to be winners. I want them to enjoy sport as much as I have. But I want them to be involved in a game like golf,' he said. I asked why. He thought for a minute and then said: 'Because it's pure.'

When questioned about his own future he said he had not retired. He is sitting down and looking at the offers on the table. He says a proper offer would get him back into Formula One but that the most intriguing invitations so far have come from America. In spite of winning the IndyCar championship you sense he has unfinished business in the States. But why risk everything he has worked for? Doesn't he state in the last line of his autobiography: 'I realise I am lucky to be alive.' He said: 'And I am. But life is not a practice lap. My career has been racing cars. Perhaps I should keep on doing that so long as I am able. Life today is what you have today. Tomorrow it will be gone.' If he does return to motor racing it will be a foolish fellow to bet against Nigel Mansell writing the closing chapter of his life story in the manner of his choosing. He fears no man. What he should perhaps consider is the possibility that next time round he might come up against the opponent who has never been beaten, the one with the long beard carrying the scythe.

Sporting Champion: Nigel Mansell – 4 British Grands Prix (1986, 1987, 1991, 1992); 1 Formula One World Drivers' Championship (1992); 1 CART IndyCar World Series (1993).

MARTINA NAVRATILOVA – THE CHAMPIONSHIPS, WIMBLEDON

VETERAN QUEEN OF TENNIS STILL HOLDING COURT

Sebastian Coe, 20 May 2003

Martina Navratilova spent her early years in the Krkonoše Mountains of Czechoslovakia which are also known as the Giant Mountains – an apt word for the colossus who went on to tower over women's tennis. With career earnings of more than £12 million (only surpassed by Steffi Graf), and still playing, the question has to be asked: 'Why are you still doing this at forty-six?'

She responds simply: 'Life. We're lucky to be here. It's about learning and our time is limited. I'm still learning, to do better, still studying strategy. I'm technically better now than I was in my heyday. You know I hit a shot against [Jana] Novotna at Wimbledon last year when I played. After the game she said, "What was that? I've never seen it before". I said I only learnt to play it a few days ago. The key was the grip but you never stop learning the game. You have to have talent, but if you haven't the heart to explore the talent it's all a waste of time.'

Navratilova turned professional in 1975 and in the early days of her career in America, her hunger to explore was focused as much on the fast-food drive-through as the court, prompting American journalist Bud Collins to describe her as 'the Great Wide Hope', weighing in at one stage at an unflattering 11 stone 13 lb. 'I defected to the States after losing in the semis of the US Open in 1975. It was inevitable. I never felt more at home anywhere than the first time I visited America. It was the space I suppose. I'd also arrived in a country where it was up to you to make something of your life – and the possibilities seemed endless. I was somewhere where you could do or say and think and feel what you wanted to,' she said. For a woman who never hid her sexuality, America was a place where she felt comfortable. 'People didn't care what you were, they just wanted to watch good tennis.'

It was another eleven years before she returned to her homeland and four years before she was reunited with her mother and stepfather, who had guided her formative tennis years. 'I missed my family, particularly my grandmother and my dog, but how could I return? I was too much of a rebel. I'm not great with authority. I don't like to be told what I have to do. I came from a repressive society. Saddam Hussein and Stalin are two peas from the same pod.'

The records show that Navratilova won fifty-seven Grand Slam championships – only Margaret Court won more and no player, male or female, has won more tournaments than her 167 or more matches than her 1,483. She was ranked number one for 331 weeks, second only to Graf. However, what the records don't show are the physical changes and mental traumas that so coloured her game and the perception of the tennis public, which in the early days viewed her with suspicion – a talented but troubled soul, prone to bouts of rage which lost her matches within her reach. With the help of Sandra Haynie, the US golf champion, she learnt to control if not entirely master the demons. In 1978 Navratilova won the first of her nine Wimbledon singles and doubles titles, defeating Chris Evert and becoming the World Tennis Association's number one only a few weeks later. Returning to Wimbledon the following year she won again, but by 1981 it became clear that her physical limitations were 'too obvious to ignore'. 'Nineteen eighty-one was a disaster. I didn't win a single final – not even on grass – I lost at Eastbourne, then at Wimbledon in the semis to Chris. I even lost in Surbiton to Betsy Nagelson, for Christ's sake. I always planned to play until I was thirty and I was now twenty-five and time was running out. I thought I'd better get serious and then Nancy Lieberman, a great basketball player, really laid it down for me. "You're wasting your time and talent and you've got to get your arse in gear".'

With ferocious purpose and a brutal conditioning programme, and a new coach in the controversial Renée Richards, and additional help from a track coach, Navratilova changed forever the physicality of the women's game and arguably female sport. 'Up until then I played tennis, and not much of that – maybe two hours a day in December I lifted weights. Then I started to work out with a track coach who could outrun me backwards. Ran lots of one hundred-metre and fifty-metre repeats, played a lot of basketball, lifted serious weights and when Renée started to work with me I'd got the conditioning and then the tennis coaching in place and started to work on the emotional. I studied the strategy and technique but not the emotional side of my game until 1989, when I started to work with BJK [Billie Jean King]. Had I done that earlier I'm sure I'd have won more. I mastered the physical side and neglected the mental.'

The physical change was dramatic. Gone were the heavy thighs, the Rubensesque arms and laboured movement – replaced by muscle definition and a new inner strength. Within a year she had won fifteen singles tournaments, fourteen doubles (which included her first victory on clay in Paris) and the first of her six straight Wimbledon championships. 'For the next five years I kicked butt, but by the end of 1986 I had started to burn out. I was playing too many matches and forgetting that you can't work out and improve if you're playing tennis all the time. It was Virginia Wade who made me realise that. I needed to peak. She recognised it and I didn't. I was in denial.' The legendary BJK also came to the rescue. 'You can go on playing like this, quit altogether or get some fun back into it,' she told her. Navratilova worries that what happened to her late in her career is now a common syndrome for today's young talent. 'You just can't work on your game when you're playing tennis week after week. Now it's just about quality over quantity. I didn't really start to play until I was fifteen or sixteen. I don't believe you have to be that good at ten. Everybody hits the ball well. Most kids now have hit more groundstrokes at the age of fourteen than I did at twenty-five, but then they don't do anything else. They're not taught to play tennis – skills or finesse. Hit hard and win at the earliest age you can and the agents will pay attention. The problem is they sign a contract but don't have a second serve.'

Navratilova is happy and comfortable in her fifth decade. But if there was disappointment it is a genuine yearning to have played the very best in any era. 'Chris [Evert] was important for me. She made me change my whole approach. I had to or I'd never have beaten her and I made her change when I thought she never could challenge me again. Steffi was sensational; Venus and Serena are not as good as they can be.' And the best? 'I really think I was. At my best I wouldn't have feared anybody.'

Sporting Champion: Martina Navratilova – 9 Wimbledon Singles Championships (1978, 1979, 1982, 1983, 1984, 1985, 1986, 1987, 1990); 4 US Opens (1983, 1984, 1986, 1987); 3 Australian Opens (1981, 1983, 1985); 2 French Opens (1982, 1984).

MARK WOODFORDE AND TODD WOODBRIDGE – THE CHAMPIONSHIPS, WIMBLEDON

THE DOUBLE ACT THAT'S CLOSE TO SYNCHRONISED TENNIS

James Mossop, 21 June 1998

The telepathic 'Woodies' have banked $13 million between them. They are going for a record sixth successive Wimbledon doubles win. And they are planning to split after a tournament where the only prize is a medal. The unique Australian partnership of Mark Woodforde and Todd Woodbridge, often seen as Mr Cool and Mr Angry, have a dream that lives beyond the lawns of Wimbledon. They want to say goodbye with a gold medal on home soil at the Sydney 2000 Olympics.

It would be the perfect way of defending the gold they won in Atlanta in 1996 and the closure of a double-act unprecedented in world tennis. The left-hander (Woodforde) and the right-hander

(Woodbridge); the sage (Woodforde, thirty-two) and the twenty-six-year-old volatile sorcerer (Woodbridge). 'These are the odds and evens that make us the Woodies,' says Woodforde, the tall one with the red hair who talks of Sydney 2000 as the end of their rainbow. They are close friends off the court. Woodforde was best man at Woodbridge's wedding three years ago. The two couples play four-ball golf, visit the theatre and often eat out together.

The Woodies' understanding on court is phenomenal, and the way in which they came together in 1990, before winning their forty-six career titles, seemed to be something handed down from the gods. Woodforde explained: 'I used to partner John McEnroe and then one day in Cincinnati he told me he was going to wind down from doubles play. He said I should find someone younger, someone who wanted to play week-in week-out, singles and doubles, worldwide. Someone right-handed, an Australian because of the camaraderie we Aussies have. And without mentioning Todd Woodbridge's name he selected the ingredients. Todd was finishing his doubles partnership and we teamed up. It's almost as though we fell into each other's arms. We played twice at the end of 1990 and we were shocking. The next year, after a couple of good tournaments, we realised we had something.'

The flourishing partnership seemed to work on an unwavering mental wavelength. It has become as close to synchronised tennis as anyone could imagine. They are different in physique, Woodforde (6 feet 2 inches) is from Adelaide and Woodbridge (5 feet 10 inches) is from Sydney, but they think and move like identical twins. Woodbridge explained: 'What didn't work immediately, we worked at and it began to gel. When we started, Mark was playing the forehand and I was playing the backhand court. That lasted about a month and in the middle of one match we were getting so frustrated because I wasn't making anything that I suggested he should have a go. We ended up winning the match and the following week we made the semi-finals of the Australian Open and never even thought about going back after that. After so many years we have a pretty good idea of what kind of shot the other is going to play. We know each other's strengths and weaknesses inside out. If Mark is missing first serves I don't need to look at him to know what he is doing wrong, and vice versa.'

There are matches when Woodforde needs to put a hand on Woodbridge's shoulder; usually when the younger man senses the bounce, the line judges, the umpire and the world in general are conspiring to put him down. On other occasions, Woodforde has been known to take on the carefree mood of a man playing from a deckchair. He says: 'After so long together, we know each other's emotions and idiosyncrasies. Todd does sometimes get a bit volatile, but that can be a positive because sometimes you need a bit of anger in a game and he inspires me, saying things like, "Come on, mate. You're too relaxed". He gees me up. I think it's great when he realises he's not playing well and gives himself a good talking to. I can have a calming effect on him and his emotional side helps me out as well. It's those kind of things that make us a decent team.'

What happens when the draw brings them together in the singles, where Woodbridge reached the Wimbledon semi-final in 1997, losing to eventual champion Pete Sampras? Woodforde: 'It's hard. We are always relieved when we see each other's names in the opposite half of the draw. Todd was upset the first few times at not winning but he has been victorious of late. You try not to let too much emotion get into it because we may have to play doubles the next day.' Woodbridge: 'These are matches I don't like playing. We have been through so much together. It's a bit like playing your wife and trying to beat her up. We have good matches with some great rallies. The points are fun, but playing him is difficult.'

Sporting Champions: Mark Woodforde and Todd Woodbridge – 6 Wimbledons (1993, 1994, 1995, 1996, 1997, 2000); 2 Australian Opens (1992, 1997); 2 US Opens (1995, 1996); 1 French Open (2000); 1 Olympic Games (1996).

ANDY MURRAY – THE CHAMPIONSHIPS, WIMBLEDON

AFTER SEVENTY-SEVEN YEARS, THE WAIT IS OVER

Paul Hayward, 8 July 2013

The most painful wait in sport is over. Andy Murray won Wimbledon for himself first and Britain second, but there was no mistaking the relief that swept the country as a seventy-seven-year hoodoo was lifted on a joyous summer day. Shaking his head and gasping for air on Centre Court, Murray became the first British men's singles winner at the Lawn Tennis Championships since Fred Perry in 1936. He is also the first British man to win Wimbledon in short trousers. The shame has passed. Frustration has been banished. Wimbledon fortnight is no longer a ritual of hope and despair. Centre Court has shed its inhibitions.

Murray's great conquest of Novak Djokovic brought David Cameron from his seat to punch the air and revived the spirit of the 2012 London Olympics as the lucky few who were there rejoiced. Alex Salmond, the SNP leader, seized his moment to unfurl a Saltire behind the Prime Minister's back and claimed Murray's win as a specifically Scottish triumph. True, he is Scotland's first Wimbledon singles champion since Harold Mahony in 1896.

Elsewhere, in an unusually festive Royal Box, Wayne and Colleen Rooney joined Victoria Beckham and Tomislav Nikolic, the Serbian president, who watched Djokovic, the number one seed, fall to the first British champion of either gender since Virginia Wade in 1977.

Vindicated and exhausted, disbelieving and overwhelmed, Murray could look back on a performance of immense fortitude. The sometimes limp, fragile and self-reproaching youth who took the torch from Tim Henman, has grown into a confident and combative twenty-six-year-old who hunted the mighty Djokovic down to win 6–4, 7–5, 6–4 in 40°C heat. As Centre Court erupted after a tense and debilitating contest of booming groundstrokes and thrilling rallies, Murray fell to his knees, wandered around the court bemused, buried his head in his towel and then climbed to the players' box to hug his entourage of coaches, physios and fitness experts, mother Judy and girlfriend Kim Sears. Forgetting his mother first time round, he had to double-back to kiss her.

We will wrap this day in Union flags, but it was really one man's victory over doubt and public negativity. To some, Murray was merely a slightly more credible Tim Henman who had the misfortune to be born in a golden era for men's tennis. Djokovic, Roger Federer and Rafael Nadal were all daunting obstacles to him winning Wimbledon, which he has at the eighth attempt. In little over a year he has been anointed Olympic, US Open and now Wimbledon champion: an astonishing revival for the Scot who was widely mocked in his early days for his monotone, his stroppy demeanour on court and his near-misses in big events. Behind that tortured exterior burned a fierce will, a determination not to be outdone by the great players of his age. Murray was a pupil at the school in Dunblane where a gunman, Thomas Hamilton, murdered sixteen children and one teacher before killing himself, in March 1996. Only in a recent BBC documentary, when he broke down and wept while trying to recall the incident, will most people have understood the impact on him of that calamity.

In much narrower sporting terms, Murray has seemed more assured in the past twelve months: less prone to fall apart under pressure. He is a model of self-improvement and persistence who the British public have been slow to love. They can hardly withhold their affections now. Murray's first roar, in victory, was to the press box. He would not say whether he meant it as a rebuke but did speak of a 'difficult relationship'. Murray finally exorcised Fred Perry's ghost, the tennis hoodoo was always the most infuriating, persistent and downright humiliating. Although Britain still lead the way, remarkably, with thirty-five Wimbledon men's singles wins, there had only been one victor since 1909: though Perry won it for three years in a row from 1934. The curse has been lifted with the 127th staging of the Lawn Tennis Championships, which began in 1877 with a British victor, Spencer Gore.

Foreign visitors to Wimbledon have observed the writhing of the home team with great amusement. 'I think with the amount of money that's invested in the sport in this country, then it shouldn't take another seventy-odd years,' Murray said. Tens of millions of pounds in profits are carted away from the All England Club every year, but there is no reliable supply of talent. Murray, who developed largely outside the Lawn Tennis Association system, has carried the weight of British failure for eight years, like Henman before him. 'For the last four or five years, it's been very, very tough, very stressful, a lot of pressure,' he said. 'The few days before the tournament are really difficult. It's just kind of everywhere you go. It's so hard to avoid everything because of how big this event is, but also because of the history and no Brit having won. I think I felt a little bit better this year than I did last year. But it's not easy. I think now it will become easier. I hope it will. I hope it will.'

In a dramatic final game, Murray dropped three Championship points but recovered to beat the more illustrious Djokovic, who was born seven days before him. The new champion paid tribute to the Centre Court audience. 'I've been saying it all week,' he said, 'but it does make a difference. It really helps when the crowd's like that, the atmosphere is like that. Especially in a match as tough as that one. The first few games were brutal. And the end, mentally. That last game will be the toughest game I'll play in my career, ever. It's the hardest few points I've had to play in my life.'

More than anything, this is a story of self-advancement through dedication, of patience in the face of let-downs. In Ivan Lendl, Murray found a coach who forced him to confront the causes of defeats. 'I think I persevered,' Murray said. 'That's really been it, the story of my career probably. I had a lot of tough losses, but the one thing I would say is I think every year I always improved a little bit, every year my ranking was going in the right direction. No, I didn't always feel it was going to happen. It's incredibly difficult to win these events. I don't think that's that well understood sometimes.' We understand it now. A colossus led British tennis out of the darkness and achieved his own immortality. It was an inspiration.

Sporting Champion: Andy Murray – 1 Wimbledon (2013); 1 US Open (2012); 1 Olympic Games (2012).

WILLIE JOHN McBRIDE – BRITISH & IRISH LIONS TEST SERIES

THE CAPTAIN WHO TRIUMPHED AGAINST THE ODDS

Robert Philip, 12 May 1997

Even now, quarter of a century after he led the British Lions to glory in South Africa, Willie John McBride fills the room like that great old armchair which bulged from the corner of your granny's front parlour; as the Springbok pack discovered when they vainly tried to shift him, the unyielding Willie John comes covered in leather and stuffed with horsehair. As a lock forward, only Colin Meads of New Zealand matched him in prowess; as a leader of men, only Henry V could rival his powers of oratory. 'Remember lads,' he told the Lions in his soft County Antrim brogue before the first Test back in 1974, 'there's no retreat. No more talk now. Just make peace with yourselves.'

The ears, cruelly misshapen by his years in the vortex of the scrum, have lost the angry redness of old, the Samsonesque hands and arms, which could hurl an irritating opponent bodily through the air, gently tend the vegetable patch of his sprawling 3-acre home in the rolling countryside of Ballyclare, and the twin pillars of teak which served as legs, now chase nothing more belligerent than his three beloved donkeys, Hazel, Molly and Jack. The memory of what the '74 Lions achieved in South Africa, however, is as sharp as ever. 'No one had ever beaten the Springboks on home soil. Not even the All Blacks and they'd been trying for the best part of a hundred years. I was very fortunate because I was around for so long I got to go on five Lions tours. To go to New Zealand and win as we did in 1971 was a bit special, but nothing I ever did on the rugby field comes close to '74.'

For three and a half months, McBride's marauding Lions rampaged across South Africa, winning twenty-one games before drawing the fourth and final Test. Has there ever been such a collection of talents? J.P.R. Williams, J.J. Williams, Billy Steele, Andy Irvine, Ian McGeechan, Dick Milliken, Phil Bennett and Gareth Edwards formed an irresistible back division in the Tests, while McBride, Gordon Brown, Chris Ralston, Mervyn Davies, Fergus Slattery, Roger Uttley, Fran Cotton, Ian McLauchlan and Bobby Windsor went to war in the forward trenches. 'The South Africans still acknowledge our superiority but they've never accepted it – even yet.'

Those '74 Lions did not depart accompanied by the best wishes of the entire British Isles because their decision to tour the Republic in the evil era of white supremacy attracted widespread criticism. 'It wasn't a popular place to go and there was a lot of anti-apartheid feeling. The protesters were entitled to their opinion just as I was entitled to mine. Living in Northern Ireland, I hadn't had much influence on the political world here, so I couldn't see me having much influence in ending apartheid. So after a lot of soul-searching, I decided to accept the captaincy.' When the '74 Lions assembled at their Hyde Park hotel, they found themselves under siege from hundreds of protesters, unable even to slip out for a training session unnoticed by the mob. 'It was as though we were under house arrest,' recalls McBride, who gathered his depressed forces to deliver an exhortation which, two decades and more on, he remembers as going something like this: 'There were obviously a lot of people who didn't wish us to go – including Harold Wilson – and I told the players that the only way we were going to survive it all was by sticking together and working together. We knew when we agreed to go on that tour we would feel a sense of isolation. But our one and only goal was to beat the Springboks.'

McBride advised anyone harbouring the slightest doubt to leave there and then, recounting horrific tales of the violence and chicanery which would undoubtedly face them on the so-called field of play. 'You know you're up against it when the ref shouts "our ball!" at the put-in. So if you're not up for a fight,' he pronounced, 'there's the friggin' door.' It was the Welsh hooker Bobby Windsor, as hard as the coalface where he worked, who replied on behalf of the party: 'Fighting? Did you say fighting? I'm going to bloody well love this, boyo . . .'

The protesters failed to stop the tour but succeeded in bonding thirty players – doctors, bankers, lawyers, labourers and miners, Scotsmen, Englishmen, Welshmen, Irishmen northern and Irishmen southern – into one gloriously defiant mass. 'When we ran out for the first Test at Cape Town,' smiles McBride, 'I could not only feel the fourteen players at my back, I could feel the fifteen players in the grandstand running out with me. I knew, I just knew, we couldn't lose and that's a funny sensation when you're about to face the Springboks in South Africa. That was the special thing about '74. The guys who didn't make the Test side – who formed the Wednesday side – played an equal part in our ultimate triumph because the first-choice XV knew they had to play out of their skins to keep their places. When the whistle blew at the end of the third Test, as one, the fifteen players on the field turned to the fifteen in the stand and applauded them. It hadn't been rehearsed, it hadn't even been talked about. It was an instinctive reaction and to this day that was the most magical moment of my career.'

Off the field, it was McBride's job to bond disparate characters such as the rascally Windsor (imagine a twentysomething Just William) with Ralston, the patrician England lock forward. 'We used to spend twenty minutes on scrummage practice every day – Test pack versus the Wednesday pack – and they often gave us a tougher time than the Springboks. Towards the end of one particularly torrid session, we pushed them back and ran over the top of them, leaving Chris Ralston lying in bits and pieces all over the place. "Are you all right?" I inquired as Ken Kennedy, who was a doctor, tried to put him back together again. "Ehctually," said Chris, sounding like Prince Charles, "the pain is absolutely excruciating". At which point wee Bobby Windsor sneered, "You can't be in that much pain, boyo, if you can think of a f****** word like that". The current players might be earning a fortune, but you can't buy memories like that.'

There were others. The recollection of the outlandish high jinks draws thunderous guffaws from Willie John. 'New Zealand '71 . . . a town called Westport where the rail-track ran down the middle of the main road – no pubs, no clubs, no nightlife, nothing to do – fifteen players in the Old Albion Hotel, fifteen players in the New Albion Hotel. "Why are they in the New Albion, when we're in the Old Albion?" bemoan I one dark night. So off we go in search of mischief. Me on an old bike I found lying by the side of the road, and another of the lads on a horse he's requisitioned from a farmer's field. When we arrive at the New Albion, we can hear the others singing in the bar. Up the stairs we creep, trash their bedrooms, throw the furniture out the window, fling the beds up on the roof – all that kind of juvenile stuff. Then off we ride again on our bikes and horses. Meanwhile, all hell has broken loose. The police have been called, and the Lions management are going bananas. To this day – well I suppose until they read this – no one knew who was responsible.'

Three years later in South Africa, it was McBride, infuriated by the biased refereeing, who instigated the notorious '99 call', whereby at the sound of the words 'ninety-nine', all fifteen Lions would stop what they were doing and belt the nearest Springbok to hand. 'There was method to the madness. You see, there were fights breaking out all over the place and some o' me lads were running a hundred yards just to get a kick at a South African – retaliation like. Now that was no use to me. If someone like Gordon Brown, say, was fighting for ten minutes that was ten minutes he wasn't playing rugby. The "99 call" ensured everyone had a chance to settle their grievances and be ready to play thirty seconds later. Even a South African referee, so I reasoned, couldn't send off all fifteen of us.'

Victory assured and their unbeaten record intact, the Lions embarked on the mother of all parties on the night of the third Test in their Port Elizabeth hotel. Much furniture was splintered ('inadvertently') and many fire extinguishers were set off ('accidentally') before the hotel manager, seeing his beloved lobby disappearing under 6 feet of water, stormed off in search of the skipper. He would have knocked on McBride's bedroom door except the bedroom in question had been without a door for some days after the captain, returning from a night on the Port Elizabeth tiles without a key and finding the night porter in unhelpful mode, removed said door – and door frame – 'with a couple of gentle dunts'. 'Mr McBride,' railed the manager, 'your players are wrecking my hotel.' 'Are there many dead?' inquired the great man, puffing contentedly on his pipe and sitting on top of the bed cross-legged and naked but for his Y-fronts. 'I want every one of you locked up. The police are on their way.' 'And tell me,' puffed McBride with a proud smile as the mayhem continued unabated below, 'these police of yours – will there be many of them?'

Sporting Champion: Willie John McBride – 3 Lions series wins (1966 – Australia, 1971 – New Zealand, 1974 – South Africa).

BRITISH & IRISH LIONS – TEST SERIES

WARRIORS IN RED RECORD HISTORIC TRIUMPH

Mick Cleary, 8 July 2013

Sydney awoke to bleary eyes and a pinch-yourself feeling, Lions and Wallaby fans alike still reeling from events of the night before. Reports that a surfer had been knocked unconscious on Bondi Beach after being tail-whipped by a whale seemed somehow apt – nobody saw any of these things coming. The dramatic deeds, though, are inscribed in the history books. The statistical ledger alone will tell you that it was a momentous occasion, with these British and Irish Lions posting a record score (41–16) and Leigh Halfpenny laying claim to landmark after landmark. Yet the facts and figures tell you nothing about the size of the heart of these men, of the coaching and back-up staff as well. They held their nerve while many around doubted them. They did not blink when the opportunity came their way, did not sink into the doldrums after defeat in the second Test nor wobble as Australia came back at them at the Olympic Stadium, closing a 19–3 deficit to just three points.

Teams without real backbone would have splintered at that point, at the end of a long season and with a home crowd scenting the kill. Their togetherness was for real, their commitment to the cause profound and their relish for the jersey all too evident. This was not a side of ten Welshmen and a few others making up the numbers out there. This was a Lions team in their pomp. There is a lot of emotion and froth that surrounds a Lions tour. Were there not, it would become just like any other national team, worthy but mundane and all too predictable.

No one, not even Warren Gatland, knew for sure that his selection punt would come off. He made an 'informed decision', as he put it, before pouring himself a stiff drink to steady the nerves. Gatland is an old bare-knuckle fighter. He likes a scrap, a bit of bother, and the chance to prove people wrong. But Gatland does seem to thrive on friction, whether self-induced or not. His preference for Jonathan Davies and/or Jamie Roberts over Brian O'Driscoll was not of that order, but he was fully aware of the firestorm that would descend. He also copped flak for taking the squad to the holiday resort of Noosa on the north Queensland coast at the start of the Test week. The players enjoyed themselves for a couple of days, having fun in the sea by day and a couple of drinks by night. It was Brian Clough-style man-management. It worked. Passion does play its part, particularly with the Lions. Gatland recognised that as well as the fact that Australia would probably not be able to replicate their intensity of the second Test. At the very time that northern hemisphere players should be on their knees through end-of-season fatigue, the Lions stormed through that period in the middle of the second half to leave the Wallabies chasing shadows. It was no fluke. 'Players have told me that they feel in the best shape they have ever been,' Gatland said. 'There was a calmness about us, knowing what we had to offer physically.'

It was not brute strength alone that tipped the balance. It was more subtle and complex than that. It began with the reintegration of prop Alex Corbisiero, who gave the sort of performance that used to be the preserve of Andrew Sheridan. Corbisiero resurrected all those old demons to the point where his opposite number, Ben Alexander, had been dispatched to the sin-bin by the twenty-fifth minute, ignominiously never to return as Australia subbed him out of the game. That platform gave the Lions so much purchase, as did the hefty, heaving boot of Halfpenny, who atoned for his last-gasp miss in Melbourne with a kick from a similar distance in the seventh minute. It soared and soared, as did the hopes of the many thousands of Lions fans among the record crowd. By that point, Corbisiero had already burrowed through for a try triggered by a fumble from Will Genia.

The Lions were of a different ilk. Toby Faletau was immense at number eight, likewise lock Alun Wyn Jones, toiling ceaselessly, articulate in deed rather than babbling unnecessarily in his new role as captain. His second-row partner, Geoff Parling, has been criticised at times but he pulled off one of the most spectacular moments of the trip with his flying tap-tackle on Jesse Mogg just before the break. Australia did get over the try-line, James O'Connor squirming through on the half-time hooter, a score, which allied to the dead-eyed goal-kicking of Christian Leali'ifano, put the Wallabies in with a shout. The mute button was soon hit on their fanciful aspirations as the Lions rattled in quick-fire tries from Jonathan Sexton, George North and James Roberts, two of which featured significant contributions from Halfpenny. It was a glorious finale, fitting that this band of brothers should respond to a spot of adversity by rallying round each other.

Northern hemisphere sides are so often mocked for being one-dimensional, forward-orientated beasts of burden. Yet here even the Aussies rose to acclaim the warriors in red, for their heritage, for their travelling army of fans, but above all for their rugby.

Sporting Champions: British & Irish Lions – 7 Test series wins against Australia (1899, 1904, 1950, 1959, 1966, 1989, 2013).

ROBERT FULFORD – WORLD CROQUET CHAMPIONSHIPS

MY LIFE IN CROQUET

Robert Fulford, 12 October 2005

Croquet is essentially an amateur sport, though I won a lawnmower in two successive years for winning the Open at Hurlingham. I spent four summers in the United States from 1990 as a professional, like a golf club pro, attached to a country club at Chattooga in the mountains of North Carolina, two hours from Atlanta. It was great, though there wasn't quite enough for me to do. But the place itself was fabulous.

To be honest, there's not a lot of high-level coaching over here. People pick up a mallet in the way they feel comfortable and develop different styles from there. Reg Bamford, David Maugham and myself, perhaps the top three in the world, are completely different in style. There are several ways of gripping the mallet. We don't have top-class coaches, like a David Leadbetter in golf. My own backswing, for example, veers to the right, though the mallet does come through straight. Reg has practised using a box-like device that forces him to swing through dead straight. He beat me in the world final this year, but I reckon I'm a better shot. I did experiment with straightening out my swing, but it caused more stress on my wrists. If there is any part of me that will wear out, it will be the wrists – I get a lot of my power from snapping them. There are still fundamentals, such as how to aim, how to generate power and making sure the mallet hits through the ball.

Unlike most sports, croquet can be played by absolutely anyone at any age, male and female, and many people who play can be quite old. Physical strength helps to a certain extent, but it is not a huge factor. Debbie Cornelius, a woman not much taller than 5 feet, has been an excellent tournament player.

My biggest purse was £2,700 for winning the Sonoma Cutrer tournament at a country club in Santa Rosa in California. It coincided with a wine auction and there were about 1,500 watching the final. Most of the spectators had, shall we say, had a good lunch, and the atmosphere was quite rowdy, completely different to the normal sedate tournament atmosphere. Not everyone was watching, but of those who did, many were betting in loud voices and I was told several times: 'You're gonna miss!' When new management took over, the annual event was stopped, which was a shame.

I have just played in the Egyptian Open golf croquet tournament in Cairo where I finished runner-up, winning £270 this time. I usually play association rules, like garden croquet, and probably win half the tournaments I enter. Over fifteen years or so at the top I suppose I have broken even financially, helped by sponsorships. It has meant lots of lovely free trips to play in the United States, Canada, Australia, New Zealand, France, Italy, Spain, Japan and now Egypt. The Egyptians prefer golf croquet – competing for each hoop in one-turn rotation. It's not a bad spectator sport at all, though the game is more physically demanding because it makes sense to strike the ball hard. In Cairo under lights the courts were much slower by our standards with their longer grass, and my wrists wouldn't survive lots of golf croquet. In fact I had to adapt my technique to cope.

People find croquet absorbing to play. It's a great de-stressor – you can't play and think about other things. With the association game, it's important to compartmentalise strokes and tactics in your mind for breaks, which can last for a long time. I started playing when I was at Colchester Royal Grammar School, where croquet was an option, with the local club just down the road.

Amazingly I made very few sacrifices at all reaching the top. It's an individual sport, and I love playing. Otherwise it would have been grim practising. It was no hardship playing all the time, perhaps two or three hours a day, testing myself in games. I was world champion at twenty-one.

Sporting Champion: Robert Fulford – 5 World Championships (1990, 1992, 1994, 1997, 2002); 9 British Open Championships (1991, 1992, 1996, 1998, 2003, 2004, 2006, 2007, 2008).

DONALD BRADMAN – THE ASHES

TRIUMPH OF BRADMAN

B. Bennison, 12 July 1930

At the close of the first day of the third Test match Australia have scored 458 for the loss of three wickets. Of this huge total Don Bradman has made 309. For five hours and fifty minutes he has defied the English bowlers, and is not out. Until his innings the distinction of compiling the highest score in matches between the two countries was held by R.E. Foster, who, twenty-seven years previously, at Sydney, made 287. This is the third three-figure innings Bradman has played against England in this country, and the fifth in his career. At Nottingham his score was 131; at Lord's, in his first innings, he made 254.

His partnership with Kippax for the third wicket, which realised 229, is an Australian record, beating that of W.L. Murdock and H.G. Scott, at the Oval, in 1888. Bradman already holds the world's record of 452. In his score here were forty-two fours. One cannot exaggerate the feat of the young man from New South

Wales, or overstate the magnificence of it. As a maker of runs, he must be numbered among the phenomena of cricket.

During the long hours he was at the wickets he paid no respect to any of our bowlers. Every one of them was the same to him. His perfect footwork, his unerring eye, his quick brain, enabled him to do almost what he willed. When it suited him to drive, he did so with power and accuracy. By an almost imperceptible twist of his bat, he would steer the ball through the slips; the excellence of his strokes all round the wicket was amazing. He reached the boundary by strikingly different routes, and there were times when he seemed to revel in befooling the fielders. Now he would drive through the covers, then he would cut with such crispness, such certainty, that we were utterly perplexed as to what stroke he would next execute.

It would be unkind to contrast Woodfull's batting with Bradman's. Had it not been for Bradman we should have been appalled and wearied by the desperate care and slowness of Woodfull. Bradman made us forget it. There were eyes only for him; it was his day entirely. See him as he has carried himself in each of the three Tests in this country, and there could be no surprise at his enormous capacity to score runs. If there is room for wonder it is that he is ever out. The wicket here, it is true, was emphatically in favour of the batsman, but to enlarge upon that would be to deny Bradman full and deserved praise. And it would be unkind to say of our bowling that it was not good enough. So long as Bradman is in this country we may build an attack as we will without the least certainty that it will triumph. Bradman, for the purpose of batting, is a whole team in himself.

The day had a dramatic beginning. Tate, with the fifth ball of his first over, got Jackson caught at forward short leg by Larwood when he had scored a single. The stroke by which Jackson got himself out was a very poor one – no more than a push, by which he sought to keep the ball out of his wicket. Jackson has yet to give us a sample of the batting by which he has become famous throughout his country. The great shout that was roared at his dismissal had scarce died away when Bradman made his appearance to the accompaniment of a rousing cheer. He settled down at once to give a masterly and magnificent display. Neither Larwood, who opened the attack, Geary, Tyldesley, nor Hammond, who were in turn employed by Chapman before lunch, appeared to cause him a moment's anxiety. He could not have been bolder or more sure of himself had he been engaged in some cricket picnic.

It was Bradman who got the first four of the day. Thereafter, it was as if he might do as he pleased. Woodfull was just Woodfull – calm, deliberate; by comparison with Bradman he was as a tortoise is to a hare. Bradman got fifty out of sixty-three in forty-five minutes with two consecutive hits off Geary, and in that number were included no fewer than eight fours. He brought the one hundred up after the game had been in progress an hour and twenty-five minutes. When he had scored eighty-one he hit a ball with considerable force to Hobbs at cover point. Hobbs stopped it and could not hold it, but it was not a catch that Bradman offered, as many of the crowd thought. Bradman put one up dangerously in the slips, and the ball was taken by Geary, but again there was no catch. Then, amid a thunder of applause, he made his score 102 with a glorious boundary to leg off Larwood. He had batted for an hour and thirty-six minutes, and had hit fifteen fours.

When luncheon was taken Bradman had scored 105 and Woodfull 29 – in two hours. It was not the stupendous difference in the rate at which Bradman and his captain made the runs that captured the imagination; it was the totally dissimilar way by which they crushed the very life out of England's attack. Bradman sparkled; he was carefree, joyous. Woodfull was grim, dour, unemotional. It took Woodfull as long as two hours and forty minutes to score fifty; in five minutes less time Bradman made 142. Woodfull had no sooner reached the half-century than he was bowled neck and crop by Hammond. The ball which beat him was pitched slightly short. Woodfull tried to hook it; it came in quickly from the pitch and hit the middle and leg stump. It is a great feat for any man to bowl Woodfull, whose defence is as elaborately arranged as it is strong. Woodfull and Bradman had raised the total from two to 194.

As soon as Hammond had completed the over in which he disposed of Woodfull he was rested and Larwood was substituted, Tate taking over from Geary. Kippax survived two confident appeals for a catch, and then Bradman banged a ball from Tate to the boundary to bring his score to 150. For a little time he was comparatively quiet, but, having indulged in a breather, he went on as merrily as ever. Driving, cutting, pulling, hooking – there was no known stroke that he did not exploit. At 254 Leyland was brought from the long field to bowl. From his first and his second ball Bradman hit a two; the third he merely tapped; the fourth and fifth he sent to the long-on boundary, and he got a single from the last. Turning his attention to Tyldesley, he completed his second hundred amid a tornado of cheers. Two hundred out of a total of 268 in three hours and forty minutes! And in those 200 runs were twenty-nine fours.

He had his first slice of luck when he had scored two more runs. He then skied a ball from Tyldesley to mid-on. A faster fielder than Tate, who ran for the ball, would have caught it. The Bradman–Kippax stand was nearly ended by Leyland, who made a brilliant attempt to catch Kippax, whose score was then twenty-four. He stopped a hard, high drive to mid-off, but could not hold the ball. It would have been an extraordinary catch. Before the tea interval the Australian total had been raised to 300, and when the adjournment was made Bradman was 220 and Kippax thirty-three.

There was a great cheer when Bradman after tea equalled his Lord's score of 254, and it was renewed again and again when he had beaten the previous highest individual score in the history of Test cricket. The enthusiasm was unbounded, and the game was held up for fully a couple of minutes so that the cheers might be prolonged. He waved his hand to express his joy, and for the first time indulged in a happy and expansive smile. When the total was 423, he lost Kippax, who was easily caught by Chapman off Tate for seventy-seven. The partnership, which lasted two hours and thirty-five minutes, realised 220 runs.

Sporting Champion: Donald Bradman – 6 Ashes series wins (1930, 1934, 1936–37, 1938 – drawn to retain the Ashes, 1946–47, 1948).

IAN BOTHAM – THE ASHES

GREATEST PLAYER ENGLAND HAVE PRODUCED IN THE LAST HALF-CENTURY

Michael Henderson, 14 August 2001

There are certain clubs that everybody wants to join. It is fascinating to discover how many people shared a jar with Dylan Thomas in the glory days of Fitzrovia; hundreds at least. Recently, it has been amusing to count all those discriminating judges of human character who saw from the first what a sharpie Jeffrey Archer was; thousands, apparently. In sport there are clubs, too, and none bigger than the association of skivers who were (they insist) at Headingley on 21 July 1981, the day that Ian

Botham joined the immortals. It wasn't really Botham's day, of course. It was the fast bowling of Bob Willis, who took eight for forty-three, that enabled England to defend a target of 130 and bring the country to a standstill. But it was Botham's match, then, now and forever. For one extraordinary day, England really did stand still.

I would love to claim membership of that Headingley club. Alas, I can't. I was present on the first three days, and vividly recall looking up from the Football Stand End when rain stopped play on Saturday night to see the famous odds of 500–1 being offered on an England victory on the electronic scoreboard above the Western Terrace. But I couldn't be there on the Monday, when Botham played what Christopher Martin-Jenkins, commentating on BBC Television, called a 'leonine' innings, the one that will be remembered so long as cricket is played. I remember quaffing in a grotty Manchester pub that night, the sort of place where drinkers take little interest in anything other than football. That Monday was different. All talk was of Botham's volcanic innings. Something miraculous had occurred, and everybody wanted to talk about it.

People still want to talk about it, which does not always impress the players who have followed Botham into the Test side. Only the other day Michael Atherton lamented that 'wallowing in nostalgia is a peculiarly English thing', an observation that could be made only by somebody who has spent little time in continental Europe. Been to Vienna lately, Michael? According to 'Macauley' Atherton, 'we continue to invite scorn as a nation that is forever looking back rather than moving forward'. He must have spent the last twenty years living in a mud hut. The most notable thing about modern English life, surely, is how novelty is venerated, for its own sake. The past has been abolished and a generation has grown up knowing next to nothing about England.

Two decades on, twenty years in which Australia have been England's masters in eight of the ten subsequent series, Botham's unbeaten 149 and Willis's eight wickets have acquired the patina of history. They are the most obvious reference points on the map of modern English cricket, achievements that people point to whenever they get lost. Disarmingly, for he is a modest man, Botham calls his famous innings 'a fluke'. Well, it may have been, but it took a cricketer of the rarest gifts to pull it off. Artur Schnabel, the great pianist, was once asked, after a daring performance of a Beethoven sonata, whether he could play it differently. 'I could play it better,' he replied, 'but it wouldn't be so good.' *Voila!* Botham did do it differently – and, from his point of view, better. The century at Old Trafford two Tests later, after he had secured a win at Edgbaston with his bowling on a barmy Sunday, was, judged by all normal standards, the greatest innings of his life. Now that one I did see, every ball, and I know, along with the 20,000 others who were present, that I will never again see an Englishman bat with such liberty. On a grim day, Botham's strokeplay dazzled the eye.

Normal standards, however, did not apply at Leeds. It is worth recalling events earlier in the year, to put 'Headingley 1981' in its true context. England had lost the first Test, at Trent Bridge, and Botham had bagged a pair at Lord's and then resigned the captaincy, bailing out minutes before the selectors sacked him. Ever since he stepped up to the big stage in 1977, on the previous Australian tour, Botham had been the golden boy. Now he was the whipping boy. On his return to the Pavilion at Lord's he was greeted by silence. Even the hardest hearts there usually soften for the captain of England, out of custom. On this occasion they did not, and Botham never forgot. The innings that altered his life began half an hour after lunch on the Monday. When Geoffrey Boycott was out and Terry Alderman dismissed Bob

Taylor, England had three wickets in hand, and were ninety-two runs behind. But somehow Botham, at first with Graham Dilley and then with Chris Old, established a modest lead. Of his 149 runs, no fewer than 114 came in boundaries. It was that brutal. If Manchester saw the innings of true class, Headingley was the ground where Botham played the innings of his life, and of all our lives.

They make a cosy pair these days, Botham and Willis. Marked for life as the best of friends, they can be found in many a restaurant between Battersea and Double Bay, scrutinising the wine list with a keen eye but invariably opening the bowling with something Spanish. Botham learnt about wine at the foot of John Arlott, whose radio commentary was the only thing that could have conferred greater honour on the heady events of 1981. He had retired the year before, after the Centenary Test against Australia at Lord's. Opinionated, never knowingly wrong on any subject, and yet as generous a man as you will find, Botham remains, eight years after his retirement, England's most popular cricketer, and the greatest player this country has produced in the last half-century. He is a force of nature and, as David Hockney has said, 'nature never lets you down'.

Willis, a Dylan man in his prime, is more of an opera buff these days, and there was something of Siegfried and his horn about the way he charged in twenty years ago. Willis blew his own horn one last time at Headingley, and England achieved something impossible. Once more, then, we must recall that unforgettable match and travel 'down the highway, down the tracks, down the road to ecstasy'.

Sporting Champion: Ian Botham – 5 Ashes series wins (1977, 1978–79, 1981, 1985, 1986–87 – drawn to retain the Ashes).

VALENTINO ROSSI – WORLD MOTOGP CHAMPIONSHIP

FUN-LOVING ITALIAN IS THE FASTEST
THING ON TWO WHEELS

Sue Mott, 12 July 2003

You have to hand it to Graziano and Stefania Rossi. When their son was born twenty-four years ago they didn't look into his sweet, little, mewling face and think 'Ah, let's call him Paolo' like everyone else in Italy; they took a gamble of heroic order instead. 'Valentino'. Just imagine how horribly wrong that could have gone. However close his birthday to Valentine's Day (16 February, in this case), you don't want to be the possessor of a fat, spotty, slow little boy called Valentino Rossi. Luckily, he wasn't any of the above. He was small and fast and positively dangerously fond of the engine-powered bike his dad built for him before his third birthday. 'I crash into everything. But it so natural to me. Like walking or breathing,' said Rossi, now grown up (ish) and four times a world motorcycle champion. Valentino is now a perfect name. Full of drama, passion and theatricality (and probably what he gets up to in London nightclubs, though that has no place in a sporting context). He is also the reigning MotoGP world champion.

So we have in our midst – a flat in Knightsbridge, in fact – a genuine, global superstar. A charismatic, fun-loving, bona fide champion with in-born talent, a sense of humour and a monstrously large shoe collection. 'I love, yes,' he admitted re: footwear. But the sentiment could apply to his life. For example, performing for his fans as a prelude to the British Grand Prix involved zooming down the Thames on a powerboat, lunch with the media and a rally in front of an adoring throng in Leicester Square. Not all went according to plan, not least the circumstance of his yellow Honda cap flying off and sinking in the murky depths of the river. No matter. He was urbane, relaxed, funny, adorable. Imagine Frankie Dettori on fast-forward. That is the general idea. His father was also a bike racer and the best piece of advice he gave his offspring was to enjoy his sport. 'Aaah, 'e say to me, treat it a little bit like a game. Is not 'undred per cent serious. Have fun.' This advice, you have to admit, has been faithfully followed by his loving son. Poor Max Biaggi. Part-real and part-hyped, one suspects, the two Italian racers have established a notorious rivalry from which the elder man, Biaggi, frequently emerges the loser. When once he went out with the supermodel, Naomi Campbell, Rossi countered by performing a victory lap on his bike with a blow-up doll sporting the name 'Claudia Schiffer' riding pillion. There was also the time, in 2001, that the simmering dislike erupted in fisticuffs after the Catalunya Grand Prix. Biaggi had to walk into a press conference with a bloodied gash on his chin. 'A mosquito bit me,' he said. It is likely that Biaggi, a Roman who worked devotedly hard for his place in MotoGP, has an intense dislike of the seeming ease with which Rossi has become a world champion. And the jester's touch of the younger man. He represents Biaggi's name on his website as XXX XXXXXX.

People still laugh about the time Rossi paused halfway during a victory lap to run into a Portaloo and the occasion a man dressed as a chicken joined him for a celebration circuit. Or 'cir-qwit', as he cutely calls it. But these are merely the ornamental offerings of a man who still understands business. He would not be paid a reputed £10 million over two years by Honda were he not the genuine article. He is mad but not crazy, nor heedless of the myriad perils of a sport that has already claimed the life of the Japanese rider, Daijiro Kato, at Suzuka this year. 'I 'ave fifteen crashes in 1996. Maybe more in 1995, maybe twenty. You 'ave to understand from your mistakes. The motorbike is dangerous. Fear is good. You must do 'undred per cent what is possible and a little bit less when not possible.' The hair's-breadth difference between safe and unsafe, title-winning and life-threatening, he seems to have absorbed with his rusks.

His phenomenal progress in the sport began in 1996 when he came ninth with the Aprilia team in the 125cc World Championship. He was seventeen. The next year he was champion. He graduated to 250cc in 1998 and was runner-up. The next year he was champion. He moved up to 500cc with Honda in 2000 and finished runner-up. The next year he was champion. In 2002, in the first year of MotoGP, this was his run of results: first, second, first, first, first, first, first, first, first, crash, first, first, second, second, first, second. This year, 2003, as he acknowledges, the other bikes are catching up with Honda. 'The battle is more close. But good for everybody. Good for the show. For sure, the machines are more equal. In South Africa we make mistake with the tyre. In France it start to rain and in Barcelona, ha, make stupid mistake. Is mistake, yes.' He paused. 'Finish question,' he grinned, moving swiftly on.

Within the sport there is feverish anticipation of a possible move to Ducati, the Italian team. 'Is like a dream,' he said, failing to damp down the speculation. Honda, in negotiations with him for an extension to his contract, will be alarmed by the comment. 'But I am basically talked to everybody,' he said. Wait a minute. He wished to amend that statement? 'No! Everybody is talking with me!' But that is not all. There is another dream he holds dear. To emulate the record of John Surtees and become world champion on two and four wheels. To be a world champion in motorcycling and then graduate in Formula One. People are always asking him about this and he is encouraging on the subject without being fully committed. 'For us is, er, dream. I dunno. Maybe is possible.

I am young, so maybe is enough time. Maybe yes. [Pause.] Maybe something. [Pause.] Or, also, maybe nothing.' He has the timing of Tommy Cooper, this boy. He certainly does not see himself continuing to race bikes into his dotage. 'Is good to retire when I am fast,' he explained.

He cannot live in Italy anymore. Such is the momentousness of his fame and popularity, it is well nigh impossible to stop his fans from pitching up outside his home and offering up their adoration. So he now lives in London during the week making excursions to upmarket shoe shops and not necessarily upmarket nightspots, and returns to Italy at weekends. 'For fun,' he said. He has two modes of being. Feverishly active or flat-out asleep. 'Ah, sleep,' he said of his favourite hobby. 'Yes, whenever possible I sleep very much. Eighteen, twenty hours, yes, yes. But when I race, I have to get up at eight o'clock in the morning.' He implied that this was ridiculously early. 'Eight o'clock,' he said in tones of outrage. 'Is night!'

Another little clue into his psyche is the fact that he proudly wears the letters 'WLF' always on the front of his riding outfit. If you ask him what this stands for, he collapses into a fit of giggles and cannot trust himself to speak. 'Is, er, is, a compliment to the female sex,' he says finally, looking sheepish. It becomes evident why Italy loves him and why the British fans of motorsport teem along in their tens of thousands to watch him in action. Such frivolity in conversation is matched by the finesse of his riding. He ought, by rights, to be deeply unpopular in the eyes of his fellow competitors, so often left in the wake of his fuming exhaust pipe. But they – with the chronic exception of Biaggi – seem to find his impish charms as irresistible as the rest of us. Indeed, Sete Gibernau was moved to take him parachute jumping. It is the only time in his life that Rossi has been petrified. He demonstrated the flutter of a parachute with his hand and rolled his eyes in mock terror. 'Is big mistake,' he admitted. 'Is my first and last time?' Did he scream all the way down? 'No, no scream,' he said. 'I already think I am dying.'

Perhaps surprisingly, one of his greatest racer heroes apart from Ayrton Senna is our own Nigel Mansell. They hardly seem ideal soulmates, one fizzing like a firecracker and the other with a reputation for being rather droningly boring. Rossi doesn't see it that way. 'I like Mansell very much because he was very aggressive, very fast and make stupid mistakes.' That, of course, explains it. Above all, Rossi is a pragmatist. The mischievous, incorrigible prankster is replaced in the saddle by a man cognisant of machine, track and his own limitations. He once vowed not to race for a team sponsored by a tobacco company, but given that the Spanish, Catalunya, Valencia, Portuguese and Malaysian grands prix are sponsored by Marlboro; the Dutch, Czech Republic and Pacific (Japanese) by Gauloises; and more or less the rest by Cinzano, the stance is tricky to maintain. 'Is 'ard,' he conceded. 'Tobacco is bad for everybody. But I always say I am a rider. If it is a choice between 'oliday or race with cigarette, I race with cigarette.' He is a breath of fume-filled air. A life-enhancer. The sport – potentially an anorak's graveyard of lap times and fuel caps – is hugely fortunate to have him.

Sporting Champion: Valentino Rossi – 6 MotoGP World Championships (2002, 2003, 2004, 2005, 2008, 2009); 1 500cc World Championship (2001); 1 250cc World Championship (1999); 1 125cc World Championship (1997).

LEON ŠTUKELJ – OLYMPIC GAMES

THE MAN WHO SHOOK HANDS WITH HISTORY

David Miller, 7 November 1998

He competed simultaneously with Paavo Nurmi at Paris 1924. He applauded poolside when Johnny Weissmuller retained his 100 metres crown at Amsterdam 1928. He shook hands with Jesse Owens, fellow national hero at Berlin 1936. He sat 50 yards from Hitler in the Olympic Stadium, and thought him 'a bit of a clown'. Four years later the Gestapo commandeered his imposing four-storey house as their headquarters in Maribor, Slovenia, and locked him up for being an alleged partisan. When the War ended, the Communists jailed him for allegedly being an anti-partisan, even stopping him attending his mother's funeral, and subsequently demoted him from his position as civil judge to the twilight world of granting market licences and building certificates.

Yet Leon Štukelj, Slovenia's most famous sportsman, with six Olympic medals including three gold, has the last laugh on them all. Liberated from the former Yugoslavia, Slovenian authorities recently returned his house. Now dignitaries from around the world gather in Ljubljana to celebrate his centenary: the oldest living Olympic champion, still at heart a teenager. He will continue doing daily exercises on the rings hanging in his bedroom doorway to make sure he is in trim for the occasion. Meanwhile, in Bled, under the auspices of the Council of Europe, there is an international scientific seminar in his honour – Sport, Health and Old Age – with keynote speeches from physicians and professors who marvel, as does anyone who meets him, at this human phenomenon. In attendance will be officials of the World Health Organisation and the International Society for the History of Physical Education and Sport. Štukelj has the demeanour, the mental agility, the physical elasticity of someone less than half his age. Studious associates are chided for inaccurate recall of dates and names. He jokes about the skin cancer on his scalp. 'But for this,' he says, 'I could die healthy.'

Last week he dined with Prince Charles. This week Juan Antonio Samaranch, president of the International Olympic Committee and very much a junior at seventy-eight, will be there to pay homage. The schedule of appointments awaiting Štukelj would daunt a thrusting, workaholic salesman in his thirties. Following the domestic acclaim, he has accepted over six months invitations to Australia, Japan, the United States, Brazil, Olympia in Greece, Austria (to present some medals) and to Kemnitz in Germany for the one hundred and thirtieth anniversary of the birth of Otto Jahn, father of German gymnastics. There will be a Slovenian stamp issue with the heads of Štukelj and Samaranch.

While the world queues at his door – 'I cannot accept anything more' – Lydia, his wife for sixty-five years, as ever demurely supports his kaleidoscopic activities though attempting to limit the number of gymnastic demonstrations requested by visitors. In a strange way, age seems not to have touched him. His suit is as neat as his step and when he thumbs through the 300-page autobiography he recently published, the years between the world wars appear still at his fingertips. 'I'd rather be fifty,' he says, 'but I'm very happy to reach this age still in good shape. Good genes, that's essential. I've been exercising all my life: swimming, skiing, skating, as well as gymnastics. No smoking, no drinking. At one hundred I can't complain.'

The gymnastics started when he was eight. In the small town of Novo Mesto (New Town), there was not much else to do. He joined the local club but was basically self-taught. He had read about the development of the sport, under Jahn during the last century, but there was no status attached to being accomplished, only personal fulfilment. His friends, those still alive, say that he had little competitive streak, was wholly without aggression: that his aim was perfection more than victory. So it was that his first competition came aged twenty-three, the World Championships of 1922, when they happened to be in Ljubljana. In the course of four championships, he was to win fourteen top-three places. 'There were no medals in those days,' he recalls, 'and the championships included swimming, athletic events, rope climbing, but as gymnastics grew in importance the additional events were excluded.' In 1922 he was first in rings, horizontal bar and parallel bars, and second in pommel horse and team event.

He had by then qualified as a lawyer, studying in Vienna and then at Ljubljana University when it was inaugurated in 1918, becoming a court clerk. In the tradition of Pierre de Coubertin's Olympic ethic of 'taking part', Štukelj has always believed that sport was ancillary to life, not life itself. 'I'd read about de Coubertin, the dedication to fair play, and this concept took root throughout Yugoslav clubs. Gymnastics strengthened our feeling of [Slovenian] national identity, helped to preserve our language where we're transit territory between Germany, Austria and the sea.' For the Olympic Games of 1924, Slovenia provided all of the Yugoslav gymnastics team. Meagre finances meant that while the national federation paid the fare to Paris, the competitors had to find their own lodgings, food and local transport. 'Our pension had only cold water, and some of the team complained about the food,' he says. 'But Paris was a pleasant new experience after the world championships.'

Štukelj gained his first Olympic medals, gold in the horizontal bar and the overall title – in spite of rope climbing being included for the last time. 'I found that a tough event,' he says, in spite of the fact that he gained a maximum ten points, though no bonus for speed. When the competition was concluded, there was no immediate announcement, in the days before computers, of the result. The judges departed for lunch and a discussion, while Štukelj and his colleagues went off to see Versailles. On returning to Paris in the evening, one of the Czechoslovakian gymnasts said to him: 'You're rather good.' Why was that? Štukelj asked. 'You're apparently on the front page of *Le Matin*,' his rival replied. Štukelj and his colleagues jumped into a taxi and dashed off to the newspaper's office to confirm the story: Štukelj first, Robert Pražák and Bedřik Šupčík, both of Czechoslovakia, second and third. 'Things weren't so organised in those days,' he says. Back home, Štukelj received the Order of St Sava (fifth class) from King Alexander Karadjordjevic, but there was otherwise little acclaim, 'just the occasional handshake, those were amateur days!'

Though becoming a judge, Štukelj continued to train for two or three hours every afternoon in preparation for the World Championships in Lyon and the Amsterdam Olympics. His great rival on rings was Ladislav Vácha, of Czechoslovakia: in Lyons, he beat him by a tenth of a point, in Paris by eight one-hundredths. Štukelj was the first in the sport to introduce the 'standing cross', the static rings position with head down and arms stretched wide horizontally, a feat even today needing exceptional muscular control. 'Vacha tried it,' he remembers, 'but he couldn't.' The French had treated the Yugoslavs so shoddily with outdated apparatus in 1924 that for Amsterdam they took their own parallel bars on the train, for practice and for competition. 'It gave us the "feel" with which we were familiar – the last time the rules allowed that,' he says.

With no first place in the World Championships of 1930 in Luxembourg or 1931 (individual, back in Paris), Štukelj sensed that his powers were declining. There was no money to go all the way to the Los Angeles Olympics, but he decided on one last attempt in Berlin. 'A new, more muscular style, was emerging,' he says. 'There were very strict rules for the exercises, tougher elements, and, at thirty-seven, there was no one of a similar age to me.' By a tiny margin, he beat Matthias Volz, of Germany, for the silver on rings behind Alois Hudec, of Czechoslovakia. 'We expected the Germans to be dominant in many sports, and they were,' he recalls. 'The organisation was excellent but the sea of swastikas everywhere was very depressing. I was sitting quite close to Hitler, Goebbels and the rest when I was a spectator. He was often shouting, not behaving normally, much the same as Mussolini, but he was a clown. Well, I suppose they both were. I ran to the exit when Hitler departed and he was still shouting. Yet the crowd in the stadium were fair, generous in their applause. I saw Owens in the long jump, his world record with his final leap was thrilling, and there was no evident discrimination by the crowd. I was able to meet him in the village. We congratulated each other though we couldn't talk much. He autographed a photograph for me. We seemed to feel a bond as champions. He was a gentle, open man.'

Štukelj was sad to retire after Berlin, but felt it best to do so at the top. 'Nowadays, the sport is less elegant, less beautiful, in my opinion,' he says. 'It is tougher and has more dangerous elements, especially on the horizontal bar. It is more acrobatic but doesn't have the same art.' Prior to the outbreak of war, Štukelj had written that Yugoslavia should use gymnastics as a preparation for invasion, but the truth was that his nature was alien to any idea of holding a gun. When the Germans arrived, the Yugoslav army soon collapsed. Losing his house in Maribor, he moved back to Novo Mesto to look after his family, declining to join the Communist insurgents, a decision which was to rebound on him in Marshall Tito's post-War regime. There remains in him an almost naïve quality. Asked if he was afraid when in prison, he replied: 'Not for one second. I knew I had not done anything wrong.' In Yugoslavia between 1940 and 1990, that was not necessarily a guarantee of safety. To this day he is a man of almost nineteenth-century habits. After all, he was born then. As before the War, he walks every day in the parks of Maribor, on Sundays with Lydia. His great grandchildren now live on one of the floors of his restored, expansive house. As he contemplates his centenary, he has the smile of a truly contented man.

Sporting Champion: Leon Štukelj – 3 Olympic Games (1924 – 2, 1928); 5 World Gymnastics Championships (1922 – 3, 1926 – 2).

SEVERIANO BALLESTEROS – THE OPEN

SEVE RETAINS HIS BEGUILING AURA OF SELF-BELIEF
Sue Mott, 24 September 2005

I t doesn't matter that he can scarcely hit a ball straight, Severiano Ballesteros is a legend. There are golfers and there are icons, there are competitors and there are tigers, there are characters and there are starbursts, there are tempers and there are tantrums. Seve is extreme in all cases. His long fall from the ramparts of golfing domination is positively Shakespearean in its nature. He was the matador of the sport, killing courses and rivals with his extravagant combination of outrageous ingenuity and downright courage. He won five majors. He was adored and adorable. He seemed possessed of gifts beyond the range of ordinary club-wielding mortals. Suddenly, it went. It must have been like Mozart waking up one morning to discover he had two cloth ears.

For ten years, more or less, Ballesteros has been searching for his own lost game. His marriage did not survive the quest but his self-determination did. He is ready. He will play again soon. He is confident. He can win again. You should hear him. No, first you have to see him. At forty-eight years old, in a cobalt blue jumper and a charismatic mood, he remains quite ravishing. This is not said in a sexist manner. You would defy any man, woman or child not to be charmed by Ballesteros at his most charming. He can appear haughty and regal and then counteract the effect with a multi-wattage smile of huge complicity. Caught in its rays, you just fry up in admiration.

On a visit to our country in his capacity as host of the Seve Trophy, he bore all the hallmarks of contentment. The day was fine, Europe were winning, people were remarking upon how well Ballesteros looked, slim and fit, after battling an arthritic back for eighteen months. But he still chose not to play in his event. 'Well, I decided not to play here,' he said, sipping a beer in the clubhouse. 'It would be some kind of disrespect to the players and to the tournament because if you don't feel you are competitive, you step away and wait for better times.' He has identified the Madrid Open as the better time. Is he excited? 'Sure.' Nervous? 'No. Everything's going to be OK. I'm very positive. I'm going to perform very good. I'm mentally convinced things are going to be very good for me. That's the key. Everything is in the mind.' He never slips – not once – from this appraisal. His face is serious and straight. He simply discounts all the experience of the last ten years when, in fact, the quixotic disappearance of his beloved game must have driven him half mad. He won't look back. 'I don't really like to remember bad times and moments. I like to think about good things. I'm not interested in talking about negative things. Or sad things. That doesn't bring you any good. Sometimes you have to go through difficult times. Golf is a challenge every day and life is a challenge every day.' He sounds strong and convinced. 'I am. I am,' he insisted. 'Golf teaches you to be. You are alone. Just you and the ball and the clubs. I live my life so far with a lot of intensity. That makes you strong.' But vulnerable too. He won't agree. 'I give a lot to the game,' he said eventually. 'But I think the game gives a lot for me.'

There has been no time in his life when his passion for golf did not exist. Born into a family of golfing brothers, the youngest, in the small village of Pedreña, on the southern shore of the Bay of Santander, he was surrounded and blessed by the game simultaneously. 'It was the influence of my brothers, the influence of living only two hundred yards from the second green, and the atmosphere of the whole village.' The second green in question belonged to the Royal Pedrena Golf Club, a prestigious bastion into which the young Ballesteros was only invited in his role as a caddie. This, of course, did not stop him. 'I used to play on the beach and I sneak on to the golf course. I just waited until the caddie masters had left. I played under the moon or in winter in the rain, with not many members on the course. My mother and father were really happy. Best for me, being on the golf course instead of the bar. All the time, I was dreaming about being a champion. I knew it was going to happen. I was having these dreams when I played the course at night or sitting in my living room or in the night when I was in bed, sharing the room with my brother Vicente. The house was an old house. We had the cows underneath in the winter to keep it warm. True.'

It is an impossibly romantic story of a humble beginning that was almost immediately superseded by stardom. He turned professional, at sixteen, in March 1974. Two years later he came second in The Open to Johnny Miller, sharing the honour of runner-up with Jack Nicklaus. That announced his arrival pretty thoroughly. That was the beginning of the building of the Ballesteros legend. 'You know at that time, golf in Spain was unpopular. Socially, it was rejected by people for being only for rich people. I did change Spanish culture a lot. Now it's very popular. We have public golf courses that become reachable for everybody. I'm very happy about that. A lot of things happened to me very quickly. In the beginning, it was fun. As time went by, it became a bit more tough. You lose your privacy, you have to learn to cope with a lot of things which are not easy to accept. Like learning how to say "no" to things.' What things? To wine and women who seduce our footballers with the tiniest crook of their painted fingernails? 'No, no, I was always very dedicated,' he said manfully. 'Now I drink wine and beer a little bit, but not then. I would not celebrate, not really, after winning a tournament. I would just get ready for the following week.'

And *señoras*? Seve was young, famous, handsome and ridiculously alluring. Presumably those were entertaining times. 'Yeah,' he agreed, not coyly either. 'But it was golf. Always golf.' You believe him. In 1979 he won The Open at twenty-two, the youngest winner of the century. He doesn't remember being nervous. 'I was pretty much in control of the situation. When I won, I took it pretty much internally. I was very much calm. The only time I break was when my three big brothers all run and jump on me.' He smiled at the fond memory. But his greatest backward-looking pleasure comes from the birdie putt on the last at St Andrews in 1984 – 15 feet, breaking right to left – to claim his second Open title at the home of golf. 'That putt was pretty special,' he said. 'From that putt, that moment, came this logo.'

He pointed to his chest where you could make out a yellow figure clenching his fist in the instant of triumph. 'And this also,' he said rolling up his sleeve to reveal a tattoo of the same freeze-framed moment on his left arm. This struck me as incredible. Footballers, boxers, athletes are always scrawling over themselves, but Severiano Ballesteros, a man welcome in every clubhouse in the world with dress codes tighter than the Royal Box at Ascot, tattooed? He saw nothing to apologise for. 'I had it done a long time ago,' he said.

It must signify how much it meant to him, the victories and the apparent vista of many more to come. It did not quite work out that way. His last major trophy was The Open at Royal Lytham St Annes in 1988 when one round of 65 was simply breathtaking. There were wonderfully dramatic Ryder Cup moments to savour, not least the hair's-breadth victory at Valderrama in 1997 when Ballesteros was the very hands-on captain, but his last tournament win was 1995. He has won eighty-seven titles and will not be satisfied with that. He wants number eighty-eight. 'Nothing is impossible. If you believe you can do something, you can. There is only one way. With very good attitude, positive thinking, hard work and dedication. With these four things together. If you are dreaming about something you want to happen, it will happen.'

Some critics, not necessarily harshly, wonder whether he is delusional. Can a sportsman of his age in a decade-long slump simply rise again in all his former splendour? They don't think so. They wish he had retired. Some even call him 'an embarrassment', especially concerned when his occasional explosions of Latin temper reach the press or cause him to be threatened with suspension on the European Tour for abusing an official. He once accused the Tour of being run like a Mafia. Not the most diplomatic of charges since he was standing on Sicilian soil at the time. 'People, they always say a lot of things. I don't really pay much attention. If people believe in you, it's good. But they cannot help you, they cannot come round the course with you. You have to believe in your own self, your own life.

'I am not worried about the game. I am not tired, looking for a rest. I don't have a reason for being upset, I look at everything as a good challenge.' Ballesteros says this slightly pugnaciously, as though daring someone to disbelieve him. But the word 'embarrassment' – no man who has stood at sport's summit can hear such a thing and not flinch at the cruelty. He is at his most regal now. 'When you try your best, it doesn't matter how you do it, you should never feel embarrassed by yourself.' Perhaps he is right and there is no Shakespearean trauma playing in his head after all.

He took time at the Wynyard to instruct a few local children and was hugely enthusiastic about their potential. 'I saw one boy and I thought he had been playing for a year or so. I said, "How long have you been playing?" He said, "Two hours".' Cue the radiant grin. 'And I saw a little girl, maybe six or seven. Fantastic. She was hitting the ball one hundred and fifty yards.' His infectious passion is undimmed. He plays sport with all his children, two boys and a girl, aged fifteen, thirteen and eleven. 'Not only golf we play. Also ping-pong, tennis, basketball.' You have a horrible feeling he is ultra-competitive, even with his children, hating to lose and vying to win at all times. He denies it. 'No, I just take the game as something to enjoy. Not to take it that serious.'

Beyond times spent with his children, he lists golf as his other activity. Either practising for it, exercising for it, working alongside it and designing golf courses with his company, Amen Corner. 'Thirty so far, we have designed,' he said. Do they have very tiny fairways? I asked and then wished I hadn't. Thank God, he laughed. 'I have been thinking about designing courses without any fairways at all,' he said, entering the spirit of the occasion. 'Make it fair for the ones who cannot hit it straight.' Self-mockery is a good sign. Ballesteros needs a few good signs, not least of that poetic, majestic game he once summoned through his fingertips at will. He refuses to consider the seniors' circuit for the time being. 'I don't think about it at the moment,' he said firmly. We know what he thinks about. 'Golf. Always. It's been my life. It's been my passion. It's been my game. I can play when I'm eighty.

That's the good thing about golf. You can play as long as you can walk.' And dream.

Sporting Champion: Severiano Ballesteros – 3 The Opens (1979, 1984, 1988); 2 Masters (1980, 1983).

NICK FALDO – THE OPEN

AGE FAILS TO DULL WINNER'S INSTINCT

Sue Mott, 9 October 2004

They say you've got to be careful what you wish for. How true. We wished for a British sporting hero with killer instinct and we got one. Nick Faldo, master golfer, of Welwyn Garden City and the world. Then we didn't know quite what to do with him. Revere him for his prowess and multiple titles? Disapprove of his waspishness and multiple marriages? We exist – still – in a state of uneasy truce.

He is bigger than you expect when you meet him. All those years of pudding-bowl haircuts and Pringle jumpers prepare you for an overgrown schoolboy. Instead, he is tall, broad shouldered and tousled (it is early morning) in a crumpled shirt and with a humour that you feel might edge towards grumpy if we are not all very careful. We are all very careful. But, to give him his due, he drinks his mint tea and makes a discernible effort. He is making the rounds to sell his autobiography. I am probably round seventeen. Keenly aware of this, I ask him what he would like to talk about. 'Nothing,' he says, heavily. But he does not mean it. When you are an only child who became the best in the world in your chosen field, there is a fantastically obvious choice of subject.

'I'm always uncomfortable talking about myself as a "great". Technically I'm a legend. Bloody hell! In my ten-year span, I won the most number of majors of any British golfer. When you think of the list of the greats: Sarazen, Jones, Snead, Hogan, Harmon, Nicklaus, Watson, Faldo, Woods. It's like . . . hello? When I put it like that I think – bloomin' hell. It's quite difficult to say I'm a legend but, on paper, I am!' Now you wouldn't catch Tim Henman saying these things, with his preternatural sense of propriety, but then he has not exactly had the opportunity. Faldo, conversely, is a roaring egocentric who has backed up his self-regard with results. We can hardly laud him for his heroism and then hypocritically wish he would shut up.

It used to irritate him half to death. Now he is more philosophical. 'I suffered from my image on the golf course. Head down, looking a right miserable bastard. People assumed that was what I was like off the course. They threw in words like "obsessed" and "cold". My commitment became "aloofness". Confidence was "arrogance". That's another thing. Golfers are taught to say modestly . . . "be nice to have another good day tomorrow". Then you get American athletes, especially basketball players, who say, "I'm the man. I'm the best. I'm gonna win". That's actually how a sportsman should be talking, but if you stood up and said, "I'm gonna kill them tomorrow on the golf course. I'm gonna win by six!" people would say, "Who the hell does he think he is?" You have to think one way, while talking all humble and quiet. It's quite bizarre when you think about it. Look, Jonny Wilkinson has to be a killer inside even if you can't see it. He must have a serious passion to kick that ball over for the whole blooming country.' He mused for a moment. 'It's great to just be the best at something, isn't it?' Frank the photographer and I looked at one another. How would we know? Frank has to take Nurofen just to play tennis and I have never won a sports event in my life. There is something touchingly oblivious about Faldo in his pomp.

But then he was forged in a world of his own. A little boy in a suburban council house back garden, contentedly playing with a set of the most rudimentary props: a shed, a ladder, a bush and the woods across the road. 'I was happy as a sandboy, playing all day. Just amusing myself. Generally it was just me and my totally vivid imagination. I didn't know it then, but I was learning how to visualise – something that psychologists now tell you is crucial to playing any sport. That started off the loner trend in me. That's why I was perfectly happy practising on my own when I left school. Belting balls all day. I was having fun. I'd sit on a log for thirty minutes and eat my sandwiches and then I'd chip and putt all afternoon. But I was always competitive. It was always me versus Lee Trevino or Jack Nicklaus. I always practised to a target.'

Rampant competitiveness sometimes took over. Under the fond, indulgent eyes of his parents, George and Joyce, his first venture towards international sporting stardom almost came to grief in the 1966 Hertfordshire County under-ten breaststroke final. 'I peed myself on the starting blocks,' he admitted. 'I choked. I couldn't handle it. But it didn't scar me for life and I ended up winning the race. I didn't sink like a stone because of it. So why not tell the world? It happened. It was a sign of how much I always wanted to win. I don't know where it came from. My parents weren't like that. But my attitude was always: if you do it, you've got to win. You've got to be number one.'

Lo, he was. His golf record is an astonishing testimony to fearlessness in the face of victory. He has played in eleven Ryder Cups and won a record twenty-three matches. He has won three Opens: in 1987 at Muirfield, 1990 St Andrews (with a scarcely believable scorecard of 67, 65, 67, 71) and Muirfield again in 1992 when he ill-advisedly sang 'My Way' at the Claret Jug presentation and thanked the media from the 'heart of his bottom'. Stuffed shirts swelled like barrage balloons. He won three Masters and reckons to this day that the single most important golf shot of his life was the putt that won his first green jacket in the sudden-death play-off against Scott Hoch in the gathering gloom and drizzle of Augusta 1989. What do you think? he asked his caddie. 'It's all a blur to me, guv,' said the helpful bag carrier. Never mind. Faldo was his own boss that day. 'I never felt a putt come off the putter so sweetly. It rolled – woosh! – into the hole and I thought, "Wow, I've won!" It was an amazing five seconds.' Golf being golf, however, and one of the most consistent reminders of human fallibility outside a cemetery, Faldo's game was not always top hole. 'You win one week and two weeks later you're thinking, "Christ! I can't play this game". Or, you miss a cut for six weeks and then win a tournament. Where does that come from? It's very, very weird.'

Before he won a major he deconstructed his swing completely under the tutelage of guru David Leadbetter. It was a brave and noble enterprise, worthy of his (alleged) ancestor Sir William Faldo, of Italian descent, who apparently came to England in the 1300s with a coat of arms representing three arrows and a shield. 'Oh, wacky,' said Sir William's famed scion. 'Must be where I get my arm from.' And, of course, had Faldo's life encompassed no more than that – victories, ego, obsessive determination and a slightly worrying sense of humour – all would have been very well. But then there were the women. Rather like Joan Collins, he seems quaintly attached to the idea of getting married with the result that he has been less-than-quaintly attached to three successive women (with the possibility of overlap, here and there). It was nobody's business, but the modern triumvirate of celebrity, media and British prurience made it so. He was hot controversial property. 'I realise now that I lived in that era when the media were pretty brutal to sportsmen. Look what happened to Ian Botham and Nigel Mansell. The brief to the golf writers was, "You write golf and you're fired". They had to find a sensational story all the time and I was on my own. You didn't go to media classes. You didn't have a PR team behind you. Look at Tiger Woods today. The media guys all tell me they hate him because he never tells them anything.'

In a slightly less combative moment he does admit to failings in his personal life which have garnered him two ex-wives, one apparently feisty American ex-girlfriend, three children by his ex-wife Gill, and fourteen-month-old Emma with his Swiss-French third wife, Valerie. 'There's a solid relationship for my children now. There's nothing worse than going through a divorce and the children not knowing what's going on. They go through that lost era. They were lost with it all. It's no good saying, "Oh, they're all right" because they weren't. It takes time to heal. I wasn't all right either. It got me in a right pickle. I couldn't make a good decision to save my life. It was a serious screw-up.'

Faldo gamely admits throughout his book to passionate torrents of tears. 'I moved through my life like the bow of a ship. Things happened behind me. Things I never saw. But, you're right, I must have rattled, upset people.' This is possibly the curse and blessing of the only child. Growing up, you rarely have your attention brought forcibly to other people's needs by a sibling with a blunt instrument. A certain self-absorption necessarily sets in. But he is not taking the full blame here. 'God dear, it's tricky. You girls!' he said. 'Working you girls out, it's incredible. Yes doesn't mean yes. No doesn't mean no. And we're supposed to understand the difference. Val's a good character though. We go from fiery moments to wonderfully good laughs. You could say there's a lot to be said for marriage.' Pause. 'Eventually.' The day he married his first wife, Melanie, he managed to play golf in the morning. 'At least the whole day wasn't ruined,' he joked cheerfully. You see what people mean about his sense of humour.

Moving swiftly on, what next? He wants to be Ryder Cup captain. 'What's the bottom line here? You want to win it? Right. OK, who's the man? The fact that I've had an argument from time to time with someone shouldn't affect selection for the job. And I don't think it will. I'll let the Ryder Cup committee decide and if they choose me, I'll be honoured.' He is also on a diet, a prelude at forty-seven to joining the Champions' Tour at the age of fifty. 'I want to do some damage,' he announced typically, endearingly untamed. 'I want to get myself fit, technically, physically, mentally. I've got five to six years mapped out. Coaching, commentary, business things. It would be kind of nice to have another baby.' He is also trying to learn French from his iPod to keep up with his bilingual toddler daughter. Being brought back down to earth by a one-year-old cannot be bad for Britain's greatest golfer. So he strides contentedly into his future, a man who achieved his mission. 'It's what we strive for. The buzz. The respect. I just wanted people to say, "I watched Nick Faldo – what a so-and-so, but bloody hell he was incredible".' Not bad, as a self-appraisal.

**Sporting Champion: Nick Faldo – 3 The Opens (1987, 1990, 1992);
3 Masters (1989, 1990, 1996).**

DOYEN – KING GEORGE VI AND QUEEN ELIZABETH DIAMOND STAKES

DOYEN IS KING AFTER DAZZLING DISPLAY

Brough Scott, 25 July 2004

The big day needs the big performance. Right on cue Doyen and Frankie Dettori powered off the turn to put this King George VI and Queen Elizabeth Diamond Stakes field to the sword with the run of the season. At the line he was adjudged three lengths clear of the international traveller Hard Buck and his own anorexic-looking stable companion, Sulamani, in the ordinary time of two minutes 33.18 seconds. But mere statistics give no indication of Doyen's superiority, nor of the thrill of the moment when Dettori tightened the reins and angled his partner towards daylight and King George glory.

Hard Buck's effort under Seabiscuit star Gary Stevens was an enormous tribute to the enterprise and skill of his Kentucky trainer Kenny McPeek, who had successfully campaigned the Brazilian ace in both the United States and Dubai before producing a best-ever performance from an American-based horse in the King George. Sulamani may show every rib and have the neck of a roe deer, but there was nothing wrong with the way he ran here. Except that he, like the rest, could not match the marvel that Doyen has become as a four year old.

It was the fourth time that Sheikh Mohammed's Godolphin operation have won what is the most important race in the calendar. But even Swain (1997 and 1998) and Daylami (1999) cannot have given more satisfaction than this supremely handsome son of Sadler's Wells, who was bred and reared on the Mohammed studs in Ireland. For the Sheikh also bred Doyen's dam Moon Cactus, who won three good races and was second in the French

Oaks for Steve Cauthen and Henry Cecil in 1990, and her own first foal was Moonshell, who won the Oaks at Epsom under Dettori in 1995. In the past the Godolphin approach has had a touch of the Abramovich about it. Sulamani, bought expensively from the Niarchos team after running second in the Arc, being a typical example. But Doyen's triumph has represented long-term planning on the track as well as off it. Entrusted to Andre Fabre in Chantilly for his first two seasons, he was a slightly baffled fifth on his only run as a two-year-old, progressed through three modest victories to run second in an Arc trial and a seven-length fourth in the Arc itself. His winter in Dubai was not wholly successful, he also took time to settle when he first came to Newmarket and his Coronation Cup second to Warrsan had a touch of ring-rustiness about it.

But now the shine is full and glorious on him. At Royal Ascot he set a two minutes 26.53 seconds track record for this demanding 1½ miles and here, in the paddock, on the way to the start and in the race itself he was never less than awesome. A bay son of Sadler's Wells he has that super stallion's trademark white star on his forehead and a smoother, and therefore firm-ground adapting action and a more forward head carriage than some of the Sadler's Wells stock. Once the stalls opened Dettori's only problem was to restrain his mount in what seemed a pretty steady opening quarter. This was set by his stable-mate, Lunar Sovereign, from Hard Buck and Warrsan. Quite why major courses like Ascot cannot install basic quarter-mile sectional timing is little short of a scandal at a time when millions are being spent on efforts to modernise racing. Maybe, as everyone watches lap times being called in the Olympics, the penny will drop that in 2004 it is wholly inadequate for an equine athletic meeting to give its viewers no more than the final clocking. That gripe had special relevance here. For at Swinley Bottom, Ted Durcan accelerated on the leader and it would have been interesting to know the increase in the tempo. Even more illuminating would have been to have the sectional clockings off the final turn. For a moment Doyen did not have much racing room, then Dettori saw the gap and the punch he delivered to go clear of his field was as good as anything we have seen in the event's fifty-five-year history. How much better if we could put a measurement on what looked like greatness.

'This was the easiest King George winner I have ridden,' a beaming Dettori said after his obligatory flying dismount from a horse who is only now maturing towards perfection. 'Now we can say it – he is one of the finest. He can only learn and get better and better.' Sheikh Mohammed added: 'The sky's the limit. We can take him to the Arc and the Breeders' Cup. He is a very special horse.'

Dettori's day had begun eventfully with a fall and his 2,000th winner in Britain when the first-time-out two-year-old Nightfall took his re-united partner to a photo-finish victory in the first. Dettori gave the public a special flying dismount to mark the occasion and then, with his unerring instinct for the hearts and minds, continued: 'I have lived here for eighteen years and the British people have taken me to their hearts as if I was one of them. I have a wonderful job and a wonderful team to work with at Godolphin and a great support from my family and friends. This was a great milestone for me.' Doyen's victory four races later was proof that there is a long and glorious way to go on the Dettori journey.

Sporting Champion: Doyen – 1 King George VI and Queen Elizabeth Diamond Stakes (2004).

JONATHAN EDWARDS – COMMONWEALTH GAMES

'UGLY' EDWARDS SEALS SLAM

Sue Mott, 29 July 2002

L ike any man who collects things – Spode, stamps, butterflies – Jonathan Edwards was out to complete a set. As he arrived in the soft evening light in the City of Manchester Stadium, wearing tight red training pants that made him look oddly like a ballet dancer, he was nursing one fierce and noble ambition: the Commonwealth Games gold medal. And now he has it. It was an ambition with which Tiger Woods would be familiar. Or Steffi Graf. Only the true sporting greats step into this rarefied territory. He was challenging likelihood and fate. He was trying to achieve the athletic grand slam of holding all four major titles: Olympic, World, European and Commonwealth at the same time. The world record holder in his sport since 1995, only the Commonwealth title had eluded him. The rest have fallen to the sprint, speed and sacrifice of one of the greatest British athletes of all time. Arguably *the* greatest if you take into account the longevity of his reign and the completeness of his dominance over an event. For a pacifist, his grip round the jugular of the triple jump is profound.

No greater favourite has entered the arena during these Games unless you count David Beckham in the opening ceremony. And no greater contrast could possibly exist between the two. Edwards is the unshowiest athlete on God's Earth. He hasn't dyed his hair, which has greyed with the years, his ear lobes are not weighed down by metalwork and his manner reminds you of an assiduous and earnest country vicar. But his competitiveness is renowned. It co-exists in his soul with his famous niceness, and pounces like a beast under floodlights and pressure. When his rivals jump he walks up and down the track beside them. Who knows how much the tentacles of intimidation reach out to them? Mugged by reputation. One competitor, Karibataake Katimiri, of Kiribati, didn't even turn up. But then his personal best was 12.15 metres, which probably wouldn't have reached the sandpit.

By his own standards, Edwards barely made it either with his opening jump, a whimper not a bang. It earned a wry grimace from the Olympic champion and his second jump was a foul. Meanwhile, Leevan Sands, of the Bahamas, was flying interestingly long and then Phillips Idowu, the Londoner who beat Edwards in Sheffield the month before, sailed into the ether with a jump 35 centimetres beyond his previous best. It is always advisable for an athlete who dyes his hair blond and decorates it with a border of red love hearts, not to mention a metal stud in his chin, to come up with the sporting goods. He had failed at the World Championships, not even breaking the 17-metre barrier. But this was home soil and the source of his inspiration. Following the moment of joyful impact in the sandpit, Idowu stripped off one shoulder of his vest in passionate celebration, to become Edwards's potential successor and a bodice-ripper simultaneously.

How would the champion in Edwards respond? With an expression of utter raptness on the runway. With a sprint that ought to have pitched him straight into the England 4x100 metres relay team. With a leap of prodigious faith and not a lot of technique. ('It was a mess. It was awful. I won ugly.') And a landing to a roar that is unlikely to be echoed in this magnificent stadium until Nicolas Anelka scores his first goal for Manchester City here in 2003. Edwards had barely landed in the sandpit before he was off and running, arms outstretched, punching the air in celebration. The scoreboard showed the toe of his spikes on the board. Clean. Another roar. Then the distance was picked out in neon. Another roar. It read: 17.86 metres. Idowu had broken the Games record. Edwards broke it again.

He has called this stage in his career 'The Long Goodbye'. Those looked like romantic words for the twilight zone for the first couple of rounds. But he was just lulling us, the old showman. The hunger was there. He had said his physical condition was fine despite the evolution of a less rigorous attitude to training and diet. But he had worried about his own motivation. However, there was motive as well as means. He may be thirty-six but there was a grand slam beckoning. He was jumping for the illusion of omnipotence and being famously God-fearing would know this accolade was in the sporting context only. Yet his satisfaction was profound. His seven-year-old son, Nathan, watching in the stands with his mum and grandparents, had been very nervous, but his nine-year-old son, Sam, had announced with confidence: 'Daddy, you're going to win.' And so it proved. 'It was wonderful,' Edwards said. 'The warmth of the crowd, the weather, the atmosphere was electric. I didn't think we in Britain could put on a show like this.'

He is such a professional. Undeflectable. As he listened to the sustained swell of ecstasy and appreciation that accompanied Paula Radcliffe's monumental run in the 5,000 metres, he limbered up, a mere spectator. What sights he has seen. At Sydney 2000, he was winning his gold medal in the stadium the night Cathy Freeman won for Australia and Michael Johnson became even more immortal than he already was. But no sight beat that of his opponents here trailing in obeisant wake. Now he has it all. His lap of honour was a long, slow, drink-it-in pleasure. In contrast to the silver medallist, Idowu, who bounced gleefully along like Tigger. The new Commonwealth gold medallist was one consonant short. 'Tiger' Edwards, we salute you.

Sporting Champion: Jonathan Edwards – 1 Commonwealth Games (2002); 1 Olympic Games (2000); 2 World Championships (1995, 2001); 1 European Championship (1998).

LANCE ARMSTRONG – TOUR DE FRANCE

A FREAKISH SPIRIT THAT CAN'T BE BROKEN

Brendan Gallagher, 25 July 2005

It was a year on, almost to the day, that Lance Armstrong treated his US Postal team and back-up staff to a banquet at a château in Burgundy on the Saturday night before his promenade to victory down the Champs Élysées the following day. The final time-trial at Besançon had been won, the opposition routed yet again and only the formalities of the 2004 Tour de France remained. Armstrong presented everybody with a signed yellow jersey by way of thanks – his fellow riders also shared his £500,000 prize money as tradition dictates – and as they posed on the marble staircase for a group photograph they raised six fingers to signify his incredible achievement. Everybody except Armstrong. He held up seven. He knew.

That mission has now been accomplished and with Armstrong heading into retirement his extraordinary achievements can be assessed. Some Armstrong myths need to be debunked, or at least modified, notably that his phenomenal success on the Tour is totally down to massive changes in lifestyle and a hardening in attitude after his recovery from cancer. Winning that war affected him profoundly and kick-started his career, but there is every possibility that Armstrong would have been a high achiever anyway. He has a resting pulse in the low thirties and nearly 7 litres of lung capacity, one of the highest recorded, and his body also produces almost negligible lactic acid, hence his ability to ride harder and longer than anybody else. In other words, he is a freak. 'People have the false impression that Lance was a regular guy who got cancer and then came back to win the Tour de France,' says trainer Chris Carmichael. 'The truth is that he was one in a million before and he's one in a million now.'

When he won the Verdun stage in 1993 he was, at twenty-one, the youngest stage winner on the Tour for fifty years. Armstrong – pre-cancer – was an outstanding prospect in a sport in which the world's best habitually peak in their late twenties. He was an exceptional, but raw athletic talent and could be consumed and distracted by anger and vitriol, the result of a disrupted and largely unhappy childhood. But nobody doubted that he was a champion in the making. By 1996 Cofidis had identified him as the man to win the Tour for them and offered him a contract worth nearly £3 million for the following season. Later that summer he started to feel breathless and feverish but even with his body, unknowingly, riddled with cancer, he finished second in the Tour of the Netherlands and runner-up in a world-class time-trial in Brussels. Within a month he was undergoing radical surgery and had begun chemotherapy. Testicular cancer with secondaries in the brain, abdomen and liver was the diagnosis – and so began a two-year fight against death. He emerged with the US Postal Team to win the first of an unprecedented seven consecutive Tour de France wins in 1999.

How can this be? What is his strange magic? There are many theories. Perhaps his brave and ultimately successful battle against cancer finally enabled Armstrong to make sense of everything and released an unstoppable life force. He was no longer frightened. 'That which doesn't kill you strengthens you', is one of his favourite mottos, along with 'Go hard or go home'. Post-cancer, no day in the saddle has been too hard when set beside the fight for life itself. Or it might be that cancer provided the cataclysmic, life-changing experience of staring death in the face and making the other guy blink first that pushed him into a kind of obsessive but controlled competitive madness. Many top road racers have, mentally, ridden close to the precipice. The trick is not to tip over. 'As long as he's pushing himself as an athlete and going fast, he doesn't have to deal with his emotions,' was the astute observation of his former wife, Kirsten.

There could be mileage in that. Armstrong might have remained grounded by his excess emotional baggage. Instead, he decided to discard it completely and fly high. Broken home, refusal to meet his natural father, rows with and beatings from step-fathers, marriage, cancer, death sentence, exhausting chemo-therapy, miraculous recovery, sceptical, often vicious press, drug accusations, courtroom fights, legal victories, celebrity status, con-stant media demands, death threats, unhappy marriage, three kids to fret over, feuds with fellow riders, relationship breakdown and traumatic divorce – 'Divorce has been harder than dealing with cancer' – love with rock star Sheryl Crow, increased rewards, dimin-ishing privacy. His life has been extraordinary and extreme. And he is still only thirty-three.

Considered a saint by some, a sinner by others and a terrorist target by the lunatic fringe, there must have been many days when the freedom and stark simplicity of the road – no matter how long or steep – and the macho challenge of riding hard and beating the 'other bastards' was irresistible. The peace, and the feeling that for five or six hours a day he was totally in control. After his stroppy early years he is now the *patron* of the peloton and largely enjoys their company and companionship, give or take the occasional feud. Armstrong never lost his 'attitude' and nothing ever comes between him and winning the Tour, but he will do a stint at the front or chase down a break to help a colleague or friend take a stage.

The conspiracy theory, of course, revolves around dark allegations of drug use from those unwilling to believe what they have seen over the last seven years. Cycling – like other sports such as athletics – is riddled with drug cheats, so such allegations are not to be treated lightly. What can be said is that Armstrong is one of the most tested athletes and has never failed a drugs test. In his defence there are many much more mundane reasons why Armstrong has won seven in a row. The world's best ever rider – arguably – has been competing in a generation of good but not outstanding riders. The opposition have rarely tested him. Eddy Merckx sums it up thus: 'When you're the strongest, the Tour is the easiest race to win because it's the hardest race of all.'

Nor has anybody approached the Tour de France with more professionalism. Armstrong does not get diverted by the spring classics or the Giro d'Italia. While others were racing eyeballs-out in May and early June to earn a crust he would be quietly training in the Alps and Pyrénées. Three or four times a day he would ascend a near deserted Alpe d'Huez or the Col du Tourmalet noting the change in road surfaces from last year, where the road has rutted, where it has been repaired and is smooth and storing away all those mountain miles in his legs.

It was 102 years since Henri Desgrange, a man of sadistic tendencies, founded the Tour de France, proclaiming: 'The ideal Tour de France is the one in which only one rider finishes.' Perish the thought, but in such an eventuality does anyone seriously doubt that the last man left, dancing on his pedals up the Champs Élysées in splendid isolation and wearing the *maillot jaune* would be Lance Armstrong? Desgrange wanted to break the human spirit. Armstrong, above all others, has proved that it cannot be broken.

Sporting Champion: Lance Armstrong – 7 Tours de France (1999, 2000, 2001, 2002, 2003, 2004, 2005 – all subsequently declared void over drug abuse).

BRADLEY WIGGINS – TOUR DE FRANCE

'LE ROSBIF' PLUNDERS FRANCE'S GREATEST SPORTING TREASURE

Ian Chadband, 23 July 2012

Paris swooned for the funny fellow in yellow; it was simply *magnifique*. Pedalling from a council estate in Kilburn all the way into legend down the Avenue des Champs Élysées, Bradley Wiggins became the first British cyclist to win the world's grandest bike race, the Tour de France. He was cheered on by thousands of fans who had made the pilgrimage from the United Kingdom because they were determined to be able to say they were there for a moment of unbeatable theatre, to salute perhaps the greatest individual sporting feat by any British sportsman in history. Indeed, as the thirty-two-year-old Londoner stood on the podium dressed in the primrose *maillot jaune* against the matchless backdrop of the Arc de Triomphe, it is hard to imagine that anything could possibly match the magnitude of his achievement in this 2,172-mile epic.

The flag-waving British fans evidently agreed as Wiggins, a very laconic English hero, told them cheerily from the top step: 'We're going to start drawing the raffle numbers now', before offering the parting salute: 'Have a safe journey home – and don't get too drunk!' Some chance of that. Here was an achievement so unfathomable that it merited champers all round, even if Lesley Garrett – swishing a Union flag dress around while offering an OTT rendition of the National Anthem next to the podium – did seem to bring a slightly pained look to the champion's face.

In ninety-nine editions of the Tour (it began in 1903, but did not run in the war years) nobody from the land of the bicycle clip across the Channel had come remotely near to winning sport's most murderous endurance test. The challenge of the British had been, for the most part, seen here as either risible or invisible. Yet on a day when Mark Cavendish, the world's greatest sprinter, won the final stage on the Champs Élysées for the fourth consecutive year, British cycling celebrated a seventh win of this Tour and two British riders, Wiggins and Chris Froome, finished first and second overall, this really had become what the hosts had dreaded as *La Promenade des Anglais*.

It was all quite surreal. Never has there been an attack of *Les Rosbifs* quite like it. Thousands had piled across on Eurostar, boats and planes for the weekend, hooked by a new cult hero for British sport. One whom even the French had learnt to appreciate. *L'Equipe*, the French sports newspaper, had already christened him as '*Wiggo le Froggy*', naturally taking a bit of credit for his victory by noting how he had cut his teeth in professional road cycling over there. They were also particularly admiring of his marvellous *rouflaquettes* – 'The most famous sideburns since Elvis Presley'. The Parisians may have been more than a little fed up about losing the 2012 Olympic Games to their neighbours but, *sacre bleu*, now it was also their greatest sporting treasure, too. Whisper it, but no French cyclist has won Le Tour for twenty-seven years. Yet for all that, they appeared to recognise a kindred spirit in this intriguing, eccentric Londoner, somebody who is a bit different, a guitar-playing, plain-speaking mod who was in love with their Tour as a boy, hanging posters of cycling heroes on the wall of his bedroom in Kilburn while all his mates were worshipping Gary Lineker or Paul Gascoigne.

Wiggins remembered how he had once come to Paris for this great sporting ritual of the final stage as a thirteen-year-old being treated by his mother. He thought to himself then that it was just a pipe dream that he could one day win the thing himself, but as he addressed the crowd from the podium, he pointed to his mother,

Linda, and said: 'Some dreams do come true. My old mum over there? Her son has just won the Tour de France!' Later, he said it must have been 'an incredible feeling' for her to watch him stand at the top of the podium. He also paid tribute to the support he received from British fans.

'Now I've come out of my bubble I start to realise what it means to all these people who've come over here,' he said. 'That turn near the Arc was just a sea of Brits and the noise was phenomenal. I'd like to think my victory stands for a lot more than just adding my name to the names that went before me. I think cycling is changing and I hope my victory goes down for the right reasons. I like to think it will be remembered in a positive sense. I hope this gives people hope and belief because this is a fantastic sport and people love it.'

It has often been a hard road for Wiggins. His father, Gary, was a hard-drinking and brawling Australian cyclist who left his first wife and baby daughter to seek his fortune on the European circuit. Wiggins senior met Bradley's mother, Linda, then a seventeen-year-old spectator, while racing in London. They married and Bradley was born in Ghent, Belgium, where his father was based. But Gary Wiggins walked out on them two years later. Mrs Wiggins and her son returned to London and lived in a flat with her parents, George and Maureen, while she worked as a clerk.

In 1992, Wiggins watched on television as Chris Boardman won gold in the 4-kilometre pursuit at the Barcelona Olympics. After his mother explained that it was his father's best event, he became hooked on cycling. But he did not meet his father again until he was eighteen when, hearing that his son was training in Australia, Wiggins senior arranged a reunion. They met again after Wiggins won a medal in the Sydney Olympics and his father persuaded him to enter a race at his local club to impress his friends. When he came only second, Gary Wiggins berated him and insisted that he had been the better cyclist. In 2008, the fifty-five-year-old was found dead in the street in Aberdeen, New South Wales. He had been assaulted and his attackers were never caught.

Wiggins reckoned that thoughts of some of those struggles – his beloved grandfather died while he was on the Tour two years ago – had preoccupied him during the time-trial to Chartres as he pedalled to victory. That win meant overall victory was already his – barring an accident – allowing the final 120-kilometre stage from Rambouillet to Paris to become the traditional ceremonial parade for the race leader. Still, he had one piece of serious business left: to help Cavendish win the last stage. 'It's a little weird to leave Paris without a party but now everything turns to the Olympics,' said Wiggins. 'I've got an Olympic time-trial to try and win.'

As well as a new generation of cyclists to woo. Wiggins is an outspoken critic of a British culture that embraces those famous for merely being famous. 'If I'm held up as an example to kids, then that's fantastic,' he said, 'because I was inspired by people like that. It's nice to be recognised and respected and have people look up to you for those reasons. And not to be like, whatever . . . Jordan, Peter Andre. Hopefully someone will see this and go, "I want to be like Brad Wiggins, I want to go and ride my local time-trial". It's nice because you are actually doing something through your life that is inspirational.' Absolutely. *Allez, Wiggo le Froggy!*

Sporting Champion: Bradley Wiggins – 1 Tour de France (2012); 4 Olympic Games (2004, 2008 – 2, 2012); 6 World Track Cycling Championships (2003, 2007 – 2, 2008 – 3).

MARK CAVENDISH – TOUR DE FRANCE

THE GENIUS OF SPRINT CYCLING

Jonathan Liew, 4 November 2013

You start a kilometre before the Poggio. Comes up slightly. Some traffic lights. Then you come back on to the cape, come round, rise up slightly, 500 metres to the Poggio, which is kind of like a bottleneck. That's 9 kilometres to go.

The mind of Mark Cavendish is a place few are capable of understanding. At a superficial level, there is something essentially disarming about him. The thin, reedy voice; a brusqueness of manner; a simplicity of vocabulary; an abruptness of tone; a truculence that is often mistaken for denseness. If you were to form an opinion of Cavendish based on his post-race interviews alone, you might indeed conclude that he was a little dim.

Then you've got a hairpin. Goes back on itself. Gradually bears round. It flattens up, then a hairpin, then slightly flat to the next hairpin. Turns right, kicks up a bit, then the steepest part of the Poggio. About 6 kilometres to go.

But Cavendish is not dim. He is a genius. The most skilful sprinter in British cycling history also happens to have perhaps the sharpest brain in the sport. Those two facts are by no means coincidental. 'If I do a circuit,' he assures me, 'then after three laps I could tell you where all the potholes were.' Cavendish cannot say when or how he developed his photographic memory. All he knows is that he possesses an extraordinary gift for absorbing his surroundings. All cyclists reconnoitre the courses they will ride, learning the cambers, getting a feel for the twists. For Cavendish, knowledge comes more naturally. When he first applied to join the British Cycling academy as a teenager, coach Rod Ellingworth asked him to describe his journey. Cavendish was able to describe his trip from the Isle of Man to Manchester in minute detail: the road numbers, the towns he went through, the times he went through them. Ellingworth realised he had an unusual talent on his hands.

> *Then it kicks up for 500 metres. That's normally where the splits go. Then it flattens off, around to the top of Poggio. Then a sharp left. You can't take it on the inside, the road drops away from you. Down to the hairpin, then the descent. Bottom of the Poggio, 3 kilometres to go.*

The last few kilometres of a sprint are where Cavendish gets to work. As the leading teams manoeuvre themselves towards the front of the bunch, Cavendish's mind starts running in slow motion. 'For me, it's like a calculation, a series of movements, a series of chess moves. Not thinking, not having to react. Just reacting. By the time we start the sprint, my heart rate is probably twenty or thirty beats slower than the other guys. So many cyclists train their bodies. They don't train their mind. I constantly do puzzle books. Smash through them. My iPad's full of them. Logic puzzles. Bridges. Slitherlink.' He pulls an iPad out of his bag. A picture of his wife Peta adorns the background screen as he opens up his latest puzzle, a variation on sudoku. 'Hanidoku. You've got this honeycomb. Every single line has to have a consecutive run of numbers. Could be one to five, could be two to six. So there's got to be a five here, because there's a four there, but it can't go with another five. Do you see?'

Does he do puzzles to nurture his cycling brain, or are both symptoms of his basic inquisitive intelligence? 'A bit of both. Like, I play Scrabble against random opponents, and if I lose that I'm as p***** off as if I lose a Tour de France stage.' Is he a genius? 'Last time I did an IQ test I was, yeah.' But a very particular sort of genius. 'You called it conscious subconscious competence,' Cavendish's agent Simon Bayliff pipes up from the back of the room. 'You know when an athlete is in the zone? There's actually a stage beyond that, where you are actually conscious of your subconscious. There's a ladder: conscious incompetence, then conscious competence, then subconscious competence, which is the zone.' 'Now I have no f****** idea what he's talking about,' Cavendish says, and we all laugh.

The closing stages of the 2011 World Championships in Copenhagen are a case in point. As the sprint wound up the finishing straight, Cavendish was aware that the wind was blowing towards the left, and that the peloton would naturally drift in that direction. So he placed himself on the right, waited for the gap he knew would open up, and surged through it to become world champion. Another puzzle solved.

> There's dustbins on the right of the road that they never, ever move. You come back down the main road, 2 kilometres to go. Then a left.

But a brilliant mind only goes halfway to making a champion. The rest is attitude, and especially for a rider as small and stocky as Cavendish, the sheer drive to put in the physical work required. 'My stepson, if he can't do something, he just says, "I'm not doing it". I was the exact opposite. If I couldn't do anything, I had to do it.' At twenty-eight, Cavendish is no longer a boy racer. Younger, bigger challengers like Marcel Kittel and André Greipel are snapping at his heels. The redoubtable Peter Sagan now owns his Tour de France green jersey. 'I feel that I'm getting older,' Cavendish says. 'I don't have the punch. I have to work on my sprint now, which I didn't have to do before.'

Brian Holm, a great friend and Cavendish's boss when he was at HTC-Highroad, once said that Cavendish rode better when he was angry. Does that still hold true? 'To an extent. Not so much angry: I've really learnt to control anger, it's a waste of energy. But when I've got a point to prove, that will still be the case. I've been relatively unchallenged until now, and now people are challenging my position as the most dominant sprinter in the world.'

After Cavendish the thinker, and Cavendish the racer, comes a glimpse into Cavendish the man. His book reveals a more mature and reflective subject, deeply devoted to his wife and daughter. It is the same unflinching, unstinting bond he shares with those who have helped him along the way: trade-team colleagues, British team-mates, friends and sponsors. Cavendish's world is a diverse, collegiate and yet fiercely loyal place. 'I don't know any different,' he says. 'I don't like being in London too long, because everybody's just looking straight forward, at nobody else. That freaks me out a little bit. I have a house in a small town in Tuscany where everybody knows and looks out for each other. That's a similar mentality to the Isle of Man.'

So, finally, a test. I ask Cavendish if he can describe the last kilometre into Sanremo, the town where he achieved his breakthrough win in 2009. Cavendish says he will do the last 10 kilometres. After about five minutes of minuscule detail, you can see his eyes glaze over as he describes the closing stages.

Left, then a roundabout, then a right. Then you come down, the
road forks and you bear left: 1 kilometre to go. It comes down, on

to the car park, they put up the road barriers on race day. The last
600 metres is straight. And there you finish.

Sporting Champion: Mark Cavendish – 1 Tour de France Points
Classification (2011); 1 World Road Race Championship (2011);
2 World Track Championships (2005, 2008); 1 Commonwealth
Games (2006); 1 European Track Championship (2005).

REBECCA ADLINGTON – WORLD SWIMMING CHAMPIONSHIPS

ADLINGTON VICTORY COMPLETES TITLE COLLECTION

Duncan White, 31 July 2011

Back in China and back at the top of the podium: Rebecca Adlington won the 800 metres freestyle gold at the World Championships here in Shanghai, beating Denmark's defending champion, Lotte Friis, in a thrilling stroke-for-stroke duel in the middle lanes. Adlington showed that her talent is now encased in armour-plated resilience. It was like a great boxer unifying all the belts: Adlington is now an Olympic, World, European and Commonwealth champion.

'No one can ever take that away from me now,' she said, having won 400 metres gold in the European Championships in Budapest in 2010 and both the 400 metres and 800 metres at the 2008 Olympics in Beijing and the 2010 Commonwealth Games in Delhi. 'Obviously I want to win again at the Olympics but even if that didn't happen I'd still be happy with what I achieved in my career. China's obviously a good-luck charm for me.'

Her vocal team-mates had stood throughout the race, urging her on from poolside. With only two medals in the pool before Adlington's race, there was pressure on her to give the whole team a lift. She did that all right, but those watching from the stands had to suffer nearly as much as her; it was an almost unendurably tense race. Adlington and Friis have been competing since their European junior days and they did not cede an inch to each other here. And it really was coming down to those kind of distances.

For the first 650 metres they had not been more than four-tenths of a second apart at each turn, as the rest of the field drifted into the background. Friis was first at the halfway point, but Adlington clung on and, while the Dane seemed to be making gains with her turns, Adlington immediately clawed back any advantage. With 100 metres to go, Adlington trailed by more than half a second and looked like she might be tiring. It was simply the calm before the storm. Adlington's last 50 metres was explosive, finally breaking Friis's resolve.

'I've never had a race that tight at a major meet,' said Adlington. 'I think when I raced Lotte at the Mare Nostrum meet in Barcelona last year we had a similar race, going head to head the whole way. But never at a major games, so that has given me confidence. I know now that if I'm out ahead or in a close race I can get the touch. I knew it was going to be between me and her from looking at the times from qualifying. I saw her pushing me at the four hundred-metre mark but I stayed in there. I didn't try to break her, I just tried to stick with her. She got ahead a bit between seven hundred and seven hundred and fifty metres but at that last turn I just put my head down and went for it. It was only in the last twenty-five metres that I saw I was getting clear. I just told myself to keep going. We've always raced against each other and it's always been one does it one year and one does it the next year, but I hope to God it's me next year.'

Having already claimed silver in the 400 metres freestyle, Adlington, twenty-two, has shown a maturity and competitive composure that bodes well for the London Olympics in 2012. She went into the World Championships in Rome in 2009 as a double Olympic gold medallist and admitted that the pressure of expectation got to her. While she swam a personal best in the 400 metres freestyle it was good enough only for a bronze; then, in the 800 metres, her strongest event, she ended fourth in a race won by Friis.

'I learn more from the bad swims rather than the good swims. It definitely makes me stronger. I'm not the sort of person who gets knocked down by a bad swim; I just get more motivated. I'm resilient in that way. I'm definitely the kind of person who can handle pressure. I have learnt to cope with it; I kind of had to after the Olympics. I want to do well, I want to succeed, I don't want to put all the hard work in every morning to turn up and not make it happen. A lot of people struggle mentally and I do sometimes. But I've got Simon Middlemas, our sports psychologist, and he's absolutely amazing. He's helped me so much.'

She added: 'I'll be back in the pool in mid-August when the season for Olympic trials starts.' Those hard yards through the cold winter will be needed, though, because she knows wherever the championships are, Friis will be waiting on the block next to her. Adlington will be prepared.

Sporting Champion: Rebecca Adlington – 2 World Championships (2008, 2011); 2 Olympic Games (2008); 1 European Championship (2010); 2 Commonwealth Games (2010).

ENGLAND – FOOTBALL WORLD CUP

TOGETHERNESS WAS THE KEY TO GLORY

Alan Ball, 9 June 2006

Every one of us who was part of the squad Alf Ramsey gathered around him that summer thought we would win the World Cup. We had players with pace, players with power, players with stamina and skill. We knew we would be extremely difficult to beat; by 1966, England had lost just four matches at Wembley in their history. But most of all we were together. The men at the Hendon Hall hotel became a family, and we still are. The man I shared a room with during those weeks was Nobby Stiles, who I still count as one of my closest friends. We were both young northern lads desperate to do well. There were no debates about what to watch on television because generally you came back exhausted. All you wanted was sleep. The team Ramsey sent out to Mexico four years later is regarded by some as better than the one who actually took the World Cup. It had more flair and panache but the 1966 team was more complete. It had no weaknesses, and we knew it.

Alf was a man considerably ahead of his time. At Hendon Hall we watched films of our opponents continually. We knew precisely how they would play, and Ramsey always knew how England would line up. We had played Spain, who were then European champions, at the Bernabéu in Madrid, and beaten them 2–0 with Nobby Stiles as a holding midfielder – a task he performed better than anyone in the world. We warmed up with a tour of Scandinavia, but we did not use that system again until the opening match of the tournament, against Uruguay. They called us the wingless wonders, but it worked because the full-backs never knew who to mark and England usually found themselves with more bodies and more space in midfield. If the opposition counter-attacked, Nobby and I were there to break things up.

It was a long build-up to the tournament. Blackpool's season had ended in the first week of May and the World Cup did not open until 11 July. We went to a training camp at Lilleshall, where we slept in dormitories, and Alf did not spare us. We expected something gentler, and instead we were worked and worked every day. It was like enduring another pre-season. There were powerful characters in that squad; Bobby Moore, Jimmy Greaves and Gordon Banks were men of very strong opinions. Jack Charlton was forever trying to clip me round the ear because of some comment I'd made out of turn. But we became a kind of family, with Alf Ramsey at its head.

Everything he did in that summer paid off. On the eve of the World Cup final he took us to a cinema to watch *Those Magnificent Men in Their Flying Machines*, although Alf was a great fan of westerns. With Sven-Göran Eriksson's 2006 squad tucked away in their German retreat, it seems incredible to think that this happened, but we were touchable, part of the everyday in a way footballers no longer are. As the curtain came down, the entire picture house rose to us and applauded and one of the lads said to me: 'We can't lose it for these people.'

It was different in 1970. England were world champions. It gave us a certain swagger in Mexico, but it also meant we were there to be shot at; the target for a lot of unpleasantness off the field. Bobby Moore being accused of stealing a bracelet in Bogotá, and the constant noise around the team hotel, the Hilton in Guadalajara, were cases in point. There, we developed a kind of siege mentality. One thing that was the same, though, was we knew how much it meant to the ordinary fan because we had been through it before. Time tended to drag at Hendon Hall and it will do among Eriksson's squad. They, like us, will be straining to get out there, desperate for the first match, the first tackle and the first win. Nothing quite prepares you for the first taste of a World Cup. Whether you play for Manchester United or Chelsea; whether you've won championships or European Cups, nothing matches that anticipation of walking out at the greatest sporting show on earth.

We were the host nation, it was the opening game, and what was uppermost in our mind was that we should not lose. When you are not playing, days crawl by. The goalless opener against Uruguay was a poor game; the crowd were flat and so were we but Alf was curiously upbeat. 'You haven't lost,' he said in the dressing room, 'and if you don't concede goals, you will win the World Cup.' Yet I was left out for the two matches that followed, against Mexico and France, both of which we won 2–0. I knew England were not going to change a winning side and I confess to feeling very low. There was nothing you could do. Ramsey was not a man to complain to and, anyway, there was this general and very real sense that what counted was England, not you. And yet Ramsey always had in mind that I would play again. He was not a man to stand by the tired adage of never changing a winning team. He knew Argentina had a full-back, Silvio Marzolini, who liked to get forward, and he told me I was the man to stop him in the quarter-finals – and we did.

The night before the World Cup final we were edgy but full of a quiet confidence. We had got to the final by conceding one goal. Against Portugal, in the semi-finals, we had produced our best football of the tournament against the best side we had faced. We were young and hungry for success, although we did not quite know how our lives were going to change by the following afternoon. When we went to bed the mood was: 'West Germany – bring them on.'

Sporting Champions: England – 1 World Cup (1966).

GREAT BRITAIN – DAVIS CUP

BRITAIN'S CLEAN SWEEP IN DAVIS CUP

A. Wallis Myers, 31 July 1935

Five matches to nil – a clean sweep! Such was the final verdict for Great Britain in the challenge round of the Davis Cup. In the last phase at Wimbledon, with two singles remaining on the card, H.W. Austin defeated D. Budge 6–2, 6–4, 6–8, 7–5, thus reversing a result at the Championships. Then F.J. Perry followed with a victory over W.A. Allison in a very fine match. The champion's score was 4–6, 6–4, 7–5, 6–3.

It is not a novelty for this country to win the international championship with a clean slate, but the precedent dates back three decades – to the Doherty era. Even American teams, with envoys stronger in skill than the present challengers, failed to capture a match in 1905 and 1906. And the total number of straight-match victories since the Cup was founded in 1900 is as high as nine, although that registered here was the first 'five-pointer' since 1925. The result reflects the great strength of the present British team in stamina as well as in skill, in *esprit de corps* as well as in sound training. It does not, of course, mean that our overseas rivals are so inferior to the defenders here that our position at the top is safe for any given period of time without relays of new talent, but it does imply that Perry, Austin, Hughes and Tuckey can look the world in the face with a confident air.

Another page has been added to the Cup's history; the name of Great Britain, the original challenger, will now be inscribed on Mr Dwight Davis's famous bowl for the eighth time. This is two more than the six wins of France and Australia, but it is two fewer than the ten of America. Long leaseholds of property do not necessarily bring prosperity to the outside world. The Davis

Cup would not have attracted the competition of more than thirty nations, nor helped to develop lawn tennis as a cosmopolitan game, if the title deeds had always been kept in the same hands. The passage of the Cup from continent to continent, from nation to nation, as the outcome of friendly rivalry, is the best guarantee of its future popularity.

The crowd was large and articulate even if it were many hundreds below the record of the first day – the largest throng, by the way, that has watched a Davis Cup match in any country. Two first-class matches were provided. There was not – there could not be – the tension either on court or surrounding it that a still open verdict would have generated. But all four players were keen; their minds and muscles were on their tasks. Only Budge, of the quartet, looked battle-worn, giving one the impression that he had to whip his will to keep up resistance. Austin, playing beautifully and well within his powers, beat him fairly comfortably in four sets. It is true the Californian took the third set and held a favourable lead in the fourth; true, too, that he sacrificed an easy chance when Austin was 40–love down, to take the ninth game and secure a lead of 5–4 with his service to follow. But Austin's ball control was so consistently good, his capacity to hit through or round Budge so freely demonstrated, that I believe, since his physical reserves were still strong, that he could have safely survived the test of a fifth set had one been necessary.

The service had little influence on the match. Indeed, breaks were so frequent that no fewer than eight were recorded in the second set of ten games. This unusual attribute was, perhaps, fortunate for Austin, since he was rarely threatened with a menacing delivery from his opponent, and could afford to concentrate on co-ordinated strokes that could command the rally by their perfection. Having put the first two sets safely in the bank, Austin could enjoy the luxury of a little holiday from sustained effort in the third. He nearly won this, too, for he reduced Budge's lead of 5–3 to vanishing point, and then, after saving a set stroke in the tenth game, went on to lead 6–5. Budge came a full 'cropper' in this game, by the way, and for a moment one wondered whether he would rise with all his ligaments intact. But he soon relieved any anxiety and proceeded to play more forceful tennis in the next three games, in which Austin's lobbing eye seemed to desert him.

The fourth set was like the second, except that, after he had forged ahead, Budge seemed to have no energy left to bid for its possession. He was, as I have said, 4–2 and was 40 up on Austin's service in the ninth game. Here he played some very poor strokes, and though he rallied to hold his service from 15, he forfeited another 40 lead in the next game, and Austin was his complete master in the final game.

Had Allison offered any nominal resistance to the champion in the second match it would not have been altogether surprising. No man fighting lost causes on a tennis court had worked harder in the last few days. Instead, Allison played his last match at Wimbledon in a fine career with all the pluck and industry of a fresh competitor. He found a rather perfunctory Perry in the opening set, needing the spur of intensive battle to kindle his energies, but, when the American had captured it, the issue was joined in a match full of glorious strokes and counter-strokes. Perry did not lose another set, but he was nearly caught in the second after leading 5–3; was actually caught in the third with the same advantage; and even in the fourth set, when Perry, leading 5–1, the *coup de grâce* was signalled.

Splendidly as Allison fought, extracting dream-shots from the champion – and there was one forehand winner from Perry across the court that for spontaneous speed will live in the memory – the American was dogged by his bad fairy of 1935 – the double-fault.

He must have lost twenty points through service lapses, and when one looks at the figures of the match one can realise their bearing on the fate of the sets. Yet even those timing mistakes could not tarnish a very brilliant display, featured by many galloping volleys, and groundstrokes and lobs that always had shrewd purpose behind them.

As for Perry, he showed conclusively why the Davis Cup remains in England by the scintillating play in the break which carried him to 5–1 in the fourth set. I have seen nothing quite so devastating as this phase after watching lawn tennis – and playing a little, too – for nearly forty years. It was a striking climax to Perry's unbeaten career at Wimbledon in 1935 – something we can store in our memories when he goes off on another tour round the world.

Sporting Champions: Great Britain – 9 Davis Cups (1903, 1904, 1905, 1906, 1912, 1933, 1934, 1935, 1936).

JIM LAKER – THE ASHES

LAKER TAKES NINETEEN WICKETS FOR NINETY RUNS

E.W. Swanton, 1 August 1956

For many nervous hours since the evening of the second day it had seemed that England would be robbed of victory in the fourth Test match. But Manchester expiated its sins of weather on the final afternoon, and it was in bright sunshine tempering the wind that the game ended in an innings win, which meant the safekeeping of the Ashes until MCC next sail in their defence two years from now. The only proper formal announcement of the result is that J.C. Laker defeated Australia by an innings and 170 runs. Unprecedented things are always happening in cricket, because it is so charmingly unpredictable a pastime. But now and then occurs something of which one feels certain there can be no repetition or bettering. Laker followed his capture of nine first-innings wickets with all ten in the second. What is left in the vocabulary to describe and applaud such a tour de force? It is quite fabulous.

Once at Johannesburg on the mat, S.F. Barnes, still happily with us at a ripe eighty-three, took seventeen for 159. That analysis topped the list in Test matches until this – when Laker, wheeling relentlessly on, left the statistical gentry without another comparison to make or another record to be knocked down. Hedley Verity took fifteen for 104 after the thunderstorm at Lord's in 1934. Wilfred Rhodes, another old hero still listening to the play, even if he cannot now see it, got a like number at Melbourne half a century ago. In the recent past, Alec Bedser got out fourteen Australians for ninety at Trent Bridge on their last visit. Great figures. Great deeds. But Laker in 51.3 overs has added a ten for fifty-three to his ten for eighty-eight against this same Australian side for Surrey. And in this Test he has actually taken nineteen for ninety.

Laker's first-innings performance was phenomenal enough, but its merit was perhaps clouded by the deficiencies of the Australian batting, as also by the palaver over the condition of the wicket. There was no room whatever for argument regarding his bowling here. He bowled thirty-six overs, practically non-stop except for the taking of the new ball, all the time attacking the stumps and compelling batsmen to play, never wilting or falling short in terms either of length or direction. Nor was he mechanical. Each ball presented the batsman with a separate problem. Laker never let up and neither for an instant could his adversary.

It is, of course, scarcely less remarkable that while Laker was building up new heights of fame at one end Lock was toiling just as zealously, albeit fruitlessly, at the other. On a wicket on which one famous cricketer captured nineteen wickets the other, scarcely less successful and dangerous, taking one day with another, in sixty-nine overs had one for a hundred. Of course if the gods had been kind Lock could have taken more. He was not, in cold fact, at his best, and if he is suffering the reaction now from all the hard bowling in Pakistan it is not to be wondered at. Still, the comparison between the figures is in one sense unarguable evidence of Laker's great performance. If the wicket had been such a natural graveyard for batsmen it is inconceivable that Lock, even below his peak, even with the other arm tied to his side, would not have taken more than one wicket.

Applause for Laker, and applause also in a scarcely lesser strain for McDonald, who, in his long vigil, rose to the occasion for Australia and fought as hard as any man could do to win his side the respite of a draw. So long as McDonald was in the odds were still fairly balanced. When he was beaten at last directly after tea the latter-end batsmen carried on in the same spirit, and there was a bare hour to go when Maddocks, the number eleven, played back and slightly across to Laker, fell leg before and advanced up the wicket to shake the hero by the hand. One of the Australian party summed up the day, as the crowd that massed round the pavilion dispersed and Laker, glass in hand, had turned from the balcony to the dressing room by saying: 'Well, it was a good scrap after all.' There was relief in his voice, just as there was jubilation in the surrounding English faces.

The captains having formally disagreed, there was a delay of ten minutes before play was continued on the fifth morning. The wicket was just about as sluggish as the previous day. The weather, however, was not so violently unpleasant, for the wind, though still quite brisk, had dropped, and the clouds were higher with even a hint or two of blue sky. McDonald and Craig, by high-class defensive play, withstood the session of an hour and fifty minutes without many moments of difficulty. They played themselves in against Bailey and Laker, who were subsequently relieved by Lock and Oakman. Runs being of no object, except, possibly, to get the two batsmen to the ends they preferred, and the ball being hard to force away, the Test became one of the batsmen's concentration and judgment as to length. In this neither was found wanting, and it cannot be said that England much looked like breaking through. May gave Oakman a try, probably because from his unusual height he might get an off-spinner to lift. He kept the ball well up in the off-side and induced some strokes off the front foot into the covers. Oakman, however, is not a digger-in, and is a relatively better bowler on a hard wicket.

May took the new ball as soon as he could, which was at a quarter to one. Bailey brought back one or two and found Craig's inside edge, and Statham and he perhaps held out slightly more hopes than the spinners. Just before lunch Evans and Lock, those tireless propagandists, when the latter was bowling tried their hardest by expression and gesture to suggest that the dormant pitch was stirring. But McDonald and Craig came in calm and unscathed, having, incidentally, added twenty-eight runs.

There were early signs after lunch that the batsmanship might be more severely tested. Craig was twice beaten by lifting balls from Lock, who naturally enough was sharing the bowling with Laker. After a quarter of an hour Craig went back to the latter and was lbw to an off-break. Thus he retired full of honour after an innings of four hours and twenty minutes, in which his stature had grown surely and steadily. The breaking of the stand was the signal for the second Australian collapse of the game. Within half an hour Mackay, Miller and Archer had all followed Craig, all to

Laker, and all for ducks. Granted the ball was doing a little more during this phase in answer to bursts of sun, these batting failures underlined the worth and value of the third-wicket partnership. Where before the judgment of length and direction had been good enough to ensure a smooth, well-considered defensive stroke, now the new batsmen were floundering about and either using their pads or offering a last-minute jab.

Mackay was surrounded by slips, silly mid-off, and short-legs, six in all within a 5-yard radius. One could hardly see how he could survive, for in going forward he plays so far in front of the front leg. This had been evident against the slow bowlers even while he was putting up his celebrated resistance at Lord's. Now Mackay probed out, and edged a short sharp catch to Oakman, the middle of the slips. I have never seen a batsman whose value rose and fell so abruptly according to the state of the wicket. On a good one he wants blasting out. When the ball is doing anything it is hard to see how he can last five minutes. As it was, Mackay here, like Harvey on the second day, bagged a pair.

One expected Miller to try and shift Laker's close leg fieldsmen as he had done at Leeds. Instead he seemed intent on fending away with the pads, using the bat only as a last resort. It was this manoeuvre which undid him, for he decided at the last moment he must put the bat to a yorker on the leg-stump, missed it, and was bowled. It was an innings singularly out of character. Laker had Archer pushing out at an off-break and steering it round the corner. McDonald, at the other end, steady and more or less serene, thus saw Australia's barometer drop from the healthy regions of 114 for two to 130 for six. He himself, it so happened, during this phase was almost exclusively opposing Lock, who was giving him the chance to indulge his feelings every now and then with a short ball which was usually hit for runs.

Benaud now got stuck with McDonald, determination in every

line, fastidious care also, for he took guard sometimes once or twice an over as though suspicious that Evans might have surreptitiously moved the position of the stumps. Benaud also gardened assiduously, which was prudent enough, seeing that the ball was taking turf. It earned him a little mildly derisory applause. May did his best to scotch the threat of a McDonald–Benaud stand by changing round his main spinners, introducing Bailey and giving Oakman another spell which he was scarcely able to justify. Benaud was nearly yorked by Bailey. However, that was as near another wicket as anyone could come.

McDonald was seemingly impervious, immovable, and this pair came to tea, having stayed together an hour and thirty minutes. Australia were still breathing. But McDonald did not take rest afterwards and it was the inevitable Laker who got the most valuable wicket of all. This was a sharp off-break which for once went too quickly for McDonald, who edged it to the sure hands of Oakman in the middle position just behind square. So ended a valiant effort lasting without a chance for more than five hours and a half. Lindwall made a steady partner for Benaud and at five o'clock these two looked ominously settled and determined: there was still Johnson and Maddocks to come. It was not yet 'in the bag'. But Benaud now went back where he might have gone forward and was bowled middle-and-off stumps or thereabouts. Twenty minutes later Lindwall, like so many before him, fell to the leg-trap. Then, with Johnson looking on, Maddocks made his entry and speedy, gracious exit. So the game ended. The post-mortems no doubt will linger on. But whatever is added, one thing cannot be gainsaid: Laker was magnificent.

Sporting Champion: Jim Laker – 2 Ashes series wins (1953, 1956).

AUGUST

SEBASTIAN COE – OLYMPIC GAMES

COE'S TOTAL CONVICTION SECURES
GREATEST PRIZE

David Miller, 7 July 2005

Twenty-one years ago, in 1984 in Los Angeles, I slowly drove back in the darkness with Sebastian Coe to the Olympic Village after he had won his 1,500 metres semi-final. For a man who, for a year and a half, had been seriously unwell, who had not even known until January of that year whether he would run competitively again, let alone defend his Olympic title, he was in an unusual mood. There was a calm about him that I had never seen before and there had been times when he would fall asleep in the passenger seat on the way to a race. It was almost as if he was on holiday rather than at the climax of six months of superhuman effort to rescue the reputation which only he and a few others believed still had credibility. As we reached the Village, he jogged casually up the steps and I could tell it was the run of a man who would sleep untroubled. The next day, he triumphantly won in an Olympic record time.

He was in exactly the same kind of mood when we talked at the end of three days of his ceaseless, intense preparation for what he calls 'the biggest last lap of my life, something on a different planet from my gold medals'. There was, he said, no anxiety, never mind that Paris were the favourites to host the Olympic Games in 2012 and London had been dismissed by countless politicians and media. He had the conviction that London could win. Now forty-eight, he just had to make not the greatest run of his career but the most convincing peroration. And that is what he went and did, turning around all the forecasts at home and around the world that Paris were unbeatable.

We talked about his presentation and I suggested to him that this was the moment when he needed to summon not the characteristics of Peter, his father and coach, with the pragmatic, technical disciplines of an engineer, but the emotion and sensitivity of Angela, his half-Indian mother, who had only recently died from a disease of the nervous system and was for so long the force of his emotional soul. He nodded. 'She understands,' he said. 'Angela was passionate about what I was attempting on London's behalf, even when she was seriously ill and I had the conflict of knowing I ought to be spending time with her. She was insistent that I press on with all the travelling to every continent to persuade the IOC what a London Games might give to young children worldwide who were future contestants of the Olympics – the same opportunity it had given to me. She knew so well what it meant. She'd been with it since I was twelve, she saw and understood this unique arena of inspiration and ambition that the Games could give to kids, and especially a Games in London. My presentation would be for London, for international sport, for youngsters everywhere, but it was also for Angela.'

Here, indeed, is a remarkable man and this is not the sycophantic view of a friend who has known him since he was barely out of adolescence. From his father, he has mental discipline that is exceptional. Their combined assault on the athletic world contributed to one of the most illustrious periods in Britain's track and field history. As a skinny schoolboy, he was unusually promising. Peter Coe recognised this but shrewdly schooled him physically, protecting him from premature expectations beyond his years. Yet so unusual was this boy that, by the age of fifteen or sixteen, he and his coach were calculating that, by his early twenties, he should be ready to break middle-distance world records. The partnership was one that invited envy, if not derision, for their extreme dedication in their area of Yorkshire (Peter then being a cutlery design engineer in Sheffield), and even had Angela wishing Seb might lose a few races to ease her social discomfort from his domination at school events. Yet this was a teenager with a balanced academic curriculum, even though he would train on Christmas Day, and who had a collection of easy, close friendships among contemporaries which remain unbroken to this day, regardless of his peerage. Those friendships continued to his days at Loughborough University.

To anyone who witnessed some of the grinding, almost unprecedented training schedules that he and Peter constructed and fulfilled amid the bare, exposed hills north of Sheffield, his ultimate triumphs were no surprise. Ahead of their own expectations, he smashed three world records inside six weeks in 1979 – 800 metres, 1,500 metres and mile – cannoning him on to the global stage. When he arrived in Moscow for the boycotted Games of 1980, there were 400 members of the media at his initial press conference. With his acknowledged private fear of Steve Ovett, whom he had never previously beaten and who was even an Olympic prospect in 1976 before Coe had matured, he famously blew the 800 metres final, starting like a tortoise at the back, only to turn the tables with a galactic 1,500 metres victory over Ovett, who had not lost in nearly fifty races. Then to his Los Angeles repeat – an 800 metres silver, behind Joachim Cruz of Brazil, and 1,500 metres gold, out-kicking Steve Cram, the previous year's world champion – and taking his place among the Olympic middle-distance legends.

Skip a few years, including a European 800 metres title, and he was running to become an MP for Falmouth in 1992, defending a modest majority. With characteristic thoroughness in canvassing, he must have shaken hands with every other voter in the town. It was an experience and a discipline he was to repeat over the past couple of years among an electorate of only some one hundred voters, but who this time were spread around the globe. It has been alleged by some that he was short on commitment, that he could be seemingly casual. Juan Antonio Samaranch, former IOC president, keenly wanted him as an IOC member, especially following a speech against drugs at their 1981 congress at Baden-Baden, where he was elected to the Athletes' Commission. Coe, however, felt he had not the time to devote to the cause when he was currently moving into politics – similarly, with the possibility that he was identified within the International Association of Athletic Federations as a potential successor to then president Primo Nebiolo, of Italy. 'I couldn't possibly have done the job properly,' he reflected.

Anyone who doubted his work capacity and application should not look merely upon his athletic dedication but at his schedule since taking over the chairmanship of the London bid from the sinking Barbara Cassani. Flying some 200,000 miles – only matched by Samaranch when he was IOC president – he transformed what threatened to be a derelict bid, condemned by all and sundry as a waste of time and public money. In doing so, he has given an enormous lift to Britain's international prestige, which far surpasses what he achieved on the track. Why did he take on the responsibility? He is crystal clear about it. 'It was a vocational task and the biggest responsibility you can have to your own country. I've been a competitor, an IOC commission member, vice-chairman of the Sports Council and this was the last lap of the odyssey, the pursuit of something in which I believe. Nothing ever dissuaded me. The instant I knew London was bidding, I thought the strategy would be tough and we ourselves made some of our difficulties. But I knew if we followed the status quo, the conventional route, London had no chance. We had to go out and grab the initiative. The message we had, that the enlistment of youth was paramount, was a risk. The presentation would be a question of tone. Yet, I've seen the problem for so long, the alternative to sport – with my children, with their friends, in athletic clubs. It becomes harder every year to engage youth in sport. I needed no persuading to take it on.'

Sporting Champion: Sebastian Coe – 2 Olympic Games (1980, 1984); 1 European Championship (1986).

USAIN BOLT – OLYMPIC GAMES

HISTORY-MAKING BOLT STRIKES AGAIN TO SEAL HIS LEGACY

Paul Hayward, 6 August 2012

There have been so many joys at these London Games that a man repeating an easy win we saw four years ago in Beijing might struggle to grab a headline. But this second lightning strike by Usain Bolt was a statement of superhuman talent in a game of one-hit wonders. The champion turned the showpiece event of track and field into a parade, minus the showboating in Beijing. The celebration started after the line, not while his rivals were still straining to catch him up. There was no time for cabaret. 'You guys doubted me and I've shown the world that I am the greatest,' Bolt said afterwards. 'This is what I do. It's fun for them and I enjoy giving them the show. On your marks is when the focus starts. It wasn't the best reaction start in the world but I executed it and that was the key. My coach said, "Stop worrying about the start because the best part of your race is the end". It worked. I said it on the track.'

Men win the Olympic 100 metres and then pass it on. The demands are huge, the reigns short. Bolt's freakish physical scale seemed to offer no defence against injury, decline or the advances made by others: principally his friend, rival and fellow Jamaican, Yohan Blake, as well as three eager Americans. Yet the anxiety was false, the doubt misleading, the progress made by others not good or fast enough to bring him down. Not since Carl Lewis in 1988 had a sprinter defended his Olympic 100 metres title and Lewis needed Ben Johnson to be exposed as a cheat before he could reclaim gold. Sensing the expansive spirit of these London Games, Bolt laid down his claim to be the greatest speedster of all time with this re-run of the Beijing Bird's Nest win. Behind his Olympic-record 9.63 seconds, Blake, Justin Gatlin and Ryan Bailey either equalled or surpassed their personal best. Gatlin (9.79) ran as fast as Johnson in Seoul. Up ahead, though, strode the aristocratic figure of Bolt, tall, erect, flowing and more indomitable with every stride. World-record holder and double Olympic 100 metres champion, despite setbacks and tremors: there is no beating that.

This global showdown between an island of 2.9 million and the 314 million people of the world's most powerful nation ended with the Jamaican flag highest on Olympia. The nightmare scenario of a victory for Gatlin, who served a ban for doping, was averted by the power and charisma of the first two home. Beijing was a conquest. This was consolidation. Even Bolt could not have been sure his body would deliver him for his traditional mid-race surge. His starts are seldom impressive. His mid-track recoveries are almost always ominous. And the lengthening of his stride over the last 20 metres is unanswerable. Afterwards he drew his imaginary bow back and fired at the London sky. 'Usain, Usain,' the crowd chanted. The pleasures never cease in this Stratford stadium.

Sent off by sixty-one-year-old Alan Bell, from County Durham, who also fired the gun when Bolt false-started at the 2011 Daegu World Championships, the Americans Gatlin, Gay and Bailey squared up to a trio of Jamaicans: Bolt, Blake and Asafa Powell. The rest of the world was meagrely represented by the Netherland's Churandy Martina and Richard Thompson from Trinidad and Tobago. Jamaica had already won the women's 100 metres with Shelly-Ann Fraser-Pryce, the first to retain the Olympic title since Gail Devers in 1996. Goaded by American sprint legends in the build-up, Bolt and Blake were both a Jamaican team and mortal rivals.

Bolt's Beijing blast carried him through the next three years after China's Olympics, but the script changed. 'Superman is coming' was London's message to the ticket-buying public, some of whom handed over £700 for a seat. In the preceding months it changed to: 'Superman is vulnerable'. Curiosity took over from outright worship. Yet as the runners hunkered down, newcomers to Olympic sprinting could sense the power, the controlled violence of straight-line running. World's fastest man remains one of humanity's most cherished titles. Camera flashes sparkled around the stadium as the eight contestants exerted psychological pressure on one another on the blocks. Olympic sprint titles are not generally won by athletes with interrupted preparations. Bolt was outrun by Blake in both the 100 metres and 200 metres at the Jamaican trials. Within days he was visiting Dr Hans-Wilhelm Müller-Wohlfahrt in Munich to address possible back-related hamstring trouble. He ran badly in Ostrava and talked of needing to sleep more before withdrawing from Monaco to concentrate on London. Fine-tuning was completed away from public scrutiny and he laid his head down in a special 7-foot bed. Long-lens snaps of him stretching or wincing after training added to the drama, real or imagined. But his jog to the line in the semi-final and his time of 9.87 said all was well in his world.

Gay was the second fastest man in history. Blake was the youngest world champion ever. Gatlin had been here before and beaten the stress of Olympic finals. Bolt held three Olympic medals as he messed about on the start line. Bailey is a rising star in America. Martina is the European champion. What more could anyone want? Another lightning blast is the answer. And they got it. They saw the phenomenon put Blake in his place and stop the Gatlin revival. They saw the Beijing reign extended from east to west. America still has no answer to his speed. Lewis, who was so grudging in his praise, has lost his place in history, where Bolt now reigns supreme.

Sporting Champion: Usain Bolt – 6 Olympic Games (2008 – 3, 2012 – 3); 8 World Championships (2009 – 3, 2011 – 2, 2013 – 3).

MO FARAH – WORLD ATHLETICS CHAMPIONSHIPS

FARAH RACES INTO A LEAGUE OF HIS OWN

Ian Chadband, 17 August 2013

Mo Farah keeps elevating himself to dizzying and dazzling new heights in the British athletics pantheon. After adding the 5,000 metres title so majestically here in Moscow's Luzhniki Stadium to the 10,000 metres crown he annexed earlier, it now no longer feels outlandish to ask if anyone actually sits above him.

The man who can win any which way decided that, for his latest unfeasible trick, he would defy a sharp pain in his side to take the long run to a fifth global title and into history as just the second man, after the peerless Kenenisa Bekele, to achieve the World Championships distance 'double' a year after achieving the same wondrous feat at the Olympics.

Talk about doing it the hard way. He had been suffering from a stitch and felt unbalanced for the last seven laps when he opted to push for home with over a lap and a half left. Thus, it was, he felt, the grandest achievement yet of his amazing three-year long-distance reign as, straining every sinew and with saucer eyes almost popping out of his head, he fended off each successive challenge from his rivals, vowing no one would pass, to land global title number five. 'I never thought I'd achieve something like this in my life,' beamed Farah with a smile that still seems like that of an incredulous kid who cannot quite comprehend the dreamlike ride he is still taking. Lord Coe, an Olympic victor in this stadium thirty-three years before, presented him with his gold medal and whispered something on the podium which Farah could not quite remember afterwards; you would like to think he was passing on his belief that he has now surpassed him as the best ever British athlete.

Once again, none of the world's best runners was brave – or daft – enough to take the race by the scruff of the neck and make a concerted attempt to run the finish out of those now legendary legs. No one, apart from a nineteen-year-old Kenyan, Isiah Koech, apparently believed he could beat Farah. The dawdling interludes and half-hearted surges of the field played straight into his hands. No one took the initiative except Farah himself. With 650 metres left, probably a good half a lap earlier than his rivals were expecting, he stretched out on the back straight leaving three Kenyans and two Ethiopians to swoop behind him, ready, they may have half hoped, to finally run down a man who, unlike them, should have had tired legs after having already run the 10,000 metres just six days earlier. There was real chutzpah in the move, that of a man with total belief in his pre-eminence. Each time his pursuers perched ominously on his shoulder, Farah deftly kept them at bay like a sweet boxer flitting away from a jab.

Then, just as it seemed possible during the strain of that 53.51-second last lap that the young Kenyan champion, the most daring of all his challengers, would muscle past off the final bend, Farah saved, as his coach Alberto Salazar demanded, one final, decisive kick down the home straight. Flying through the field came another teenage prodigy, Ethiopian Hagos Gebrhiwet, to snatch silver from Koech by the merest fraction as they both clocked thirteen minutes 27.26 seconds. The kids were too late. Their time will come but they may have to wait because three strides ahead was a sight their elders have learnt to live with: a man shouting 'yes!' five times, blowing a kiss with either hand, and doing that weird thing called the Mobot. Farah was clocked at thirteen minutes 26.98 seconds, signifying how this had been another in the long line of slow, 'tactical' global finals. Who the heck cared? Not him. Super-swift times can wait. He values his career in medals.

For Farah is making the truly extraordinary seem quite workaday. He had told BBC viewers to chill out and 'have a cup of tea 'cos Mo's on the track'. It may have carried eyebrow-raising echoes of the day Dave Bedford, all red-socked and Zapata-moustachioed, had told *Sun* readers to 'sit by your TV and watch me win a gold medal for Britain' before finishing sixth. No chance of a repeat here. Farah rarely lets us down. With Farah that sort of relaxed mischief-making is one of his weapons now. Barry Fudge, the physiologist who looked after his preparations here, says he walks around the hotel and you can see a man who knows he is a winner. Yes, and his opponents can see it, too.

In the 10,000 metres, the Ethiopians' plan, Farah was told afterwards by silver medallist Ibrahim Jeilan, had been to take turns in injecting hard bursts, at unexpected moments, to drain his legs in the fierce heat. Instead, they did not hit him powerfully enough, nor hard enough, and it was the same again in the 5,000 metres. There was no teamwork, nobody prepared to sacrifice themselves.

The first championship distance legend created in this stadium was at the 1980 Olympics, when the world was left agog by a little Ethiopian, apparently aged thirty-three who looked about forty-three, as he scattered both the 10,000 metres and 5,000 metres fields. There may have been mystery about Miruts – 'Yifter the Shifter' – but there is none anymore about his modern-day successor. Give that man a nickname. All hail 'Farah the Arrer!'

Sporting Champion: Mo Farah – 3 World Championships (2011, 2013 – 2); 2 Olympic Games (2012 – 2); 3 European Championships (2010 – 2, 2012).

MICHAEL PHELPS – OLYMPIC GAMES

PHELPS SHOWS THE GREATEST WILL TO WIN

Brough Scott, 17 August 2008

Not just too close to call, too tight to touch. With fifty, twenty, ten, five, two, one metre to go, Michael Phelps could not peg back the speeding Milorad Cavić to win the 100 metres butterfly final and his place alongside Mark Spitz in Olympic swimming immortality. But he did. Only he will know why. History, and the wonders of electronic sensory timing equipment, will state that he beat the feisty California-based Cavić by only one hundredth of a second, 50.58 seconds to 50.59. Replays seemed to show that the Serbian's fingers were actually on the wall first but it was Phelps who beat him to apply pressure. It was something else, too. It was as great a display of will to win as this Olympics or any Olympics will ever see.

We couldn't believe it. The Serbians couldn't believe it so much that they made an official protest that they only withdrew after being shown the timing videos. Phelps was most unsure. 'When I saw the race afterwards I was shocked,' he said. 'I took short fast strokes to try and get my hand on the wall. All I can say is that I raced as hard as I could and swam my best and that the scoreboard shows that I got my hand on the wall first.'

But forget all the statements. Forget the million-dollar bonus Phelps now gets from Speedo. Forget the protest and that Cavić, despite being smilingly gracious in defeat, said: 'If we raced again, I would win it.' The real story here is that reports of Phelps being superhuman are an insult to him. He may have developed an astonishing physique, huge powers of concentration and an almost dolphin-like technique, but he bleeds all right. At the 50-metre mark, a full six tenths of a second down on Cavić, and lagging seventh of the eight finalists, it looked as if he was to face the full haemorrhage of defeat. In the high, wide and wonderful blue vastness of Beijing's Water Cube swimming complex, there was a throat-gripping sensation that all our Olympics had led to this. From the first time that Phelps had marched out for the 400 metres individual medley, his first final, we could not keep our eyes off him. The strange white dressing gown, the trance-like look, the ritual towelling down of his starting block, the sinking stretch of first one long leg then the other, the final disrobing of those 6 feet 4 inches and 14 stone of hard, sculpted muscle, and then the moment when he shakes that 6 feet 7 inches wingspan long and loose below him ready to plunge into the element he has made his own. We had seen it four, five, six times. But now the enormity of the seventh was upon us.

It was not lost upon Cavić. He was in lane four. He was even bigger and taller than Phelps. He had clocked a faster time in the semi-final and as Phelps stood flexing his thigh downwards with one huge foot on his starting block, Cavić turned towards him to do exactly the same. The two dark-goggled figures stared at each other, two testosterone-fuelled amphibians about to battle it out in the water. High up in the stadium we held our breath. Right away we could see it was going to be difficult. Once he surfaced from his dive Phelps was clearly being outpointed. He was working with his normal intensity but his whirling arms had no more bite, rather less, than the others. As he came to the wall he was even further down than in the semis. When he surfaced from the turn, he was a full length behind Cavić.

It was impossible but he would not accept it. Deep inside a true champion there is a will that refuses to accept defeat. It is why he accepts the early mornings, the impossible training sessions, the carbo-loaded diet, the unrelenting routine, the feeling that without winning there cannot be air to breathe or eyes to see. You see it with them all, just as much with Rafael Nadal in tennis as with A.P. McCoy in the racing game. In press conferences, Phelps smiles and speaks serenely of noble things like 'taking the sport of swimming to where I would like it to be'. But right at the core he is a champion because he has an ingrained rage against the possibility of defeat.

Up out of the water it screamed at us now. He was closing but Cavić would not weaken, Phelps wasn't closing fast enough: he was still almost half a body length behind as they went under the

5-metre wire. It had to be Cavić, but with one last titanic thrust Phelps asked the ultimate question. He turned and could see the numbers 50.58 and 50.59 up on the scoreboard. He pulled his goggles down to check his number was at the lesser one. Then the roar raged out. When he finally came through from the poolside he was still fired up enough to give very direct answers. No flannelling about records or sporting legacies, no stooping to cheap jokes about rivals. 'It just shows,' he said, 'that if you put your mind to something and really focus, anything is possible.'

What Michael Phelps did here has defined this Olympics. But his records will be matched, his marks will be passed; what matters more is the impression he left when it looked as if the ambition of seven gold medals was beyond his reach. That is the one Olympic dream that should never die.

Sporting Champion: Michael Phelps – 18 Olympic Games (2004 – 6, 2008 – 8, 2012 – 4); 27 World Championships (2001 – 1, 2003 – 4, 2004 – 1, 2005 – 5, 2007 – 7, 2009 – 5, 2011 – 4).

KATHERINE GRAINGER – WORLD ROWING CHAMPIONSHIPS

SIX AND A BIT MINUTES CHANGED MY LIFE

Judith Woods, 10 December 2012

In the Hollywood version of the life of Olympic gold-medal winner Katherine Grainger, she would surely be played by Kate Winslet. The *Titanic* actress has the requisite broad shoulders and athletic physique to portray the Glasgow-born rower, the long, intelligent face, the air of gritty determination. But much more saliently, only an Oscar-winner – pipped at the post many times previously – could possibly empathise with the highs and lows of a sportswoman who is, for many, the embodiment of the indomitable Olympic spirit.

'Sport is a strange, selfish pursuit in some respects,' mused Grainger, thirty-seven. 'But when you witness the outpouring of emotion from the crowd and see the hugely positive impact your win has on the team and the nation, you feel reassured that your achievements have a meaning that goes beyond you.' Quite so. Grainger's backstory was well known in the run up to London 2012, and her sheer indefatigability captured the imagination of the public; having memorably won silver at three previous Olympics and notched up six world championship titles, she continued, single-mindedly, to strive for Olympic gold.

She had received her silver in Sydney with astonished delight. At the Athens Games, where she took silver in the coxless pair, her joy was more confined. In Beijing, she and her team-mates were so devastated at coming second in the women's quad that they couldn't stem their tears as they stood on the podium. 'When you want gold, winning silver is a failure,' she said. 'It might sound ungrateful, but that's the truth of it.' And so the stage was set for Grainger's performance in the double sculls at Eton Dorney. Would she finally triumph after years spent dreaming of nothing else? Mercifully, she did. To the deafening cheers of the home crowd, she and team-mate Anna Watkins passed the line first. Their response was a study in dignified delight; no weeping or histrionics, just arms raised in victory and broad smiles. 'I was joyful at a cellular level,' said Grainger. 'When I sobbed at Beijing and looked so composed at London, they were visceral responses I couldn't control.'

Confident and articulate, with an entertaining line in self-deprecation, Grainger was made an MBE in 2006. She is just the

sort of enthusiastic sporting ambassador who encapsulates the
ethos of the much-vaunted '2012 legacy', a point she made when
she became the first sports person to deliver the Royal Society
of Edinburgh Christmas Lecture. 'Sport teaches you so much;
how to manage success and negotiate failure, how to be part of
a team, how to be the best leader you can be – and how to make
your dreams come true,' she said. 'My message is to set yourself
magnificent goals and work hard to achieve them.'

Even as she radiated can-do positivity, Grainger was frank
enough to admit that there were many dark moments when
she was beset by doubt and hopelessness. 'After Beijing, I felt as
though I had suffered a bereavement,' she said, quietly. 'I had
been living for that moment for years, and when I lost it was like
a death. Coming through that was the most challenging and the
most interesting aspect of my career. I couldn't bear the prospect
of possibly failing on such an epic scale again, but I felt that this
was unfinished business that I was compelled to complete.'

The perfect arc of Grainger's story cries out for filmic
treatment, not just because there's the added dimension of her
academic excellence, but also the distinctly unusual absence
of sporting flair or even world-class competitiveness in her
childhood. 'I never grew up thinking sport was my future, and
I never had the kind of parents who took me to the pool and
threw me in,' she said. 'My parents are both teachers, my sister
is a social-worker-turned-teacher and I was happy to follow
a conventional path to university to study law.' At Edinburgh
University fresher's week she signed up for activities such as
skiing, trampolining and juggling. She wasn't in the least bit
tempted to row, but accompanied a friend to a meeting, where she
was told she had the right build. 'There were fifty-four women in
the room, and the coach said they would choose sixteen to join
the team,' remembered Grainger. 'I suddenly, urgently, wanted

to be one of the sixteen they picked.' She was duly picked at the trials. Her sheer muscle power earned her a place in the squad, but she gradually learnt that brawn isn't enough to win at an elite sporting level; the brain needs to kick in, too. 'Strength can only get you so far, then you need to harness it in the service of technique,' she said. 'I was getting my head around that when I overheard my coach tell someone else that I was good enough to row for Scotland – that had a real effect on my mindset.' At the age of twenty, in her third year of study, Grainger did indeed row for Scotland. In her fourth year, it was suggested she should go to the British trials, where the Olympic team would be selected. 'It was a real OMG moment,' she laughed.

In between doing her law finals and graduating, she made the British under-twenty-three rowing team – and almost immediately won the 1997 World Championship coxless pair, in a first for the team and a breakthrough for women's rowing. During the next two years she gained a Masters in medical law and ethics from Glasgow University and then moved south to row full-time with the British team. 'I can't overstate the importance of National Lottery funding, which had just been introduced,' she said. 'Without it I would have had to work to support myself and squeeze training in around that.'

Sydney 2000 was Grainger's first Olympics and she was overwhelmed. 'If only you could bottle it,' she sighed. 'We didn't expect to do anything much at Sydney, and to get the silver was a complete shock.' Fast-forward twelve years and two more silvers and the run-up to London saw her living and breathing her sport. From 7.30 a.m. to 4.30 p.m. every day she focused on reaching peak condition; her diet was monitored, her heart rate recorded, blood samples taken from her ear to gauge her metabolic performance. 'You are constantly competing with your team-mates for a place on the Olympic squad – and they are going all out to beat you. The coaches pit you against each other. It was like *The Hunger Games* without the death.'

She pulled off a double World Championship coup in 2010 and 2011. Only Olympic gold remained tantalisingly out of reach. Grainger was 'gutted' to miss the opening ceremony – her event was too close for her to be out late – so she and her team-mate dressed in their strip and watched the coverage on television. Then, forty-eight hours later, the eyes of the world were on them as they rowed to victory. 'It will always be there. Those six and a bit minutes that changed our lives are part of sporting history.'

Now she has a PhD in homicide at King's College London to finish and her social life to catch up on. Her single status has been described as something of a sacrifice in her effort to be the best. Grainger disagrees. 'It's a choice. People make career choices all the time and have to live by them. I'm fortunate to have been doing a job I love. You need to be in a happy place to find a good relationship, so who knows what will happen now that I'm on dry land for the foreseeable future.' She cannot say whether she will ever practise the law she studied so hard: 'I'm still trying to decide what I'm going to do when I grow up. But the great thing I have learnt is that life always has more it can teach you – if you're prepared to listen.'

Sporting Champion: Katherine Grainger – 6 World Championships (2003, 2005, 2006, 2007, 2010, 2011); 1 Olympic Games (2012).

STEVE BACKLEY – EUROPEAN ATHLETICS CHAMPIONSHIPS

BACKLEY TAKES CENTRE STAGE AGAIN

Michael Calvin, 29 August 1990

Steve Backley produced, against a suitably portentous backcloth of thunder and lightning, confirmation that he has a champion's flair for the dramatic. The Briton's first European javelin title was guaranteed when he produced a final throw of 87.30 metres to reinforce his dominance of a discipline that demands mastery of both technique and temperament. He had imposed himself on his rivals with a first-round throw of 85.78 metres in what he termed 'awful conditions' that led to the competition being suspended for forty-five minutes here in Split. 'That last throw was just a release of tension,' he reflected, his face softened by a grin. 'I knew I had a big one in me, but I was too tense, too eager.'

Backley tried hard to conceal his nervousness before he left the team hotel, but spoke a little too fast and laughed a little too readily to be convincing. The European Championships were the focal point of Backley's summer, such a title has a permanence beyond the world records he set over an eighteen-day span in July, in Stockholm and Crystal Palace. He had spent the afternoon visualising his first throw, which is a barometer of his form. As thunder rolled around the stadium, and lightning was etched against the mountains, he proved he could also handle the unexpected.

It was oppressively hot and humid until torrential rain began to fall as the competition began. Like most throwers, he abhors such conditions, yet he had spoken, over lunch, about preparing himself for any eventuality. The runway was slippery, he had spent twenty minutes sheltering under a giant striped umbrella and was determined to defy officials who wished to suspend the event. His challengers, forced to retreat to their call-up room beneath the stand even as the crowd roared approval of Backley's initial effort, were immediately intimidated. Not for the first time, they had cause to rue the Briton's sense of occasion.

Comparisons with Nick Faldo are compelling. The technique of hurling a javelin has many similarities with the golf swing. The key to a successful throw is contained in Backley's final seven strides, the 'crossover' in which he is running, sideways, before launching the javelin at an angle of between thirty and thirty-five degrees. Faldo will recognise the importance of rhythm and feel, of the need to harness control, power and speed of delivery. He will also appreciate the role of John Trower. Backley's coach is the David Leadbetter figure. He has worked with Backley for five years, cultivating a singularly single-minded athlete. Like Faldo, Backley has a finely tuned appreciation of his technique. He is a perfectionist, and agreed with Trower that a slight adjustment was necessary to make the javelin fly in a little higher trajectory.

Einar Vilhjálmsson, the Icelander, failed even to qualify for the final three throws, leaving Backley, aware of the need to stay mentally sharp, to fight a growing sense of fatigue. He regarded Patrik Boden, considered physically the strongest of the throwers, as the biggest danger, but the Swede could summon nothing better than a third-round throw of 82.66 metres. That was sufficient to pip Mick Hill, Backley's room-mate, for a bronze medal. The silver was won by the Soviet Union's Viktor Zaitsev, who threw 83.30 metres. 'That first round took the pressure off me,' summed up Backley. 'It's been a difficult year to adapt to, what with the Commonwealth Games coming so early, but this is what I have been aiming for.' No one was about to argue with Trower's first words to his athlete as he clambered on to a television gantry. 'Steve, son,' he said, 'this was always going to be your day.'

Sporting Champion: Steve Backley – 4 European Championships (1990, 1994, 1998, 2002); 3 Commonwealth Games (1990, 1994, 2002).

. SURREY – COUNTY CRICKET CHAMPIONSHIP

SURREY CHAMPIONS SEVEN YEARS IN SUCCESSION

E.W. Swanton, 30 August 1958

The summer of 1958 will be recalled as among the most liquid and gloomy within memory; but it will be notable at least for one thing – the victory yet again of Surrey, under P.B.H. May, in the County Championship. For this win by Surrey is their seventh in a row, and therein they have written a new page of history. Since the Championship began in the early 1870s, no county has had such a run. Between 1930 and 1946 Yorkshire won eight years out of ten. In the last century Surrey in nine years had seven outright wins, and once shared the title. Those distant feats are the nearest approach to what Surrey have achieved in the 1950s.

It is not easy to find anything new to write in praise of Surrey. The foundation of their strength lies in the bowling, and once more they have won despite the frequent absences of Laker, Lock and Loader, in addition to the captain, during Test matches. Here, too, they were additionally handicapped by the serious illness of Alec Bedser, which kept him off the field altogether until July, and forced Surrey to nurse him to a considerable extent after that. Bedser has had his days of success, and he has been of great value as leader when May was otherwise engaged. But the number of times Surrey have been at completely full strength has been small.

Perhaps the main difference between the present Surrey and that of the W.S. Surridge days has lain in the great attraction of the batting. In the Championship sense Surrey are not a formidable batting side; nor have they been since the cycle started in 1952. But May, of course, is a host in himself, and he nowadays sees a fast batting rate as a tactical end, apart from the concrete value of the bonus points. These they have picked up time after time, as a matter of course. McIntyre, I think, should be mentioned specially in this connection. He has come in in several recent games when runs were needed against the clock, and hit extremely well. His wicketkeeping has been as reliable as ever, and once again Stewart, Barrington and Lock have set a high standard of catching close to the wicket. That Surrey are far and away the strongest side goes without question. Yet at the start of August Hampshire were well in the lead. Since the bank holiday matches they have failed on the wet wickets, whereas Surrey have been in their element.

[Alongside Swanton's commentary was a report by R.A. Roberts of Surrey's match at the Oval against Somerset]

Surrey did not have to bowl a ball to maintain an astonishingly and unique sequence of Championships stretching back to 1952 – but they made sure by bustling out Somerset for sixty-six to take first-innings points in a shortened day's play. Once Hampshire's game was rained off, the Championship was secured because they could not do more than equal Surrey's points total. Page 1,005 of the current *Wisden* points out: 'The team with most bonus points take precedence in the table. The actual Championship could be decided this way.' Lord's confirmed that if Hampshire were not in a position to catch up in bonus points – as they could not – Surrey therefore were top men again.

It would have been a pity if the issue had been settled in this way, not least because bonus points would, in a sense, have counted twice. Surrey, however, settled matters forthrightly by bowling out Somerset inside the two and a half hours' play that remained possible. Somerset, who had already lost two wickets for four runs, slumped to twenty-nine for seven within an hour. The pitch was surprisingly lively considering it was recently underwater, but it was not responsible for the early batting disasters.

At fourteen, Gibson knocked out Wight's middle stump with a full-toss. At the same score he yorked Alley and bowled Lomax with successive balls. On each occasion the middle stump was uprooted, and McCool played and missed at the hat-trick ball. Eele and McCool fell to balls from Loader that lifted, and once Palmer, who stayed with his captain for three-quarters of an hour, had been dismissed, there was little to delay the celebrations. Tremlett, who defended resolutely, was last out after fifteen minutes of the extra half-hour. Gibson finished with five for twenty-one, a further indication that in time he will take over as one of Surrey's main bowlers.

May said after the match: 'I feel this has been one of our very best performances in view of the absences through the Tests and injuries, and the uncertainty of the weather. We missed Alec Bedser for much of the season, and, in fact, did not field the full side until the middle of July. There were times when all four of our main bowlers were absent. I would, however, like to congratulate Colin Ingleby-Mackenzie on a fine season. Hampshire played entertaining cricket, and made things difficult for us.'

May emphasised the team effort, but paid a special tribute to McIntyre, who retires at the end of the season. 'I suppose since the War there has not been a more consistent county wicketkeeper. He has ended with a jolly good season, particularly in the runs he has got quickly when we've needed them. I am sorry to lose him, but we will have his help as coach.' Of Surrey's prospects of winning the Championship again in 1959, May commented: 'We must have a very good chance, but a lot depends on *Anno Domini*. The Bedser twins will be forty-one next year, and four or five of us will presumably have just got back from a hard tour of Australia and New Zealand.'

Sporting Champions: Surrey – 19 County Championships (1890, 1891, 1892, 1894, 1895, 1899, 1914, 1950 – shared with Lancashire, 1952, 1953, 1954, 1955, 1956, 1957, 1958, 1971, 1999, 2000, 2002).

SEPTEMBER

IVAN MAUGER – WORLD SPEEDWAY CHAMPIONSHIP

MAUGER – THE GREATEST GOLDEN OLDIE

Robert Philip, 18 August 2005

Back in speedway's golden days, when cinder-track racing was the nation's biggest summer spectator sport and many millions were addicted to the snarl of engines and the unique, intoxicating smell, beneath every helmet was another legend: New Zealanders Barry Briggs and Ronnie Moore, Ove Fundin, Björn Knutsson and Göte Nordin of Sweden, England's Peter Craven. Great riders all, yet when readers of *Speedway Star* and *Vintage Speedway Magazine* were invited to vote for their Man of the Millennium in 1999, the result was all but unanimous: Ivan Mauger. A generation on, Sweden's Tony Rickardsson stands poised to equal Mauger's haul of six world championships.

Although Mauger's record has stood for quarter of a century and you might think he would guard his achievements jealously, he phoned Rickardsson from his home on Australia's Gold Coast to wish him 'good luck'. 'If I have one regret in speedway,' said Mauger, 'it's that I never won a world title in front of my own folk in New Zealand; I won all six on the other side of the world and I really hoped Tony would do it in his native Sweden.' Even Rickardsson would agree that it is somewhat easier to win the world championship under the present nine grand prix format which rewards consistency than in Mauger's era when riders had to qualify for the grand final at Wembley, say, via an arduous series of qualifying rounds during which a single fall or engine failure could mark the abrupt end of your entire campaign.

Mauger recalls: 'While everyone in Britain was freezing in January and February, we were busting our asses Down Under competing in the various qualifiers. That was how we qualified for the British qualifying rounds which didn't start till April. Our world championship lasted nine months; these days it lasts nine meetings. I'd have loved to have ridden under the grand prix system as, I'm sure, would Ove Fundin [a five-time world champion]. Ove and I worked it out once that if you added up all the World, European, Inter-Continental, British, Australasian and New Zealand championships I won, or in which I finished in the top three – plus the World Team Cup and World Pairs racing against all the very best riders – it would have made me world champion something like twelve years in a row. But I think the word "champion" should mean exactly that. When Sebastian Coe won his two Olympic 1,500 metres gold medals, he didn't line up thinking, "I don't feel so good today, I don't like this particular track, I don't like the stadium, and the hotel is s***, so if I get third or fourth then I'll be quite happy. Next week is London and I'll win there, followed by Glasgow the following week and although I don't like Sweden in a month's time, a fourth place there and I'll still be Olympic champion". You don't get second chances in the Olympics.'

Now sixty-five and a millionaire, Mauger first arrived on these shores as a fresh-faced seventeen-year-old aboard the SS *Rangitoto*, which docked at Tilbury in 1957, with his teenage bride Raye, renting a one-bedroom flat in Wimbledon around the corner from Plough Lane where Moore and Briggs reigned as the twin 'kings of the cinders'. 'Without Ronnie, there would have been no Briggo and no Ivan Mauger; whenever he came home to New Zealand it was like the arrival of Elvis. He was our Pelé, if you like.' Inspired by the deeds of Moore, from the age of twelve Mauger dedicated himself to becoming speedway's champion of the world, working as a delivery boy for a local chemist in Christchurch after school and in the holidays to save money for his first racing machine. 'Everyone thought I had wealthy parents because I could afford to buy a bike before I was sixteen, but for three years I never bought an ice-cream, a Coca-Cola or anything like that. After I left school I had two jobs – as did Raye – and that's how we saved enough money to come to England when we were little more than children.'

Mauger's great adventure began at Plough Lane where he rode in the second-half 'faces of the future' races and assisted Mac the groundsman. 'I never, ever felt I was going to work for the simple reason that I just loved the atmosphere of being in Wimbledon Stadium. I cleaned the dressing rooms, the toilets, the pits and the workshop. I helped Mac work on the track, I weeded the tulip beds and on Monday afternoons I had to cut the grass out in the centre before the speedway meeting. And not just any old cut would do for Ronnie. It had to be mowed in one direction then the other, just like Wembley. Over the years, many, many people have said, "What a s****y job", but I loved it. It was my education and it stood me in great stead throughout my career; when I went to Wembley for a world final, I didn't simply go out and ride round and round the track, win another title and go home. Whatever the weather conditions, I knew everything there was to know about that track. Because we didn't have a television or a wireless, speedway was my life for twenty-three and a half hours a day.'

After winning his first world championship in 1968, Mauger ruled for a decade, gaining renown as 'the greatest of all time'. 'Speedway is still a great sport but to my tired old eyes there isn't a single rider around who could cause the excitement of Pelé coming to play at Portsmouth, Celtic or wherever. Every team in those days had one and maybe two superstars.' As dominant as he is, Rickardsson will never replace Mauger in the hearts and minds of speedway fans. 'I'm very proud of the fact it's taken a rider of Tony's ability the best part of three decades and a more forgiving system for my record to be equalled, as it most surely will,' said Mauger.

Sporting Champion: Ivan Mauger – 6 World Championships (1968, 1969, 1970, 1972, 1977, 1979); 3 World Long Track Championships (1971, 1972, 1976); 4 European Championships (1966, 1970, 1971, 1975); 1 Intercontinental Championship (1975); 5 World Pairs Championships (1969, 1971, 1972, 1978, 1981).

ROGER FEDERER – US OPEN TENNIS

SUPREME FEDERER PROVES HE IS NO SPENT FORCE

Mark Hodgkinson, 9 September 2008

There was a retro feel to the tennis in the Arthur Ashe Stadium, but it wasn't the sight of the first British man to win a Grand Slam title since Fred Perry in New York in 1936. It was the sight of Roger Federer scoring a Slam trophy for the first time for a full year. There were some moments of silvery brilliance off Federer's racket as he defeated Andy Murray, in the Briton's first Grand Slam final, to win a fifth consecutive US Open title. So it was the Swiss who was rewriting history at Flushing Meadows, not the Scot. Federer was the first man since American Bill Tilden in 1924 to win five in a row in New York. Federer became the first man in history to win two different Slams five times in succession, having also been a quintuple Wimbledon winner. So Federer hasn't had all his yesterdays; he remains a Grand Slam-winning force. This was his first Grand Slam title of the season, having previously drawn a zero at the Australian Open, Roland Garros and Wimbledon. It also took his tally for major trophies to thirteen, which means he is just one short of Pete Sampras's record. How could anyone have doubted Federer? He has owned this city for five summers now. This 6–2, 7–5, 6–2 victory extended his winning streak to thirty-four matches on the Big Apple's fast cement. 'It definitely feels great. After this year, to take this home is incredible,' Federer said. 'It means the world to me.'

This was Murray's chance to end a dry streak for British tennis that had been running, or should that be staggering, for seventy-two years. Some of Manhattan's steakhouses boast of having been in business for a quarter, or a fifth, of that time. Several generations of British tennis players have come and gone in that time. Less than twenty-four hours after beating Rafael Nadal, the world number one, in the semi-finals, Murray couldn't quite do the one-two double when he came up against the class of the second-seeded Federer. Still, this has been a superb tournament for Murray, to make the breakthrough into his first Slam final, and the indications from his run here suggest that the Perry record may not survive for long. Here in New York over the past fortnight, the Big Three have become the Big Four. Federer, Nadal and Novak Djokovic have some company. 'I had a great tournament, but I came up against, in my opinion, the best player to have played the game,' said Murray.

This was a hot day in New York City, but by the time Murray and Federer walked into the Arthur Ashe Stadium, at just after 5 p.m. local time, the blue concrete court was almost all in the shade. Federer strolled out looking as groomed, plucked, tweaked and as moisturised as a Broadway star, while Murray obviously hadn't taken a razor to his beard, just like Björn Borg never did on the way to winning all those Wimbledon titles. The players may not have had a burning sun to contend with, but there was a wind swirling around the arena. And while Murray's game wasn't firing in the early stages, Federer was striking the ball off his honey-spot. Suddenly, this looked like the Roger of old. Most in tennis had felt that Federer, who had dominated for four-plus years, had dipped in 2008. But Murray hasn't been one of those to buy into that argument. Murray's view was the competition in tennis has improved, not that Federer has regressed. And while Murray had won two of his previous three encounters with Federer, this was their first meeting at a Slam, let alone in a Slam final.

Federer was all over Murray in that first set. Federer's first break came for 4–2 when Murray misdirected a forehand wide. Murray used up one of his Hawk-Eye challenges to take a second look at the shot on the video screens, but the call stood. And a second break for Federer two games later gave him the set. The crowd were evenly split between Murray and Federer. But there was growing concern among Murray's supporters when his serve was broken for a third time in succession, in the second game of the second set. Still, Murray has never been one who likes to crawl into a racket-bag, and he steadied himself to break back in the next game, and to love, when Federer's volley spilled off his strings and didn't make it over the net. Murray could have broken Federer for a 3–2 lead when he had the Swiss at 0–40 to hold three break points. On the second of those, Murray would have won the point and the game if he had stopped the point to ask for a Hawk-Eye replay. Unbeknown to Murray, a video simulation shown on television suggested that one of Federer's mid-rally shots had bounced beyond the baseline. Federer broke Murray to love for the set when he whipped a forehand winner down the line. At one stage it seemed as though Federer was going to accelerate through the third set like a manic New York taxi driver. But Murray kept fighting until the end.

Sporting Champion: Roger Federer – 5 US Opens (2004, 2005, 2006, 2007, 2008); 7 Wimbledons (2003, 2004, 2005, 2006, 2007, 2009, 2012); 4 Australian Opens (2004, 2006, 2007, 2010); 1 French Open (2009).

OSCAR PISTORIUS – PARALYMPIC GAMES

BLADE RUNNER'S STORY NOW READS LIKE A CAUTIONARY TALE

Paul Hayward, 15 February 2013

Oscar Pistorius is the Blade Runner who united disabled and able-bodied sport. He bestrode the Olympic and Paralympic Games of London 2012 like an advert for the human spirit. But his cartoon hero status will be inadmissible when he appears in court charged with murdering his thirty-year-old girlfriend. The death of Reeva Steenkamp from gunshot wounds at Pistorius's home in a gated community in South Africa was a tragedy with only one true victim: the law graduate, entrepreneur, television presenter and model who died at the hands of perhaps the most famous runner after Usain Bolt. Whatever the eventual outcome of the case, one of the most romantic sporting tales of modern times has been engulfed by darkness. Pistorius was emblematic of London 2012. He was an inspiration who had defeated those who tried to stop him running on the main Olympic stage. He was the man who bounced across the gap between the two London carnivals. Now, the world convulses in shock at the follow-up story.

Memories of Pistorius in London remain vivid. Few nights

went by in the media zones of the Olympic Stadium without his excited chatter moving along the line of cameras and voice recorders. Often he would tell his uplifting tale for an hour before finally padding away on his carbon fibre blades. We stage-door johnnies would marvel at his appetite for publicity, his willingness to answer the same question endless times. Some nights he would give twenty interviews. Whole races would go by and Pistorius would still be talking. The tone was always the same: buoyant, affable, proud. Pistorius was his own PR department for the amazing story of how he broke down the barriers of Olympic sport. 'I'm not disabled, I just don't have legs,' he liked to say. This was a personal movie about one man's refusal to be held back by a physical calamity. But it was also a broadcast to the world: to amputees and people with other debilitating conditions. He was throwing open the doors of sport to all. He was a symbol, a moment in history, a one-man parade of the human will. He reached the semi-finals of the Olympic 400 metres before moving on to win silver in the T44 200 metres, gold in the 4x100 metres relay and gold in the T44 400 metres at the Paralympics, where he was a combination of poster boy and elder statesman. His voice box was always working, his smile never extinguished, except for the day he stirred up controversy by accusing fellow Paralympian runners of adjusting the length of their blades to gain an edge. Even then he managed to present himself as the guardian of the sport, a fierce advocate of fair play.

Born without a fibula in either leg, he lost both to amputations. A prodigy of Paralympic running, Pistorius won a major legal battle in 2008 when the governing body of athletics, the IAAF, allowed him to compete against able-bodied athletes. At London he became the first amputee sprinter to compete at the Olympics. With the filmic grandeur of his story came a celebrity profile, not only in South Africa but across the world. A large PR industry grew up around him and he became a billboard regular. Advertisers loved him because he conveyed a message deeper than money or medals. Here was an athlete on the cutting edge of science, propelled not only by technology but his own courage. London 2012 was his chance to join Bolt and company in the worldwide consciousness and he expended every ounce of spare effort to make his story heard.

With all this swirling in our heads, the news that Pistorius had been charged with the murder of Miss Steenkamp at his home in the Silverlakes complex in the Boschkop area of Pretoria arrived as two possibilities: accident or crime. Either way it has wiped out the sporting narrative. To leap from recollections of Pistorius sharing the London stage with Usain Bolt, Mo Farah and Jessica Ennis to an image of fatal gunshot wounds was indeed a shock. Whatever the truth, this is one more good reason to stop thinking the lives of top sportsmen and women are somehow superhuman and blessed.

Paralympic sport was desperate to find a way out of its minority status. Pistorius led it by the hand into the big time. London 2012 was its great leap forward, drawing record television audiences and establishing a new crop of heroes. Pistorius was the one the whole world knew. But he will no longer be known as the Blade Runner: the man who led disabled sport into the bright lights. His global renown will be much darker now. He will always be the man on 'cheetah blades' who picked up a gun and, whether by accident or deliberately, dispatched a woman to oblivion. In that sense his part in London 2012 already reads less like a triumph over adversity than a cautionary tale.

Sporting Champion: Oscar Pistorius – 6 Paralympic Games (2004, 2008 – 3, 2012 – 2); 2 Paralympic World Cups (2005 – 2).

ELLIE SIMMONDS – PARALYMPIC GAMES

FAMILY SACRIFICES PAY OFF

Oliver Brown, 15 September 2012

Does the label 'dwarf' bother Ellie Simmonds? I ask simply because, in conversation at the back of this Park Lane showroom, it is easy to forget that our Paralympic poster girl stands at just 4 feet 1 inch – until, that is, she shifts in her giant swivel chair and is unable to stop it from spinning. 'Not really,' she replied, steadying herself. 'I have grown up in a positive household. I'm a normal person, just a lot smaller. I get on with it. Everybody should do that. You only live once and you need to enjoy life, to go out and achieve whatever you want to.'

She could scarcely have expressed such a credo more eloquently than at the Aquatics Centre during the London Paralympics. Her first and most abiding gold-medal moment there, engineering a late surge to eclipse American rival Victoria Arlen in the final of the S6 400 metres freestyle, set off an ear-splitting cacophony. Simmonds had projected a vulnerability on the starting blocks, but the subsequent eight lengths of the pool proved how she offset her diminutive stature with gigantic force of will. In the immediate aftermath of her victory she cried, and it is all she can do to stop dissolving again here. 'When I was on the podium singing the National Anthem, and the crowd were all singing it, it was definitely . . .' Her voice quavered slightly. 'It was a moment to remember, and I'm going to remember it for the rest of my life.' As well she should, for Simmonds is astute enough at seventeen to recognise that such unprecedented fervour, where even recent converts to the Paralympic cause set their watches by her swims, is never likely to happen again. 'I must have taken about a thousand photos,' she admitted. 'I've taken it all in.'

Her anxiety, such as there is in so energetic a character, concerns what comes next. You will often hear triumphant Olympians talk of a desire to escape their bubble of fleeting celebrity, to embrace the quotidian rituals of domestic life once more. But Simmonds, fresh from her haul of two golds, a silver and a bronze, is desperate for her post-Paralympics glow to endure. The disjuncture between national heroine status and her routine reality as a Swansea schoolgirl is almost too disorientating to deal with. 'I don't want it to end, I love all the opportunities I have,' said Simmonds, who recently passed her driving test in a specially adapted Mini. 'When all those stop, there's nothing much to look forward to, apart from a holiday. At times it's easy to feel, "What have I got to motivate myself?" I suppose I have to enjoy this success first, and return to the water gradually.' Simmonds is not ready for her final year of sixth form at Swansea's Olchfa Comprehensive, or at least not yet. Such were her pre-London swimming pressures that she did not perform as strongly in her AS levels as she expected, receiving a C in world development and a U in history. Already her mother Val, sitting outside for this interview, has called her head of year to arrange for her to retake history classes. 'School was quite hard in the run-up to London,' she said. 'It had to take a back seat, but I love the place to pieces. My school have been so supportive in the balance between my sport and my studying, ever since I won the two golds in Beijing. I couldn't have asked for better support through what was the biggest year of my life.'

But it is the backing from her parents that has involved the greatest sacrifice. When young Ellie first became serious about swimming from the age of five, Val would prise her out of bed at 5.30 a.m. five mornings a week, in time for two hours of training before lessons and another ninety minutes afterwards. So onerous was the regime that, to support her ambitions, the family split in two, Val and Ellie moving to South Wales, so that she could use Swansea's world-class 50-metre pool, while her father Steve, brother and three sisters stayed at home in the West Midlands. The decision was an emotional wrench, but Simmonds's relationship with her father, an environmental consultant, has deepened as a consequence. 'I text my dad a lot. I live with my mum from Monday to Saturday morning and when I see my dad it's very special, because we don't have much time with each other. We do lots together at weekends, though. I would say I'm closer to my dad but I love my mum the same.' Her support network was firmly intact in London, where she was watched by thirty immediate family members, all of whom shared in the febrile atmosphere that her four medal-winning swims generated. Sweetly understated, Simmonds said: 'They don't show too much feeling in front of me. I just hope that they're proud of me.'

Never was the mood in that 15,000-seat arena more fervid than for Simmonds's opening gold, when she overhauled Arlen after trailing for three-quarters of the race. The distance between the two had never been more than a body length but, as Simmonds hit the 350 metres mark eight-one-hundredths of a second clear, she seized an advantage she was never prepared to relinquish. Her abbreviated, frantic swimming action, requiring frequent lungfuls of air, appeared to capture a philosophy she had practised almost from the cradle: that in spite of her size, she would simply try twice as hard as everyone else.

Her victory was doubly impressive for the fact that Arlen, paralysed below the waist after a devastating virus, had only been confirmed as an S6 swimmer four hours before. Arlen had been in a vegetative state for two years, but the International Paralympic Committee questioned whether her disability was severe enough to warrant inclusion in Simmonds's category. The controversy, ultimately, did not distract Simmonds, but it underlined the fiendish difficulties inherent in the classification system. How, to put it bluntly, was one supposed to draw direct medical equivalence between a dwarf and a paraplegic? 'They see us all as having the same ability in the water,' Simmonds explained. 'I have two shorter arms, which in their eyes equal one big arm, and two shorter legs. Victoria's two big arms work out as roughly the same. I think they get it right.' Simmonds, it transpired, did not simply weather the dispute over Arlen but flourished, knocking an extraordinary five seconds off the world record in the 400 metres freestyle.

Overnight, she became the emblem of a transformative Games, meeting the Prime Minister and helping to extinguish the Paralympic flame alongside sprint star Jonnie Peacock. Who is to tell what she could accomplish in Rio in 2016, or even beyond? 'I'd love to be a role model and inspire people in Paralympic sport. I don't want just to be a swimmer – I want to go to university, maybe get a job as well.' The future is a concept with which Simmonds grapples constantly. 'It keeps changing what I want to do when I'm older,' says this unabashed home girl, who has admitted to a weakness for carrot muffins. 'Maybe something in baking.'

Sporting Champion: Ellie Simmonds – 4 Paralympic Games (2008 – 2, 2012 – 2); 13 World Championships (2009 – 6, 2010 – 4, 2013 – 3); 5 European Championships (2009 – 5).

LEE PEARSON – PARALYMPIC GAMES

I FEEL LUCKY THAT I HAVE FOUND MY TALENT
Robert Philip, 30 December 2004

When Lynda Pearson gave birth to the youngest of her three sons by Caesarean section in 1974, she was kept sedated for thirty-six hours after the operation. When she finally regained consciousness, Lynda knew something was worryingly wrong when she heard one nurse hiss to another: 'Sssshh, she's coming round.' Having been told of the subsequent events when he was of an age to regard the incident with black humour rather than mortification or anger, Lee Pearson takes up his mother's tale. 'The nurses wouldn't reply to any of her questions and although mum's very passive, when riled, she's a force to be reckoned with. "If I've got a live child – whatever the circumstances – I want to see him or her right now," she demanded. "And if I haven't, then I want to be told".'

What happened next is a shameful scene from the Dark Ages. 'She was put in a wheelchair and pushed down a corridor surrounded by a team of about ten doctors, nurses and psychologists. Finally they stopped at a broom cupboard and there, in the middle of the pile of mops and buckets, was a crib with a cloth over the top. Remember this was 1974 not 1874, but I suppose I was not a pretty sight; my right foot was wrapped round my left knee, my left foot was wrapped round my right knee, my arms and hands were horribly twisted and I had an ugly birthmark covering half my face and the top of my head. Mum took a gulp, picked me up and gave the first of a million cuddles.'

Born with arthrogryposis multiplex congenita – 'the muscles in my arms and legs grew as scar tissue in the womb' – which left his matchstick limbs bent and warped, the baby in the cupboard has grown into one of the nation's most successful sportsmen. Wearing plastic splints running from his backside to his heels, Pearson has won six Paralympic Games dressage gold medals (three apiece from Athens and Sydney), five World Championship and three European titles, plus a notable victory in an able-bodied national championship event at Hickstead. 'That meant a lot to me, as did being voted BBC Midlands Sports Personality of the Year, because it's nice to take on and beat athletes without disabilities.'

Lee Pearson, who lists his hobbies as quad bikes, jet skis, clubbing until all hours and delivering more double entendres than Julian Clary, first came to public attention at the age of six. By that time he had already undergone fifteen operations, and when Margaret Thatcher carried him up the staircase of 10 Downing Street to receive his 1980 Children of Courage Award, he melted the Iron Lady's heart with his cheeky grin and delighted chuckles. 'I don't know why, but she just took a shine to me. When she bent down to pick me up my dad said, "I'd better carry Lee, he's heavier than he looks", to which the Prime Minister replied firmly, "I'll carry him".

At that time, young Lee attended a special needs school near his home in the Staffordshire village of Cheddleton, until Lynda and Dave Pearson cajoled a local mainstream school into accepting their son. 'Mum and Dad were determined to make my life as normal as they possibly could. After all, what is a disability? Sitting here in this restaurant, you need glasses to read the menu, which makes you more disabled than me at this moment. If you try singling me out to my mother, she'll be down your throat. She has three sons and she's equally proud of us all. That's why when I went to mainstream school at the age of nine, I thought it was no big deal. When the school asked if I would like an adult minder to carry my bag around Mum snapped, "You must be joking. He'll either make friends who'll carry his bag around or else he'll carry his own bloody bag".'

And did he make friends or was he the victim of the playground bullies? 'I'm afraid to say I was Mr Popular at school. I went out with all the girls in my year – I quite liked girls back then – and even dated ones in the year above.' By then, he was also an accomplished horseman, having started riding as a tot when, banned from joining his two elder brothers on their BMX adventures, his parents bought him Sally the donkey on which to romp around the paddock. 'My great grandfather had been the neighbourhood "horse whisperer" so I've probably loved horses since I was an embryo. Whenever I watched cowboy films as a small child I wasn't watching the hunky cowboys – which I'd probably do now – I was watching the horses. Even now I love sitting in the field just watching the way they move.'

Alas, the child of courage grew into a frustrated young man, hidden away in the back room of a supermarket where he stuck prices on jars, tins and packets. 'If I hadn't discovered the possibilities of a full-time career in sport through watching the 1996 Paralympics in Atlanta, I'd have committed suicide. I hated the job so much I was on anti-depressants. If I'd worked on the checkout at least I would have been meeting different people every day, but I got to talk to nobody. It's the people who are stuck in jobs like that who deserve a bloody medal, not me.' Horses were to be his salvation; seeing Lee aboard the mighty Blue Circle Boy (affectionately known as 'Gus' in the stable) in the Athens dressage arena was to witness a true master at work. 'I feel lucky that I found my talent, not unlucky that I was born with a disability. When I'm on a horse I'm more worried about what the riding hat is doing to my hair than what my bent legs and arms are doing. What riding has given me is respect. When I compete in an able-bodied event, I'm not seen as an "Aaaah, bless . . ." factor, I'm seen as an "Oh, s***, why does he have to be in my class?"'

Though Lee loves his boys' toys – motorbikes, tractors, his high-speed 7.5-ton lorry and horsebox and sports cars (he is trying to persuade Mercedes to 'lend' him an SLK roadster) – it is in the saddle on Gus, a handsome golden giant with four white stockings, that he enjoys the greatest thrill. 'I'm a nutter for speed but horses give you the freedom, movement and energy that pushing a wheelchair certainly can't. Gus is hard work because he was bottle-fed after his mother died and can, therefore, act like a spoiled brat. He's got a strong, awkward personality. What we have is a bit like a marriage – we argue as much as we get on. Obviously I don't love him as you do your wife and I do my partner but we have an understanding. I can get on him and walk two steps out of the barn and think, "Oooh, he's in one of them moods".'

Only Lee Pearson could admit that when he arrived in Sydney to compete in his first Paralympics his initial sensation was one of disappointment. 'I'd always liked to think that I was unique and there I was, suddenly surrounded by hundreds of athletes with far more severe problems than me. I may daydream occasionally that I've got a gorgeous, muscled body, but I don't have a choice about my disability just as I don't have a choice about being gay [what about those teenage conquests at school? 'Times change . . .']. I love who I am and certainly don't have a problem about being gay.' Certain sections of society do have a problem with gay men and women, however, so was it difficult to reveal himself as he truly was? 'Mum and Dad wanted to lay on a major, major twenty-first birthday party for me but I thought, "What's the point in people celebrating my coming of age when they don't know who I really am?" I used to pretend I thought a woman was absolutely gorgeous but inside I knew her boyfriend was far more hot tottie. Mum thought I was dating a girl called Jane who collected glasses in the pub – in fact I was seeing the barman, Vincent. You can control the way you think but you can't control the way you feel. It was difficult for my mum and dad because they had the normal expectations of marriage and grandchildren so there was a period of adjustment. Anyway, I'd already come out of the closet once before, hadn't I?'

Sporting Champion: Lee Pearson – 10 Paralympic Games (2000 – 3, 2004 – 3, 2008 – 3, 2012 – 1).

ALISTAIR AND JONNY BROWNLEE – WORLD TRIATHLON CHAMPIONSHIPS

AT HOME WITH THE BROWNLEE BOYS

James Cracknell, 9 June 2013

Alistair and Jonny Brownlee just seem too nice to be world-class sportsmen. If natural-born winners are supposed to be aggressive, selfish and arrogant, then the Brownlee boys are an exception – unless, of course, that is just their game face. And yet they are the most successful brothers in British, and perhaps even global, sport: serial medal winners in triathlon, one of the most brutal and unforgiving events of all. An Olympic triathlete has no heat or semi-final to find form: there is one final and it is a case of go big or go home.

How do these homely Yorkshire lads – who still pop up the street to their elderly neighbour to fix her internet – deliver under that pressure? That is what I wanted to discover. The boys have invited me to their home in Bramhope to see how they train and live, and meet those closest to them. Somehow, they have even persuaded me to go on a bike ride on their beloved fells. I want to talk to them, sportsmen to sportsman – OK, ex-sportsman – to unpick their champion DNA and explain their astonishing successes.

They say the best way of truly finding out about someone is by meeting their friends and, in Yorkshire, the Brownlees have plenty. One of their best, Alec Duffield, meets me at Leeds station. He grew up competing against Ali on the fell-running circuit and now lives with them, becoming indispensable to their operation. On one occasion, he was even dispatched to fetch their Olympic medals, which they had forgotten to take to an interview. Alec drives me to Leeds Metropolitan University, the brothers' training base and a place where the mere mention of their name to campus security is enough to gain access and a prime parking spot. The boys are finishing off a weights session – unlike the pool or the fells it is not a place they particularly enjoy – and at first they are hard to pick out among the hulking bodies belonging to Leeds Carnegie rugby club. 'If we want something heavy lifted at home we call Edward,' Jonny admits with a smile. Edward is their youngest brother and, almost unbelievably, given his siblings' build, a prop forward.

The boys appear utterly at ease: with their work, each other and, crucially, the environment in which they live and train. Not even Ali's Achilles injury, which ruled him out of a world series event in Madrid, won at a canter by Jonny, can make the shutters come down. That should not come as a surprise. The last time I interviewed Ali he had just crossed the line after winning gold in London. Jonny had taken bronze and was on a stretcher being given oxygen. I asked if seeing Jonny in that state took anything away from his moment. 'No, it's a hard sport, he'll be all right,' was his ruthless reply.

In one sense, the Olympics changed everything for the Brownlees. There was relief for Ali in winning at home, despite an injury-ravaged season, and satisfaction for Jonny earning bronze.

It made sponsors take notice, and the world suddenly wanted to hear from them, a point underlined by the fact they have recently worked on a book – together, of course – about their sport, how they conquered it and the part that luck plays along the way. But it is remarkable how much has stayed constant. They still eat at the same bistro after training – I asked if there had been a post-London legacy menu upgrade, but they insisted not. And, most pertinently, Ali still wins: in all their senior races, Jonny has still to get the better of his elder brother in a race where both have been injury-free.

What I wanted to hear from Jonny was if there is a part of him that believes he simply cannot beat Ali. 'I guess there's a small percentage of me that thinks he's better,' he says. 'The fact is he always beat me growing up and, when he's one hundred per cent fit, he's faster at the moment. But I get more out of training with him every day.' I can relate to that. When I left school I went to row at the club where Steve Redgrave trained. My rationale was that if I could beat him one day a month, then one day a week and then every day, I would believe I had it in me to win the Olympics. The complication for Jonny is that he is up against not just a rival but family. You can sense his struggle when I ask him if he would have the same attitude to competing against Ali if he was German, and not his brother. His response was immediate: 'I'd definitely beat him.'

As we left the restaurant to collect the bikes for our afternoon ride, I was looking forward to seeing the house they used to share until Jonny moved out in September. It is not hard to spot among the row of terraced houses, with the Dales beyond. There is an infinity pool – or, as the neighbours call it, the spaceship – in the front garden. It may be a four-bedroom place but, with running kit, wetsuits and bikes taking up three of them, you can see why Jonny craved his own space. As the younger brother, I thought Jonny would possess the stereotypical younger sibling characteristics: a freer spirit as the elder brother has already fought certain battles growing up. And yet it is Jonny who is more punctual, wanting to be at training early to prepare himself, whereas Ali takes his time. The only arguments they had in the run-up to the Olympics occurred when Ali had injured his Achilles tendon and had to put on a protective boot, a process that took ten minutes. When he was not ready in time, Jonny simply left him behind. As my old German rowing coach put it: 'You wait for them once, you'll always wait for them.'

He may have more space and nobody using his swimmers, but Jonny must miss Ali's neighbours. When they were away racing, an elderly lady up the road used to come in, move the post and make it look like people were home. She also provided an endless supply of homemade cake. The only catch was that she wanted help with anything technical round the house. This is not a place of gated communities and high wire fences. Ali and Jonny are familiar faces in Bramhope's streets, which is just the way they like it. 'We used to explore the area as kids,' Jonny explained. 'We went to a school that had a good reputation for running, went to a swimming club with convenient training times and cycled ten miles to school and back every day. It's the same now in terms of exploring – we just do it a bit faster than when we were kids!'

It is just Jonny and I heading out on the bikes – Ali stays at home with his feet up, resting that Achilles tendon – and, as we cycle through the Dales, it is clear he misses his brother being alongside him. Even so, it is a stunning ride – stunning, and punishing. You learn soon enough when out riding with a Brownlee that someone's 'short easy ride' is another's 'two-and-a-half-hour blast' and a southerner's 'brutal hill' is a Yorkshire lad's flat. The boys train thirty-five hours a week – twenty of those on the bike – but make light of the punishment. 'We only do that schedule for a few weeks at a time, so it's not too bad,' Jonny said. 'And training is interrupted by racing, which is the fun part.'

'Fun' is not the word that comes to mind, as I fight to keep up with Jonny, but he seems entirely at ease. 'They're getting bigger every time I come past,' he said as we whizzed past some lambs. It all feels a long way from London 2012, the awards ceremonies and VIP areas. But this is home – the place that always welcomes them back, and where they want to give back. After they have squabbled over the World Championship in London, they host a Super Sprint Triathlon in Fountains Abbey, North Yorkshire. 'The distances aren't daunting and it's beautiful,' Jonny said. 'We want people to experience triathlon the right way.' I do not doubt him for a moment, but I get the feeling that beating Ali in the fells, their own playground, would mean everything to Jonny – payback for the battles they had growing up. By the end of our ride, I am ready for home – but not Jonny. As a frustrated Ali lies on the sofa, his brother leaves for yet another run. Earlier, I had asked Ali if he felt on borrowed time in dominating Jonny. 'In the future he may win one and I'll win one, but there's only one race that matters,' he said. His tone made me feel he believed the big one would be his. But one thing is for sure: Jonny will not be far behind.

Sporting Champion: Alistair Brownlee – 1 Olympic Games (2012); 2 World Championships (2009, 2011); 2 European Championships (2010, 2011).

Sporting Champion: Jonny Brownlee – 1 World Championship (2012).

ENGLAND – THE ASHES

PIETERSEN SECURES LITTLE BROWN URN AT LAST
Derek Pringle, 13 September 2005

It used to be the dream that disappeared on waking, the yearning that had no release, and the trophy that England teams could neither win, borrow nor steal – at least not since 1989. Then, amid tumultuous scenes at the Oval, the Ashes fell back into English hands, the little brown urn finally secured after an astonishing century by Kevin Pietersen made the final Test safe from one last Australian ambush. Pietersen's high-octane innings did not prevent the moment being sealed with a whimper though, after Australia openers Justin Langer and Matthew Hayden accepted the offer of bad light. With the visitors needing an impossible 338 runs from 17.2 overs, the move simply sealed the draw prematurely.

Michael Vaughan, perhaps wanting to savour the moment in front of another capacity crowd, seemed more than a little aggrieved. His annoyance was short-lived and once he had given the replica urn a peck on the cheek and held it aloft to roars of delight, he and the team appeared overjoyed as they did a lap of honour to renditions of 'Jerusalem' and 'Land of Hope and Glory' – a combination that with all the flags and confetti made the occasion feel like a cross between a Wembley Cup final and Last Night of the Proms. Eight Ashes series had been lost before this 2–1 win. It has been fully deserved, too, and after their defeat in the opening Test at Lord's, England's has been the bolder and more persuasive cricket, a combination that has relied on finding the right man at the right time. Here, that man was Pietersen, who since he brought his combination of bling and bluster to this England side has threatened to produce something sensational, though thrill-seeker that he is, he left it until the attention of the entire country, as well as the insomniac parts of Australia, were on him before producing it.

In the context of the game, which England needed to make safe by batting out most of the day, it was a reckless but glorious ride, most of it at breakneck speed. By the time Glenn McGrath ended it, clean bowling Pietersen with the second new ball for 158, he had struck seven sixes and fifteen fours, nearly all whistle-clean off the middle of the bat. Given the extraordinary events of this series, it would be easy to be blasé about Pietersen's deeds. But as they have done since they got their noses in front during the Edgbaston Test, England once more faltered as the main prize hove into view as McGrath and Shane Warne probed for scar tissue in England's collective psyche one last time.

But Pietersen is wired up differently to most and does not do caution or self-doubt, as he revealed when hooking 93mph bouncers from Brett Lee high into the crowd at long leg. Although he is more likely to reveal the dark roots in his blond streak than the English ones in his make-up, he clearly cares, though perhaps not to the extent that he chokes up as some of his team-mates have done. Arriving at the crease after McGrath had removed Vaughan and Ian Bell in successive balls to leave England sixty-nine for three, Pietersen survived the hat-trick ball, but only just as the bouncer missed his glove by a whisker before striking his upper arm. With the whole team appealing for the catch, the pressure on umpire Billy Bowden was enormous, but his intransigence proved to be the right decision – one of several hairline ones the umpires got spot-on during the day.

If that near-miss could be put down to Pietersen's skill, he also enjoyed some luck, being dropped on nought and fifteen. The first chance came off Warne, as Pietersen edged to Adam Gilchrist, and the second to Warne, as he edged a drive off Lee to first slip. If the first was tricky the second was standard fodder and shouts of 'Warney's dropped the Ashes' echoed around the Oval for the rest of the day. While it is indisputable that the mistake cost them dear, without Warne Australia would have been pole-axed during the summer. Worrying times for Australia then that he and McGrath, who took three for eighty-five here, are into the last phases of their careers. Warne finished with six wickets to bring his tally to forty for the series. While that is not an Australian record for an Ashes series (Terry Alderman took forty-two and forty-one in the 1980s, and Rodney Hogg forty-one before that), he did beat Dennis Lillee's record for the most Ashes victims over a career, now set at 172.

He almost rallied his team for one last attempt to claw back their proud Ashes legacy, following the dismissal of Marcus Trescothick and Andrew Flintoff, caught and bowled after Warne had lured him into an indiscreet drive. The double strike left England looking distinctly insecure on 126 for five at lunch. Fortunately for them Warne's mastery of Pietersen here was limited to the first innings only. While others groped and smothered his spin, the skunk-haired one treated him with disdain, twice sweep-slogging him for six over mid-wicket before biffing him straight for another two sixes as the mood took him. It was the stuff of fantasy, ably abetted by a sturdy fifty-nine from Ashley Giles, who added 109 runs with Pietersen for the eighth wicket, an Oval record against Australia. Although both eventually perished and the team were bowled out for 335, all threat had been defused and the game, and with it the series, was in the bag. England have won the Ashes – a statement that has a magnificent ring to it.

Sporting Champions: England – 18 Ashes home series wins (1884, 1886, 1888, 1890, 1893, 1896, 1905, 1912, 1926, 1953, 1956, 1972, 1977, 1981, 1985, 2005, 2009, 2013).

RICHARD FAULDS – OLYMPIC GAMES

FAULDS IS GUNNING FOR GLORY

Simon Hughes, 31 January 2000

There's trouble on't hill. Southside Hill, Longparish, North Hampshire. A young lad is going around shooting pigeons nineteen to the dozen and disturbing the peace in a tranquil Test Valley village. Well-heeled residents are up in arms and trying to get him stopped. Why should this concern anyone outside the vicinity? And what, you may wonder, has this got to do with British sport? Quite a lot actually. The lad in question is twenty-two-year-old Richard Faulds, the pigeons he's shooting are of the clay variety, and until recently he was a world record holder. He is one of Britain's major medal hopes for the Sydney Olympics. Faulds's special discipline is double-trap clays, so called because they are released not one at a time, but in pairs. You give 'em both barrels. This is a quickfire sport with a capital Q. 'We've timed the process,' Richard says. 'From the P of my "Pull" to the firing of the second shot is less than half a second.' When Faulds broke the world record in May 1998, he hit 193 out of 200 of these moving targets. He's a crackshot with a capital C.

Faulds lives with his parents on a farm above Longparish, a sleepy village of wisteria cottages close to Andover. Half a mile from the farmhouse, well out of sight of the nearest dwelling, his father has built a small range for Richard to practise on. The clay traps are housed in a concrete bunker like a football dugout, and are voice-activated: microphones are located beside Richard's shooting positions. Earthmovers trundle about building sound-proofing embankments with imported dirt. That's the cause of the local disquiet. Although Richard only practises for about half an hour every other day, the regular rat-a-tat of 100 rounds echoes round the area like, well, gunfire. It seems to have become too much for some local residents, whose eardrums are already assaulted by low-flying Army helicopters, night-time drills on nearby Ministry of Defence land and widespread pheasant shooting. They have made life uncomfortable for the Faulds family. 'I stay away from the village because I'm not sure whether the people I'll see are with us or against us,' says Mrs Faulds.

Richard, a tall, spruce chap with a benign air, is unperturbed by the dispute, and the uncertainty of his Lottery funding for the Olympics. At the moment he is preparing to pay his own way. Fortunately, with a steady job as a clay-shooting instructor in west London and an entrepreneurial father, he can afford to. Sitting in a living room festooned with silver trophies, he talks with disarming modesty about finishing fifth at the Atlanta Olympics, in front of a crowd of 20,000, and the elation of breaking the world record, also in Atlanta, two years later. 'It was a nice day, no wind, warm, sunny and the clays looked like the proverbial dustbin lids to me.' His 193 out of 200 was the equivalent of knocking a second off the 100 metres world record, yet it barely caused a ripple back home. He received a medal, a small loyalty prize from a gun manufacturer, a few backslaps in shooting magazines, and little else. He still has to buy all his practice clays (he destroys about 15,000 a year) though at least he gets his cartridges free. He talks enviously about his government-sponsored Italian rivals, one of whom, Daniel Dispingo, eclipsed his world record by one last year.

He can't entirely explain why he's such a sharpshooter. 'Actually, I'm almost afraid to analyse my ability too closely,' he said, implying that, if he did, his prowess might unravel in front of his eyes and he wouldn't be able to put it back together again. He can't read the extra-small print on an optician's card and he hasn't got an exceptionally steady hand. 'I like the adrenalin of competition, though. It brings the best out of me.' His weakness is concentration – 'stupid, irrelevant things come into my head and I miss a few' – and he's working with the sports psychologist Peter Terry to improve it.

Even before his father, Bruce, bought him six shooting lessons for his tenth birthday, he had an affinity with the sport. 'I always used to do a spot of "pest control" on the farm,' said Bruce, 'and when Richard was very young, he used to have a go, resting the gun on my arm and pulling the trigger.' Having had some proper tuition, he won his first trophy at twelve, and went on to win a sequence of British and European junior championships. Through his teens he had to travel two hours to Cambridgeshire to practise 'double-trap'. Once he'd qualified for the Atlanta Olympics, his father constructed the layout at home. It is slickly designed on the Olympic model, with six different shooting positions above the traps bunker. You sense they have ambitious future plans for it.

'Pull!' Richard said. Two little orange frisbees flew out and away from the bunker, one slightly higher than the other. Two almost simultaneous pops from his Beretta shattered them. 'Pull!' he said again. Same result. He hit nine out of ten in the space of a minute, and he wasn't even concentrating. 'I try and ambush the first clay, get it as soon as it appears from the bunker, then I've got a fraction longer to focus on the second,' he explained. It looked easy. I tried it. I missed six out of six. 'You hold the gun and I'll point it,' he said standing next to me, in an apparently hopeless aiming-position. 'When I say "now" you pull the trigger.' I hit two out of two. His party piece is to shoot them from the hip. You wouldn't want to be a rabbit or a pheasant in that neck of the woods.

Clay-pigeon shooting is largely a summer sport, so for now Faulds is keeping his practice to a minimum. 'If I overdid it, I'd get mechanical.' He'll step it up in advance of a couple of pre-Olympic competitions. You sense he has the natural ability to win gold, but does he have the mental fortitude? 'I know if I have a really good day, I can win it if I want to,' he said. 'I do want to.' It would, of course, be a spectacular British achievement. But it probably wouldn't silence the neighbours.

Sporting Champion: Richard Faulds – 1 Olympic Games (2000).

BEN AINSLIE – OLYMPIC GAMES

OPTIMIST TURNED GENIUS

Brough Scott, 16 July 2000

It was Christmas Eve in the Cornish estuary of Carrick Roads. When eight-year-old Ben Ainslie had finally gone to sleep his parents, Roddy and Sue, tiptoed into the bedroom and rigged up the little wooden Optimist dinghy they had bought from the local garage. It had cost them £100. 'The most expensive £100 we ever spent,' said Sue. For that was the start of a waterborne journey, which in fifteen years has taken Ainslie to the very ends of the Earth and his family to the edge of bankruptcy. But at Sydney Harbour in September 2000 he sets out with a very real chance of Olympic gold in his Laser and the parental sacrifice has been worth every cent. Because the boy has a sort of genius in him. The boy can sail.

It was Jill Slater who first realised it. She and her doctor husband had just started a youth training scheme at the Restronguet Sailing Club which has now produced a whole string of internationals. 'Ben was very quiet and shy and had the oldest, slowest boat,' remembered Jill, 'then after six weeks we had our first little race. Ben won by a mile. I told Phil I'd seen something.' Phil

Slater is more practical than mystical. He recalled the obsessive dedication of the boy who would sail across the Carrick Roads by himself to join the fleet. Of how Ainslie overcame his early racing inexperience by sleuthing astern of major rivals. Of how he 'was in the right place at the right time', because of the inspirational work of the Royal Yachting Association's Jim Saltonstall in setting keen children the racing challenge. Of how this was a winner from the very start.

By 1992 Ben Ainslie had won his first title, the Optimists National Championship in Wales. Twelve months later his parents were getting him rather further afield. Victory in the Laser Radial (smaller sail) World Championships in Auckland, New Zealand, and in subsequent years gold medals and senior world and European championships, have followed as dad Roddy first sold his wood-fashioning business and then mortgaged his house literally to keep Ben afloat. Now the promised Lottery cash and sponsorship from Winchester Life and Henry Lloyd maintains the finances on an even keel but, after Ainslie's silver medal in Savannah at the 1996 Olympics, money was again so tight that when £10,000 was offered for a special race in Kuwait, Ben was off there in a flash with losing not an option. Money was needed then and now, but one look at him on Lymington River told you that money was not the key.

On land he is a tall, shy, slightly willowy figure. On the water he is a lean, hard, dominant extension of the tiny craft with which he skims and slices the estuary chop as we make our way out into the windy Solent. The Laser is the most brutally uncomplicated of all the dinghies: just a 4-metre, 59-kilogram fibre-glass hull with a centre-board and 7 square metres of sail. Same boat, same rig for everyone. Just you and up to one hundred others against the wind and tide and weather. 'I love the competition,' Ainslie had said earlier, his brown eyes flashing in a momentary abandonment of modesty. 'There's nothing I hate more than losing.' And nothing he loves more than the sensation of the boat responding to his every move. For the cameras he now runs downwind straight at us, sheering away at the last moment and jibing the sail round as if it were a ball on a string. Any ordinary mortal would be in the drink, but in an instant he is tacking ferociously up beside us, his whole 6 feet 1 inch, 79-kilogram frame arced way out beyond the gunwale as he locks his body in balance against the power of the wind. That is when you appreciate the physical side of seeking this sailing gold. The Olympic test is spread over eleven races, two a day of up to fifty minutes each, one after the other with less than half an hour in between. With almost a hundred competitors from a variety of different countries this is about as different as you can get from the gentle, boozy weekend jaunts espoused by the fleets of cruising boats on the Lymington mooring lines. This will take you to the limit and beyond.

So it is to the gym and to the road bike, not to the bar that Ainslie hightails off to after his three-hour daily stint with training partner Paul Goodison on the water. 'The Olympic level is unbelievably demanding,' said the RYA's team manager John Derbyshire, whose use of Lottery money to hire a specialist exercise physiologist and physiotherapist has paid off with what may well be the most successful and the fittest team to hoist a sail. Of course other nations' stars are hardening up too, most notably the Brazilian Robert Scheidt, who took gold to Ainslie's silver in Savannah in 1996. Scheidt got another decision over his young rival at the World Championships in Mexico in the spring, but Ainslie has previously laid the Savannah ghost, most notably by winning the pre-Olympic Regatta at Sydney over Christmas 1999. It is to Sydney that Ainslie went intent on familiarising himself with every foible of wind and tide in the famous harbour. With lighter breezes expected than on the open sea his fitness routine has included dieting down from 83 kilograms to what is perceived as an optimum 79 kilograms of bodyweight. Of all the sportsmen and women we send down to the Olympics none will be more focused than this latter-day amphibian.

But that does not explain it. To win the way Ainslie has done, to receive the ultimate accolade of Yachtsman of the Year at the ridiculous age of twenty-one, has to be through something more than just determination and a gift for pushing a sail boat fast through the water. 'I think it's a bit like understanding the angles, like in snooker,' he said in a surprisingly revelatory moment as we dry off afterwards. 'You have to have a feel for the boat and the sea. But you need to read the wind changes to put yourself in a better position. It's a mind game, a chess game and you have to pin your opponent down.'

His present ambition is Olympic gold in the Laser, but there are bigger boats ahead. Recently Ainslie helmed a 45-foot cruising yacht into second place in the IRC National Championship and when asked for the ultimate he calmly opted for the most ruthless and complicated yacht race of them all. He would like to bring the America's Cup to Britain. Through all this Roddy Ainslie looks on with something more than mere slavish paternal pride. Push him hard and he will admit he did a bit of sailing too. Push him harder and he will own up to the first Whitbread Round the World Race in 1975. And of course ten years later he and Sue spent a few quid at the garage to give Ben a chance of following the flag. It may have proved an expensive £100. But after the Sydney Olympics it could be rather more than Ben Ainslie's parents who think that their son's fame and fulfilment have come cheap at the price.

Sporting Champion: Ben Ainslie – 4 Olympic Games (2000, 2004, 2008, 2012); 8 World Championships (1993, 1999, 2002, 2003, 2004, 2005, 2008, 2012).

STEVE REDGRAVE – OLYMPIC GAMES

TAKING IT TO THE LIMIT

Michael Calvin, 27 November 1995

The engraved wooden box containing Steve Redgrave's three Olympic gold medals, crafted by a childhood friend, was passed around the room with a reverence reserved for holy relics. 'It all starts with a dream,' he told his sober-suited audience of health insurance executives, who struggled to subdue an adolescent sense of awe and anticipation. 'I never thought I'd get a chance to see one of these,' murmured one. 'Can I hold them? Are they really gold?' Redgrave had heard all the exclamations and entreaties before. His medals from Los Angeles and Seoul are, in fact, gold-plated silver. Barcelona's token of global esteem contains 13.5g of gold, and has an altogether more appropriate purity.

If all goes according to plan, his collection will be extended in 1996. Another pairs win, in the company of Matthew Pinsent, will install him as the first endurance athlete to win four successive Olympic titles. 'The only medal that means anything to me at the moment is the one from Atlanta,' Redgrave reflected as he squirmed in an alarmingly narrow window seat on an ageing Balkan Airlines Tupolev 154. 'It is the only one I have not got.' He had rushed to Heathrow from his motivational seminar with those executives in Andover, pausing only to purchase ten boxes of Jaffa cakes for his British team-mates existing on a diet of institutionalised mush in Bulgaria, his destination.

Time has stood still at the Belmeken Sports Complex in the Rila mountain range, 100 miles south-east of Sofia. Built by the East Germans to prepare athletes for the 1968 Mexico Olympics, it is a decaying outpost of Communism's sporting empire. The floors of airy gymnasiums have not been varnished since the fall of the Berlin Wall. Paint peels from swimming pool walls and first-generation multi-gyms stand rusting into obsolescence. Belmeken is principally populated by ghosts but is now colonised by British rowers, German biathletes, Greek hammer throwers and terrifyingly young Russian swimmers. All sought the physiological benefits of four training sessions a day at altitude in the Bulgarian mountains.

Redgrave and Pinsent estimate they will train for thirty-four hours for each of the 240 strokes they will use in the Olympic final. They will have lifted more than six million kilograms in the four years between Atlanta and Barcelona. Such statistics were placed into stark relief when the sun streamed through the cracked windows of a gym once used by Eastern bloc boxers. The pair's pre-lunch ergometer test, involving the equivalent of a 20-kilometre row, revealed the hidden cost of those medals.

Pinsent, disconcerted by the luxury of a day off while Redgrave made a whistle-stop return to England, struggled to find his rhythm. He was sweating profusely, leaving parallel lines of moisture on the chipped wooden floor. All that could be heard, apart from the occasional violent exhalation, was the insistent whir of their machines. Pinsent was blank-eyed but instead of concentrating on personal discomfort, he summoned images of his rivals. 'When it hurts, you think of the other guys around the world,' he reflected later. 'You think, "I wonder where the Australians are training today? I wonder what the French are doing? I wonder if the Germans are getting a quick pair together?" You think how you are going to row in that final. You never consider Barcelona. That's gone. Memories of past victories give you no kick. In some ways, you even feel guilty about looking backwards.' Redgrave, listening intently, interjected. 'You can be sure they're working, right now, on a plan to try to beat us,' he said, the urgency of his words exposing a champion's cocktail of perfectionism and paranoia. 'I don't think you ever really switch off in this sport. An Olympic final is only one day, every four years, but it is with you for every day of those four years. It is always there, in the back of your mind. You might be pushing a trolley around the supermarket, but you'll start to drift off. You'll think to yourself, "What happens if we make a bad start? How will it feel if we are two metres ahead after five hundred metres?" You cover all eventualities.'

Part of the psychological process is to reduce the scale of the challenge. Times tend to improve by four seconds during an Olympic cycle, and Redgrave calculates this involves an improvement of five 1,200ths of a second for every hour spent training. 'That's a fifth of the time it takes to blink an eye,' he said. 'It helps to remember that on days when you feel like skipping a session, having a bit of a skive.' Indolence is hardly in their nature. They are lifting bigger weights, more consistently, than their rivals.

Physiological tests prove that Redgrave, at thirty-three, is stronger and fitter than ever in his career. No one, least of all British head coach Jürgen Gröbler, doubts he will have sufficient mental fortitude to withstand the stresses of approaching an achievement that will confirm him as Britain's greatest all-round athlete. 'There is pressure there,' Redgrave acknowledged. 'Some days I ask myself, "Can you do this?" But I know, deep down, that I will respond. All I can do is forget the hype and make sure my training counts.'

Redgrave will take his medals to a Christmas lunch in Atlanta. Pinsent, whose medal is still in its velvet presentation pouch, understands the significance of the gesture. 'It's funny,' he said. 'The medals almost mean more to other people than they do to us. They are a symbol of what we have achieved but winning the Olympics is not about the medal. It is about how you feel, deep inside, at the moment of victory. It is about how your name changes, from "Matthew Pinsent" to "Matthew Pinsent, Olympic champion". It is about the unbelievable attraction of history . . .'

Sporting Champion: Steve Redgrave – 5 Olympic Games (1984, 1988, 1992, 1996, 2000); 9 World Championships (1986, 1987, 1991, 1993, 1994, 1995, 1997, 1998, 1999); 3 Commonwealth Games (1986 – 3).

NICOLE COOKE – WORLD ROAD CYCLING CHAMPIONSHIPS

MAKING THE IMPOSSIBLE HAPPEN

Sue Mott, 24 July 2004

You may have to hold on to something. A British athlete is smoothly contemplating winning an event at the Athens Olympics. The road race? The time trial? The points race? It doesn't really matter. Nicole Cooke will be under the fierce Grecian sun, pedalling like fury and burning with ambition, bumping down the cobblestones from the Acropolis at breakneck speed, radiating elbows and intimidation, driven by single-mindedness and fear of failure, our up-and-coming star of women's cycling. 'I've already identified a fountain near the finish of the road race,' she admitted. If she wins, at the ludicrously young age of twenty-one, she will make a splash in more ways than one.

Cycling is modern-day chariot racing, and about as merciful. 'There are riders who I hate. I don't like certain riders. Not because of their characters. I just don't like them because they're my rivals. I do pass the time of day with those I secretly hate. But they're very short exchanges. Just to acknowledge them. Just to say, "Yes, I know you're there".' Who can we expect to see locked with her in mortal two-wheeled combat, spoke to spoke, as the 120-mile road race roars round the foot of an Athenian mountain and back? I don't expect her to tell me. Athletes invariably grow coy about naming names, fearing mass antagonism. Not Cooke. 'Right, there's the Swedish rider, Susanne Ljungskog, who won the World Championship last year. She's a nice person. But she's one of my rivals. There's Mirjam Melchers from Holland. Those two. Then we've got the Lithuanian team, they're very strong.' But their strength may be neither here nor there with Cooke in their draught, waiting for precisely the right moment to pounce and sprint away. She loves the tactical aspect of road racing, the psychological ferocity. And then, of course, she can pedal. 'I like to call myself a complete rider,' she said. 'Only the very pure skinny mountain goats can beat me on the climbs. Only the purist sprinters can beat me on the flat.' What she really means is that not many have the credentials to beat her overall. Perhaps none.

This kind of unflinching self-confidence is a joy to hear compared to the cacophony of athletes wondering if they might dare to come fourth. It is a genetic inheritance, no doubt. Cooke's father, a cyclist himself and a parent in the 'pusher' category, placed his daughter on the back of a tandem at six and the whole family cycled round the Isle of Wight. Another year it was Devon (almost all of it). Nicole started competing at eleven. At twelve, she came fifth at a popular tournament in the Netherlands (against boys). At thirteen, she came third. At fourteen, she won. 'Once you learn how to win, you never forget. It's partly about ruthlessness. You have to be selfish. My dad's ambitiousness rubbed off on me. He would say to me, "Well, why can't you be the best? Someone's got to win this title. Why not you?" That's the type of mentality he tried to instil in my brother and me. I think Dad gets up people's noses and I think he knows it as well. But why not be ambitious? I remember when I told Chris Boardman's coach, Peter Keen, that I wanted to win three world junior titles in 2001 in track, road and mountain bike, he said, "I don't think you can do it, Nicole. I just don't think it's possible. Don't waste your time". Definitely, there was a conflict of opinion. But I was able to come through and show that I could do it.

'There have been doubters along the way. Yes, Dad and I were dreaming up quite extravagant ideas, but why not? We put the work in.' She laughed suddenly when she remembered how British sport is perceived in other parts of the world, something she has witnessed first-hand while riding with the Italian team, Safi-Pasta Zara Manhattan, for whom she has just won the prestigious Giro d'Italia. 'The secretary of the team lived in London for a few years. One day he said, "I loved the Saturday and Sunday in England watching sport on television. They have sports you just don't see in Italy". I thought he was going to say rugby, or Arsenal, or something.' She had to break off in temporary hysterics. 'But then he named them. It was darts, snooker and . . .' (she was now crying with laughter) 'sheep herding! He thought that was British sport!' It took a while to collect herself, thrown back in a leather couch, shaking with mirth. She made an effort and resumed her dissertation. 'I think we're too reserved in this country. Why should we be?'

Cooke is making up for our squeamishness in the spotlight. She would have done so sooner but was controversially not chosen for the Sydney Games on the grounds that, at seventeen, she was too young. 'We were sent a letter from the president of the British Cycling Federation saying they would discuss it at the next panel meeting which was a month after the Olympics. It was like, "What a clown".' She has – just about – stopped being enraged by this decision. 'My mantra to myself whenever I'm riding now is, "Four years is a long time to wait".' She is not going to the Olympics to have her photograph taken with Lance Armstrong. 'I'm only going to get one chance to do the Athens Olympics. If I don't win or don't get a medal, I'll know it was because I was beaten by someone better as opposed to being too busy autograph-hunting or sightseeing. I probably won't be going to the opening ceremony either. I went to the one at the Commonwealth Games. It was OK but I don't think I woke up refreshed and raring to go the next day. Yes, I saw David Beckham running round the track but that's not the experience of a lifetime for me. Anyway, I am going to the Olympics now. I wouldn't say I was excited. I'd say there's a fear in me. A fear of failure. But that's what drives all athletes.'

This is passionate stuff. At first you think it must be the Celtic blood in her veins, our conversation taking place in Cardiff and she being Welsh Sports Personality of the Year. But she has no Welsh genealogy at all. Her mother and father are both English, they just chose to live in a house in Wick, Mid Glamorgan, where she grew up and which currently contains her old mountain bike, cycle-cross bike, racing bike and going-to-the-shops bike, like a living museum. It is that focused attachment to her sport that makes her so forthright on the issues that beset it. Drugs, for instance. No sport in the world, with the possible exception of professional wrestling, has a worse reputation for the administration of performance-enhancing substances. 'Last year I got to know an American lad. He was twenty-five and had come to Italy to try out for one of the top amateur teams. They said, "OK, but we need to have a chat with you. We've got one spot. We've got our doping programme, how far are you willing to go?" He said he wouldn't do anything. He was clean, he wanted to say clean. They asked him again the next week. He still refused. In the end he had to give up his spot on the team – and his dream. He knew he couldn't have lived with himself. Same with me. Everything I achieve is because I'm the best on the day not because I've had help from any doctor. It's depressing that the pinnacle of my sport appears to be so riddled with drugs, but at least in women's cycling, there's such awful prize money we're not motivated by money.'

Many think the Tour de France is hugely corrupted, almost destroyed, by the taint of drugs. 'It is,' agreed Cooke. 'The biggest problem is that ex-riders stay in the sport. They become the new directors of the next generation of riders. The habits continue.' Cooke had little sympathy for the British time-trial world champion, David Millar, who was sacked by his racing team after admitting taking the blood-booster EPO in 2001 and 2003. 'I can't believe the world governing body haven't asked him for his gold medal and his jersey back. I think that is disgraceful. It shows the governing body aren't really taking it seriously. It's like condoning it. Maybe they know an overhaul of their anti-doping policy will kill the sport, but people don't want to see cheats. People don't want to see fake competition. They need to make the punishments a lot harder. Whole teams should be suspended for at least six months. They should pay one huge hell of a fine.'

Never mind competing in the Olympics. This girl should be running them in twenty years. She is capable of more unflinching sense at the age of twenty-one than most of our administrators have managed together in the past twenty-one years. As for the distractions of youth, the ones that get our footballers locked up, written up or divorced at depressingly regular intervals, she seems impervious to them. 'Cycling's a good sport because my training partners have to be young lads. That's quite a plus. So I mix with quite a lot of lads, but I have never met one who's really taken my fancy. I know how much time I've got to give to cycling. If I had a boyfriend, I don't think it would work. But there's plenty of time. It's not like I'm coming to the end of the line.'

Far from it. Cooke is pedalling up to the start line in terms of global attention. But neither fame nor money are her goals.

'I love the sport because it's an expression of my own natural power. That's what drives the machine, that's what makes me go so fast, makes me climb that hill. It feels like flying sometimes. And it's such a sense of achievement. If I was driving a Ferrari I'd get some type of pleasure but it wouldn't be the same. It wouldn't be generated by me.' Meanwhile, she owns a Volkswagen Beetle. Driving a Ferrari isn't quite an option. Yet.

Sporting Champion: Nicole Cooke – 1 World Road Race Championship (2008); 1 Olympic Games (2008); 1 Commonwealth Games (2002).

EUROPE – RYDER CUP

THIS WAS NEVER-SAY-DIE SPIRIT AT ITS GREATEST
Paul Hayward, 2 October 2012

They said they had 'belief', but nobody took it seriously. They claimed they had 'momentum' from a Saturday evening flourish, but it looked like whistling past the graveyard. The source of all Ryder Cup drama, though, is pressure: entertainment's cruel little brother. The United States lost golf's most gripping competition because they had already won it. So often in sport we see the presumption of victory open a gap through which a determined opposition can still stampede. Perhaps the finest example in recent times was Liverpool's victory in the 2005 Champions League final after being 3–0 down at half-time.

The sense around the Medinah Country Club early on the last morning was that Europe would be dispatched without fuss: especially after Rory McIlroy, the world number one, confused

Central and Eastern time and required a state trooper to flash him through the traffic to make his tee time. The sight of Europe's best player being delivered to Medinah in an Illinois police car sharpened the quills of those expecting to write condemnatory reviews of José María Olazábal's captaincy. At the back of the first tee at the start of a miraculous day of golf, Pep Guardiola, the former Barcelona football coach now on sabbatical, revved up the crowd and jabbered to his wife and young children. Lionel Messi's former manager hugged Olazábal and Miguel Ángel Jiménez, one of Europe's vice-captains. Nice. But surely Guardiola's enthusiasm would be a mere footnote to a humiliating day. McIlroy had been ten minutes away from sinking the whole European effort. A no-show would have brought disqualification, ignominy and an American victory.

Yet there was a strange energy around that patch of grass, with its competing galleries of boisterous fans. Up ahead, Ian Poulter had recorded his sixth consecutive birdie at the first hole, following his five at the end of the fourball the previous day. That victory had sparked a European party. Players, assistants, families and fans joined in spontaneous rejoicing as Poulter and McIlroy pulled the score back to 10–6 heading into the singles. In the stands I turned to a colleague and said: 'You'd think they'd won this Ryder Cup.' The trophy, regained by Europe in the quagmire of Wales' Celtic Manor, would not pass quietly to Captain Love, to the wild-eyed rookie, Keegan Bradley, to the rabble-rousing Bubba Watson. This much was obvious. Before the greatest comeback in Ryder Cup history commenced there was a late-night team meeting, inevitably, in which the spirit of Seve Ballesteros was invoked and the mantra of 'belief' recited by Olazábal. Oh, sure. What else is there for a beaten team to do than summon the old standby of defiance? Olazábal's men, though, were not trading hollow slogans. 'There was something in that team room which ignited everybody, and it was inspirational, just to see everybody's personalities change and the atmosphere change in that room,' said Poulter, the new monarch of Ryder Cup golf. 'And I knew there was a glimmer of hope.'

Sergio García and Paul Lawrie were there at Brookline in 1999 when the United States overturned the same 10–6 deficit. They knew it was possible and they remember how it felt to enter the singles matches in such a commanding position. García could hear the echo as Europe's five-man hit squad set out to snatch the first five matches and stun the Americans. Luke Donald beat the Masters champion, Watson, in match one. Poulter won the last two holes to flatten the US Open champion, Webb Simpson. McIlroy ended the unbeaten run of Bradley. Justin Rose took the last two holes to see off Phil Mickelson. Paul Lawrie destroyed Brandt Snedeker with a 50-foot birdie and an eagle.

Lawrie's return from the wilderness to Ryder Cup assassin was another compelling storyline. 'Some of us were there in 1999 and we knew we needed to put the American team in a situation where we could see how they felt with a bit more pressure on,' García said. 'Obviously everything was going their way throughout the whole week. You know, they were making the putts, they were getting the good breaks here and there. We were just waiting to change that a little bit and see if we could do the same thing they did to us in '99 and see how they could react to that. Obviously a lot of the matches were won because some of my team-mates played amazing; and in some others we took the possibility or the opening that they gave us. I have been in that position, Lee [Westwood] has been in that position, José has been in that position. We know how it feels, and it's not easy. We wanted to see how they would react and see if they could hold it. It was a combination of playing great and maybe then that little bit of pressure getting to them.' Olazábal knew all right. He had watched from the seventeenth green in Massachusetts as Justin Leonard rolled in a 45-foot birdie putt. The 'Miracle at Brookline' was sealed when Olazábal missed his own birdie putt. Ryder Cup golf is unlikely to script a finer example of redemption, or revenge, if you prefer. As a contest, the Ryder Cup is on a golden run of European domination, to which America now need to respond.

Across the gamut of this Ryder Cup, however, Lawrie was made to look a boy again, by his own brilliance; Jim Furyk was cast as a broken man, hands on knees; Tiger Woods lost the last of his credibility as a Ryder Cup contestant; Nicolas Colsaerts made a name for himself on day one as a genius putter; Rose (three points) came of age as matchplay aristocracy; and Martin Kaymer sank the winning putt to alleviate the stress of his mediocre strokeplay form. If one European's eyes sparkled with the light of revelation, it was Colsaerts, who shot eight birdies and an eagle on the opening day in the best round by a Ryder Cup rookie. 'Undescribable [sic],' he said. 'When I was given a chance to be part of this experience I never thought it was going to be this intense. I've had so many dreams about being part of experiences like these, but this has just been mind-blowing since the practice rounds on day one. Hanging out with all these guys, discovering all different personalities, and seeing them deliver on a day of the highest pressure like this in front of the whole world, is, like I said, it's just undescribable.' With four wins from four outings, punkish, proud Poulter was Ballesteros's representative on the field, while Olazábal is the spiritual guardian of his legacy. The star of this amazing Chicago show, Poulter found the heart of it. 'This Ryder Cup,' he said, 'is not for the faint of heart.'

Sporting Champions: Europe – 10 Ryder Cups (1985, 1987, 1989 – shared, 1995, 1997, 2002, 2004, 2006, 2010, 2012).

OCTOBER

BETH TWEDDLE – WORLD GYMNASTICS CHAMPIONSHIPS

TWEDDLE POISED TO SOAR

Sarah Edworthy, 21 July 2004

As a child, Beth Tweddle was such a whirlwind of energy her parents sought to channel it away from domestic confines. 'I was always charging around the house, jumping on beds, climbing up walls, swinging on the banisters,' she laughs. 'We were originally a hockey family so I was brought up with that, but I didn't take to it. I tried ballet – but that was too girly girly, I was more of a tomboy – then swimming. I also tried gymnastics and straight away the coach picked me out.' She was seven. Two years later she was ranked second in the country in her age group. That was it. No more rattling the foundations of the family home in Cheshire: Tweddle embarked on the training schedule of an elite athlete, first at Crewe and Nantwich Gym Club (three hours a day after school) before moving at the age of twelve to the City of Liverpool Gym Club in Toxteth (4.30 to 8.30 p.m. every day after school, plus two extra 1 to 4 p.m. weekday afternoons, 9.30 to 4 p.m. on Saturdays and 9.30 to 2 p.m. on Sundays). At fifteen she was Commonwealth Games youth champion. Since 2001 she has been British national all-round champion. Recently she has emerged as a strong European rival on the asymmetric bars for Svetlana Khorkina, the queen of international gymnastics. After years of expending energy on warm-up mats, floor, beam, vault and the bars, at nineteen, Tweddle is ready for the Olympic Games.

Romanians, Ukrainians, Russians, Belarussians, Americans and Chinese have long dominated the world of somersaults and twists, leotards, chalk dust and high pony-tails, but Tweddle is the first British female in modern times who has a genuine chance of a gymnastics medal. Her bronze on the asymmetric bars at the 2003 World Championships placed her firmly on the list of potential individual apparatus champions. As her coach, Amanda Kirby, said: 'On that piece of apparatus, if you're good, it stands out. Beth was always going to be a bars specialist. She can flow very well.' Kirby maintained Tweddle's sense of purpose made her stand out. 'As soon as she walked through the door, I could see she was determined. She would always make sure you were watching her. When she was younger, she appeared nervous in competitions only because she was almost too desperate to do well. She's become more confident as she's got older. She's ready.'

Tweddle displays a phenomenal perfectionist streak. She insists on a handguard manufactured by one company for her right hand and one from a different company for her left because the difference in the stiffness of the leather feels 'right' for her grip on the bars. She uses a video camera with instant playback to tidy up technique. She grew up not wanting to emulate anyone, but it is no surprise the gymnast she does mention – Lilia Podkopayeva – was uncompromising, too. She won the all-round title at Atlanta in 1996, boosted by a 9.887 score earned for a floor routine that had been choreographed by prima ballerina Svetlana Dubova. 'I am a perfectionist,' Tweddle agreed. 'If I get frustrated with something, Amanda can tell and she'll say, "Leave it", but I won't walk out through that door until I've done what she'd first told me to do. And I won't just do it – the other girls will say, "That was good", and I'll say, "But not good enough", and keep wanting to do it better. At home, I can't leave my room unless it's tidy. And when I was doing my homework I had to have everything neat and precise.'

With a place to study sports science at the Liverpool John Moores University, homework was obviously very neat and precise. How did she manage to fit it in? 'My schedule made me disciplined,' she said. 'My brother had all night to do his homework. He'd get home at five, or whatever, didn't start it until eight, whereas I'd get home at 9.30 knowing I had to do it before I went to bed, so I used to walk in, get my books out on the table and do it while I was eating my tea. It didn't seem strange – it's how I grew up.'

A number of injuries and setbacks punctuated her teenage years, any one of which a less doughty character would have turned into a full stop. Not Tweddle. She interprets a broken left ankle six years ago as a motivating factor. 'Most people tend to stop at the age of thirteen or fourteen and think about retiring to have a social life, or whatever, but I had a serious injury at that age. People said, "Don't you think you ought to retire?" but my reaction was to turn around and say, "I can get back from anything". I'm quite stubborn.' The ankle was an ongoing concern. Pins, inserted to help recovery, had to be removed. 'As I stretch it more, little bits of bone flake off so I have to go and get them taken out. I've struggled with the pain.' When it comes to Athens, Tweddle will be doing her usual routine – just sharper, tighter, faster – as if she were in the gym. 'I really try not to go to sleep thinking about it, but, of course, I do. I'm not imagining myself at the Olympics, just working out how I can do it better in the gym to make it better for performing out there.'

Sporting Champion: Beth Tweddle – 3 World Championships (2006, 2009, 2010); 6 European Championships (2006, 2009 – 2, 2010 – 2, 2011); 1 Commonwealth Games (2002).

NEW YORK YANKEES – WORLD SERIES BASEBALL

YANKEES CLASS OF '98 REOPEN 'GREAT' DEBATE

David Mankelow, 23 October 1998

Even in baseball, a sport in which just about everything that happens on the field can be crunched into a statistic, arguments rage as to who are the greatest team of all time. Brooklyn's 'Boys of Summer' of the 1940s, baseball's first racially integrated club, and Cincinnati's 'Big Red Machine' of the 1970s would both have their backers, but the discussion invariably narrows down to one of the teams to have sported the pinstripes and navy blue cap with the white interlocking N and Y of the New York Yankees.

The Yankees team who won five consecutive World Series from 1949 to 1953 in the twilight of the great Joe DiMaggio's career, and the 1961 team, with Roger Maris hitting sixty-one home runs and Mickey Mantle adding fifty-four, have their supporters, but undoubtedly most votes would go to the 1927 team. They won 110 games in the regular season and four more in the World Series to sweep aside Pittsburgh, with Babe Ruth clobbering sixty home runs, more than any other team, let alone individual, in the American League.

But now there is a new contender to be judged the greatest: the 1998 Yankees, who capped a remarkable season in which they won a record 125 games by brushing aside the San Diego Padres 3–0 to take the best-of-seven World Series in four games. It was the Yankees' second success in three years. However, this Yankees team are a vastly different proposition to the legendary 'Bronx Bombers' of the past who crushed the opposition with home runs and then spent the night on Broadway celebrating. The 1998 team are more inclined to hold clubhouse prayer meetings and dedicate their victories to sick colleagues, like Darryl Strawberry, who has colon cancer and whose number, thirty-nine, was stitched on to all the Yankees players' caps. And, in the year of the home run, when Mark McGwire, of St Louis, hit seventy to shatter the single-season record set by Maris, the most homers any current Yankee could manage was twenty-eight by Tino Martinez.

Yet there are more ways than one to win games and the Yankees showed how in Game Four as they scratched out three runs against the outstanding Padres pitcher, Kevin Brown. After five innings without a run, the Yankees finally got on the scoreboard when Derek Jeter, their nearest thing to a superstar, reached first base with a single that never left the infield. Paul O'Neill's two-base hit advanced Jeter to third base and he dashed home in the time it took for a chopped hit from Bernie Williams to reach a Padre fielder's glove. The Yankees added two 'insurance' runs in the eighth inning and again it was Jeter who got things going with a walk. O'Neill, whose anonymity is such that his sister Mollie – a cookery writer – is more famous in New York than he is, followed with another infield single. Both runners moved along when Williams bounced yet another of Brown's sinking deliveries into the clay infield and both scored after successive hits from Scott Brosius and Rick Ledee. Meanwhile, Yankees pitcher Andy Pettitte limited the San Diego line-up to five hits with a succession of curving deliveries and, when he finally tired, Mariano Rivera came in to preserve the shut-out. The game ended with Brosius, voted Most Valuable Player of the Series for his two home runs in Game Three, diving to field a well-struck hit and throwing to first base to retire Mark Sweeney and clinch the Yankees' twenty-fourth world championship.

The greatest ever? The Yankees manager, Joe Torre, whose deep-sunk eyes and five o'clock shadow conceal one of the sharpest minds in baseball, was loath to make comparisons, but said: 'It's the best team I've been around in forty years. The Yankees are baseball. Even if you're not a sports fan you know who the Yankees are. The 1927 Yankees may be a better team, but we won more games. We take a back seat to no one in my lifetime.' David Cone, one of the Yankees' gutsy pitchers, summed up: 'Maybe we're not the greatest but at least we're in the argument, and that's a pretty good place to be.'

Sporting Champions: New York Yankees – 27 World Series (1923, 1927, 1928, 1932, 1936, 1937, 1938, 1939, 1941, 1943, 1947, 1949, 1950, 1951, 1952, 1953, 1956, 1958, 1961, 1962, 1977, 1978, 1996, 1998, 1999, 2000, 2009).

MUHAMMAD ALI – WORLD HEAVYWEIGHT BOXING CHAMPIONSHIP

ALI'S ARTISTRY AND POWER CRUSHES 'BEWILDERED BEAR'

Donald Saunders, 1 November 1974

If anyone has $10 million he would like to invest in a worthy cause he should get in touch with Muhammad Ali, now restored to his rightful place as king of all the heavyweights after six frustrating years among the commoners. After climbing back on to the throne when George Foreman's brief reign came to a spectacular end in the eighth round at the 20 May Stadium in Kinshasa, Ali let it be known he was prepared to listen to offers of that magnitude for a contest with Joe Frazier, the only man to beat him in a championship bout. Henry Schwartz, of Video Techniques, who were heavily involved in staging Africa's first heavyweight title fight, called that figure 'ridiculous'. Schwartz, probably, will not be the only prospective promoter to hold that view, since $10 million is twice the purse received by each boxer for the contest here. Even so, somewhere not far short of that total could be the starting point for negotiations.

The sweet truth is that Ali is no ordinary heavyweight champion. Most of the world is now coming round to his long-held view that he is the greatest of them all. That is why he will almost certainly abandon pre-fight plans to retire. Though his wife, Belinda, may suggest when they reach their Chicago home that, at thirty-two, it is time to quit a young man's sport, the new champion is unlikely to say farewell without making at least one defence. This remarkable man's pride would not allow him to leave the stage he loves so dearly until he has enjoyed again the champion's privilege of entering the ring last in a title fight and leaving it with the crown still firmly on his head. For the moment he is confining himself to the promise: 'I will be around to haunt the heavyweights for six months, then will decide.' Let us hope his answer will be: 'Yes, I am staying.'

Ali is not just a superb athlete. He is a symbol of hope to millions of less privileged and less gifted members of his race. Surely no one else from any sport, with the possible exception of Pelé, could bring a city to the fever of excitement he inspired in Kinshasa – and at day break at that. I refer not only to the well-heeled ringsiders and their poorer relations out on the bleachers. News of Ali's great victory spread like wildfire to the modest homes of citizens who can only hope the future will be brighter than the past has been. As those who had been privileged to watch the champion demonstrate his magic drove home through the grey dawn, barefoot boys and girls, nursing mothers and off-to-work fathers lined the new champion's expected triumphal route to the city in their thousands, chanting, not mindlessly, but with joyful relief, 'Ali, Ali, Ali'. In these days when so much of sport is a business planned to obtain the maximum money from the public for the minimum return, that was a scene well worth travelling to Africa to see.

So was Ali's victory. I have been present at more than my fair share of great sporting occasions and am satisfied that this one will remain at the top of the list for a long, long time. Of his dozen high-standard championship performances over the past ten years, this was easily the most accomplished. We saw not the arrogant dancing master indulging himself, but the dedicated artist producing a boxing masterpiece. Ali stripped the massive Foreman of his frightening power by refusing to follow the expected path to the inevitable slaughter. Instead of running away until his legs were drained of stamina, he backed slowly on to the ropes or into corners, smothering, spoiling, slipping or simply absorbing the champion's heaviest punches and countering with jolting accuracy and bewildering speed.

Poor Foreman, whose mind worked as ploddingly as his feet and hands moved, just could not understand what was happening. Though, initially, he thumped away to the body with the clubbing blows that had destroyed Joe Frazier, Joe Roman and Ken Norton inside fifteen minutes, this opponent would not crumble at his feet. When he tried to reach Ali's jaw he usually made contact only with gloves, forearms or, to his even greater embarrassment, thin air. True, there were moments in the second and fifth rounds when many ringsiders thought Foreman's strength and power would crush an ageing challenger who did not have the speed to escape. By the sixth, we knew Ali was neither trying nor wishing to escape. Minute by minute it became clear that the battle was being conducted the way he dictated.

As the points gap between them widened and Foreman's face began to swell, his will to pursue a rugged course of action showed signs of faltering. So, through the seventh and into the eighth it continued, with Ali, tying up his cumbersome opponent at close quarters, forcing the champion's head down with both gloves, hurting him with flashing jabs and hooks and all the time taunting him with the sharpest tongue in boxing history. Then Ali let loose a decisive barrage of short punches, finishing with a right that sent Foreman sprawling to the blue canvas like an exhausted, utterly bewildered bear. The fallen champion lay on his back, his right knee bent, trying desperately to gather this senses. At six he stared pleadingly at his corner, at eight Dick Sadler signalled him urgently to rise, and at 'out' he was still struggling upwards. One or two champions of the past might have beaten the count and gone on to meet painful defeat. Foreman could only explain that he had never been knocked down before and did not know what he was doing.

So, soon, Ali was fighting off hysterical fans inside the ropes and rolling helplessly in the dust of the canvas until his handlers and riot police brought much-needed aid. Then, with peace restored, the new champion of the world left the ring for the bedlam of the dressing room, where honour was duly paid him by those who had doubted his ability to become the second heavyweight to regain the title. Floyd Patterson shares that distinction, but little else, with the man whom I am more than happy to call the greatest heavyweight of my time.

Sporting Champion: Muhammad Ali – World Heavyweight Championship (1964–67, 1974–78); 1 Olympic Games (1960).

NOVEMBER

TONY McCOY – NATIONAL HUNT JOCKEYS' CHAMPIONSHIP

I'M NO GENIUS, I'M JUST DOING WHAT I LOVE TO DO

Tony McCoy, 8 November 2013

At last I have got to the stage where I am happy with what I have done. Riding 4,000 winners is the one achievement in my life I am proud of but, to be honest, I felt quite humble that so many people came to Towcester to be part of the day. Most days I leave for work in the morning like any other father and husband. I leave my family at home, but having them all here, my wife Chanelle, daughter Evie, son Archie Peadar, the 'real A.P.', my father Peadar and brother Colm, has truly made it one of the best days of my career. Evie is the person who cheers me up after a bad day at the races because it does not make any difference to her day, although now, aged six, she is more aware of what constitutes a good or bad day for me. At only a few months Archie can now assume the role of Daddy's happy-maker. As long as I read him a story that is all that matters to him, not whether I have had a winner. Evie cancelled her sixth birthday party to come and did not want to cancel it for no good reason. Part of her was wanting a few more days off school following me around but there are limits.

I could never have ridden 4,000 winners without loving my job and if I ever get to the point where I am not loving it, I will stop.

But, at this rate, someone might have to tell me when to stop. I hope I will be sensible enough to quit on my own terms, but my biggest problem is that I enjoy it too much. If I was ever granted one wish it would be to come back as another person and be able to start this all over again.

Of course there have been low points. The lowest was probably when jockey Richard Davis died after a fall at Southwell. I was a conditional with him, rode in the race and can remember getting the call as if it was yesterday – I just burst into tears. There have been others since and the last two weekends I have been to see J.T. McNamara in hospital. He was a big part of the team run by my boss, J.P. McManus, and his life-changing fall at Cheltenham affected us all. When I go out there to ride I just take the view that if I fall I will get up again – until I am in an ambulance on morphine. I am not so tough then. Then when horses get killed it can hit you hard. The loss of Synchronised, Gloria Victis, Darlan and Valiramix each left me numb for days.

I am always relieved to win and the race here at Towcester might not have been the biggest, richest or best I have ever won, but it was fantastic how it happened; riding a horse in the gold and green silks of J.P. that is trained by Jonjo O'Neill. Doing that means as much to me as the actual number and, not that you can stage-manage these things, I was determined that it was the way it should happen. I was also very pleased my agent, Dave Roberts, could come and he was the first person to greet me on the course, as he was when I got to 3,000 at Plumpton. He booked me on every one of those 4,000 winners and has been a huge part of my career. His father died the day before and he must have been looking down on me. I remember watching Adrian Maguire ride five winners in a day at Plumpton when I was starting out and I turned to Dave and said: 'I want that.' I hope I have not let him down. We had a great celebration back in Marlborough and

I was very impressed to see Graham Lee, who had come all the way down from Wolverhampton, where he had been riding in the 7.20.

I know the win was going to happen at some stage, but I thought the race had got away from us at the third-last. Sometimes, 4,000 winners or not, you have do what is right by the horse and I wanted him to finish his race well. It was not the best ride I have ever given a horse, but he ended up making me look good. He was a bit inexperienced, there were a few more people than at the point-to-point he won in the Irish countryside, and all this was a bit new to him. I never for a moment felt any pressure or thought about the crowd or family watching. Until five strides before the winning post, it was just a normal race at Towcester. Then it hit me.

Really racing is about the horses, not me. You cannot do it without the horses and they are the big players, as are the lads who look after them, and they rarely get a mention. They are fantastic animals and most people come to see them not us. I am very lucky to have spent my life with them. Someone was saying I was also the most experienced jump jockey ever because I have had the most rides. But never a day goes past when I do not learn something new and the person who reckons any different is wrong. There is no place for arrogance or complacency in racing because you are up there one minute and on your backside the next. I feel like I am one of the lads in the weighing room and, I hope, they feel the same about me. It is a tough game and longevity needs a lot of luck. The sportsmen I admire are the ones who have stayed at the top for a long time. In racing it is Lester Piggott and Vincent O'Brien, who were global icons. I am not. Do not compare me to them. I am just a normal mortal ploughing a few fields round the countryside. They were geniuses.

Essentially I am a dreamer. I have been dreaming all my life.

When I started I dreamt I would be champion because it is a sport that is all about the people who win the most and I have a fear of not winning. You need targets in life and, luckily, I have a few left.

Sporting Champion: Tony McCoy – 19 National Hunt Jockeys' Championships (1995–96, 1996–97, 1997–98, 1998–99, 1999–2000, 2000–01, 2001–02, 2002–03, 2003–04, 2004–05, 2005–06, 2006–07, 2007–08, 2008–09, 2009–10, 2010–11, 2011–12, 2012–13, 2013–14); 1 National Hunt Conditional Jockeys' Championship (1994–95).

JOE CALZAGHE – WORLD SUPER-MIDDLEWEIGHT BOXING CHAMPIONSHIP
CALZAGHE WINS HIS MOMENT AS KING OF THE CITY
Kevin Garside, 10 November 2008

There he stood, tape across the bridge of his nose, mouth a little swollen, addressing a post-fight conference in a cavernous anti-chamber beneath Madison Square Garden. Joe Calzaghe had waited an awful long time to feel as good as this. Before him the elite corps of American boxing writers who had cast him barely a glance during his ten undefeated years as world super-middleweight champion. But now they had come to pay their respects. One suggested Calzaghe might make boxer of the year. That would be an honour, he said.

It is not that you go down but how you get up, is how Calzaghe began his speech. Let that be the epitaph on one of British boxing's finest careers. Calzaghe silenced New York. By the close an American audience, drunk on the motif of the moment, 'Yes we can', understood that Barack Obama's winning words had no application for their man, a boxer whose time had long since passed. As beautifully as Calzaghe performed – better than ever, according to his father – there was little joy in the sight of a bloodied Roy Jones Junior shuffling into a blizzard of Welsh leather. This was car-crash boxing. For three rounds we had a fight. By the fourth Jones was spent. Thereafter, intensity drained from the contest; Jones rendered a human carcass by the terrible superiority of Calzaghe. Jones's obvious decline does not diminish Calzaghe's achievement in the round. His gift, his courage, his substance deserved a night like this. America, always suspicious of records built on foreign soil, finally got to see Calzaghe as we always had, as a gold-standard boxer made in Britain.

A crowd numbering fourteen thousand-plus had a hefty British profile; they were not hard to spot: young men drowning in aftershave supported by women tottering on high-street heels. West 33rd Street had acquired the aroma of Cardiff on a Saturday night. It was not always thus. So much of Calzaghe's career has unfolded unseen by a mainstream audience. Terrestrial television viewers who a generation ago forged attachments to the likes of Henry Cooper, Ken Buchanan, Charlie Magri, Barry McGuigan, Chris Eubank, Frank Bruno and Nigel Benn have been denied emotional access to Calzaghe, whose sporting narrative has been woven on subscription channels. This has led to a recognition deficit. Praise has come late in his career, evidenced by his Sports Personality of the Year Award fourteen years after he threw his first punch as a professional. But too few people were exposed to Calzaghe when it mattered. There are some influential voices in British boxing who would not have Calzaghe in their domestic top ten. Others, like McGuigan, argue that he is the best boxer we have produced. Ten years a world champion, forty-six wins and no defeats, is a powerful counter.

As well as the issue of visibility, Calzaghe has been hurt by a lack of critical mass when he was at his peak. There were simply too many Tocker Pudwills and Will 'Kid Fire' McIntyres in the ring with him when he should have been trading with Bernard Hopkins and Jones at their peaks. There were electric nights, too, not least those against Eubank, against whom he won his first world title, and Robin Reid, against whom he dug deepest to retain it. That quality was again in evidence in New York. Bert Sugar, the cigar-toting high priest of Limey-bashing, was animated to the point of seizure in the press seats as Calzaghe picked himself off the carpet in the first round to unleash his awesome fury. Until Jones connected with a left-right combination from his past, Calzaghe was winning the first round, as he would the eleven that followed.

Over he went, just as he had done on his American debut against Hopkins five months earlier. And, reprising the funda-mental elements of that Las Vegas night, up he got, visceral juices pumping. It was the fourth time he had been down in forty-six fights. The experience triggered the caveman in Calzaghe. His fists became clubs, fed by a primal heart-pumping pure adrenalin. It was the best and the worst of starts for Jones. He returned to the corner at the sound of the bell a pugilistic Eric Cantona, chin up, chest out. I'm the man. Lumping Calzaghe on his backside as he did enhanced Jones's fairytale thinking when the reality was something brutally different. The truth of that would be tattooed in blood across Madison Square Garden. Calzaghe came out for the second round reconstituted, punches falling on Jones. The American's response was to cock that chin high, shake his head, stick Calzaghe with rogue single punches and return to the corner gesturing: you ain't hurt me, baby. But he had.

The third round was the best of the night, pure rock 'n' roll. Jones tried to keep up with Calzaghe, threw punches in clusters, offered his chin provocatively with hands by his sides. The action detonated the crowd; 14,000 people were out of their seats.

Calzaghe was loving it. This was the kind of night he had longed for, a big house responding to him under the same roof where Muhammad Ali fought Joe Frazier. The bout would last a further nine rounds, but the fight was over. Before the final bell tolled for their man, Jones's supporters were filing into the New York night, leaving him, the lid of his left eye gaping, to negotiate his own end. We hope that Jones is not seen in a ring again. His day was over four years ago when first Antonio Tarver and then Glen Johnson routed the myth. Calzaghe, considering his own future after a victory that told us little we did not already know, should take heed. Go now, as the king of New York, not on your knees, humbled by a younger man.

Sporting Champion: Joe Calzaghe – World Super-Middleweight Championship (1997–2008 – undefeated).

COLIN McRAE – RALLY GB

THE CHANCER WHO TOOK ON THE WORLD

Derick Allsop, 16 September 2007

The statue of William Wallace gazes down on the town of Lanark from the steeple of St Nicholas's Church, but Colin Steele McRae was the Braveheart of modern times. McRae wasn't just a rally driver, he wasn't just a world champion. He stirred the emotions as few sportsmen have done. He was a chancer, but then that was precisely what made him an irresistible hero.

He was the youngest world rally champion when he won the title in 1995, at the age of twenty-seven, and the only frustration for him and his followers was that he never became champion again. But therein lay the allure of the man. It wasn't championships or even rally wins that made him the icon he was. It was that spectacular, seat of the pants, and, yes, risk-taking style that set him apart from the rest. At his peak he was acknowledged as the fastest man in rallying, and he brought a buzz and sense of expectation to his home event, the RAC Rally, now Rally GB, comparable to Mansell-mania on the track.

McRae was born to compete. His father, Jimmy, was five times British rally champion. Colin's younger brother, Alister, also became an international-class rally driver. But the real star of the family was Colin. He never missed an opportunity to try his hand on his dad's motorbikes, and as a young teenager explored the limits of a mini around the old mineshafts near his home in Lanark. He had his first rally in 1985, at the wheel of an Avenger, borrowed from a friend, and although he flew off into a peat bog, he managed to continue and went all the way to the pinnacle of his sport. He paid £850 for his own first rally car, a Sunbeam. He entered the British Championship in 1989 and had his first experience of world championship competition, driving a Ford Sierra, the same year. He also made his debut on the RAC Rally.

His frequent excursions earned him the nickname 'McCrash', but he reasoned that he could harness his natural speed once he'd found the limit of his, and his car's, capabilities. He was signed up by Subaru and became the youngest British champion in 1991. He kept the title in 1992 and the following year became a full-time world championship driver. His first win came in New Zealand that same year, and also in 1993 he became the first British driver since Roger Clark, in 1976, to win the RAC Rally.

In 1995 he won an intense and sometimes controversial duel with his Subaru team-mate, Spain's Carlos Sainz, to become champion, clinching the title on home ground. He went close again, both with Subaru and Ford, but was thwarted by a combination of unreliable machinery and his own fallibility. In 2000, that fabled bravado almost cost him his life. He went off the road in Corsica and was suspended, upside down, in a ravine. According to his physio, he was within fifteen minutes of death. McRae admitted that was his greatest escape, but his appetite for the challenge was undiminished. The following year the championship was again within his grasp, but McRae couldn't resist the prospect of finishing the job with a flourish, and instead crashed out at Rally GB. His demise effectively handed the title to his English rival, Richard Burns. McRae often taunted Burns, insisting he took the cautious, boring approach. McRae was ever the cavalier. When he had a few beers, McRae would ring Burns and tell him the Englishman knew he loved him really.

McRae wasn't always known for his humour, and often he could be awkward and uncooperative in public. But those close to him saw that other side, the lad from Lanark who just wanted to have fun. He still believed he could cut it at the top, but admitted that, at the age of thirty-nine, it had to be next year or never. He was preparing for another Dakar Rally in the new year, yet he would have loved one last chance in the World Championship. His hordes of fans would have loved that, too. Instead, they have the memories.

Sporting Champion: Colin McRae – 1 World Rally Championship (1995); 2 British Rally Championships (1991, 1992).

MICHAEL SCHUMACHER – FORMULA ONE DRIVERS' CHAMPIONSHIP

ALL THIS PRAISE IS OVERDUE – I PRAY HE GETS TO HEAR IT

David Coulthard, 31 December 2013

The outpouring of concern for Michael Schumacher's well-being, not only from the world of Formula One but from the wider sporting, and indeed non-sporting, community has been wonderful to see. In my opinion it constitutes long overdue recognition of Michael's status as a true sporting great. I only hope and pray that he pulls through to see what nice things people have been saying about him. The truth is I do not believe that Michael has ever truly received the praise or recognition that his stunning achievements merited. And I say that now with the benefit of hindsight.

For years Michael was the perfect pantomime villain, particularly in this country: German, of course, ruthlessly efficient, ultra-aggressive. Whereas previous greats such as Sir Jackie Stewart or Juan Manuel Fangio left the door open to their rivals when racing, for fear of making what could easily have been fatal contact, Michael went all out in his pursuit of victory. Sometimes he overstepped the mark – Jerez in 1997 and Rascasse in 2006 spring to mind – and those indiscretions made him unpalatable to the sporting purist. He was marked down by some, including me, as a tainted champion. But you cannot argue with his achievements. At the end of the day he had the same rules and the same race marshals as the rest of us. And he destroyed us.

He could be infuriating. I had numerous run-ins with Michael, most famously at Spa in 1998 after we collided on a wet track and he stormed over to the McLaren garage and accused me of trying to kill him. I asked him later, in exasperation, whether he had ever been wrong about anything at any point in his life. 'Not that I can remember,' he replied. To me that summed him up. He had complete and utter self-belief. It was what made him a champion.

And what a champion: ninety-one grand prix victories and seven drivers' world titles. I can say now, and again it is with the benefit of hindsight, that I was never on his level. You cannot admit that, even to yourself, during your career because you need to have self-belief, but I have no trouble admitting it now. Michael was the reference point for me. I can see that now. If I beat him to a win or a podium, I knew I had done a very good job. He gave my career credibility.

As I said, we did not always see eye to eye but there were two sides to Michael. He was a ruthless competitor, but at the same time he was a family man, generous, kind. If you were part of his trusted circle then he was loyal. If you were not, he could cut you off completely. I never knew exactly which camp I belonged to but our shared relationship with Mercedes-Benz meant that we were thrown together regularly. I can vividly recall being invited to Michael's private parties after the German Grand Prix and staying up smoking cigars with him, late at night after a few drinks, talking about just how lucky we were to be doing what we loved.

There was always that underlying respect. When Michael retired at the end of 2006 he approached me and suggested we swap helmets. It had never even occurred to me to ask him. Why would he have wanted my helmet? But he knew that I collected them and I was honoured that he offered me his. It remains one of my prized possessions and I know he keeps mine at his home in Switzerland.

I think Michael might have got more credit before now had he not burnt his bridges so completely with the British media, to whom he was completely closed, at least during his first career.

I think Sebastian Vettel may have learnt from that experience. In any case, Michael's comeback with Mercedes showed he had a more human side. And in a funny way, it cemented his legacy rather than harmed it. Watching him struggle to match Sebastian and Lewis Hamilton and Fernando Alonso, not always through fault of his own, proved that time waits for no man. It was too easy during his first career to assume that he simply swept all before him. Those struggles with Mercedes gave us, certainly me, a newfound appreciation for the unbelievable levels of consistency he achieved in his first career.

This skiing crash has connected Michael to the rest of us on a human level once and for all. Here is a father, like any other, his wife and children at his bedside praying for him to pull through. It is something to which we can all relate. The awful thing is that so often it takes something like this before we say what we truly feel about someone. I hope that in this instance, Michael is going to emerge victorious once again. And when he does he is going to realise in what esteem he is held.

Sporting Champion: Michael Schumacher – 7 Formula One World Championships (1994, 1995, 2000, 2001, 2002, 2003, 2004).

SEBASTIAN VETTEL – FORMULA ONE DRIVERS' CHAMPIONSHIP

WELCOME TO KERPEN, BIRTHPLACE OF A CHAMPION

Tom Cary, 8 October 2011

To the wider world there is nothing remarkable about Kerpen; a small and not particularly attractive town in former mining country roughly 18 miles west of Cologne where the land runs flat towards the Belgian border. Yet in motorsport, and particularly Formula One, the place is a byword for excellence, known to every petrolhead with a pulse. Michael Schumacher, born a stone's throw away in Hürth-Hermülheim, was a junior champion at the celebrated Graf Berghe von Trips kart track at the age of six. We all know what he went on to achieve. Now another graduate of the Kerpen kart club is a multiple Formula One title winner.

Sebastian Vettel may hail from Heppenheim, 125 miles further south, but Kerpen is where he started racing as an eight-year-old in 1995. Kerpen is where Red Bull's blond-haired, blue-eyed *wunderkind* first made a name for himself, both on and off the track, hanging around the charmingly rustic paddock 'pestering' his hero Schumacher for an autograph. Perhaps most importantly, Kerpen is where Vettel met Gerhard Noack, president and part-owner of the circuit. The man who 'discovered' Schumacher. A former hobby karter himself, Noack recalls that first race in 1995. 'Suddenly it started to rain,' he said. 'Everyone else went on to wet tyres with only Sebastian driving on slicks. He really stood out.' As well he might. Vettel had been karting since the age of three, when his father Norbert gave him a 60cc machine to 'keep him off the streets'. In one of those quirks of fate which enter into sporting folklore, Vettel Senior had to spray the front drive with water since the only way to handle one of the corners was by skidding around it. All those hours spent lapping an artificially soaked courtyard had paid off.

Noack kept a close eye on Vettel, making sure he got the right equipment and met the right people, just as he had for Schumacher. It was Noack who facilitated Vettel's meetings with Red Bull, for whom he signed as a thirteen-year-old, and BMW, for whom he first raced in 2007 before they let him go to Toro Rosso. 'I put a lot of time and effort, ten years, trying to pave the way for Sebastian,' Noack recalled after Vettel claimed his maiden title in 2010. 'In 1997, I even rented my business to have more time for Sebastian. I was convinced that he would be a world champion. It is a moving moment when you say, "Yes, the investment was worth it".' And had he become rich off the back of it? he was asked. 'No and nor do I want any [money]. Because then it's business, then perhaps it's no fun to myself.'

What it has done, though, is make Noack uniquely qualified to comment on the rise and rise of Formula One's latest superstar. We met in early autumn sunshine, at the track in Kerpen where Noack still runs a bambini-karting team, searching for more little Schumachers. Somewhat surprisingly, given his relentless schedule, the real deal is here. Schumacher is wandering about the place with his shirt off, wheeling a mountain bike. Fans and locals mill about in the sunshine. No one bats an eyelid when the great man walks past. 'It is one of the few places Michael can really relax and be himself,' Noack remarked. It turns out Schumacher, a millionaire hundreds of times over, is actually staying in a camper van in a field just behind the circuit. Only a gleaming red Ferrari parked incongruously outside hints at the van's illustrious occupant. It says a lot, both about Kerpen and Schumacher, that the seven-time champion should choose to spend a rare weekend off in this fashion.

Vettel visits less often these days, Noack said, but not because he is a big shot. Yes, he lives in Switzerland now but he has not forgotten his roots. He, too, stayed in a camper van with his dad, his brother and a friend at winter testing earlier in 2011. He still attends Eintracht Frankfurt matches, incognito, with old school mates. Vettel was back in Kerpen for the first time in two or three years to celebrate the fiftieth anniversary of the club. Schumacher beat him in a ten-lap exhibition race. 'I guess Michael showed me who's boss,' Vettel said afterwards.

'He hadn't changed a bit,' Noack smiled. 'Very humble. That is a product of his family. They were always there – father, mother, sisters – at every race, in the family camper van. They never had any airs.' Just a strong work ethic apparently. The young Vettel printed out a Lance Armstrong quote and put it on the wall next to his bed: 'For every single victory I paid with gallons of sweat.' Once, so the story goes, Vettel became angry when his sister Stephanie went quicker than him in the family kart. He refused his lunch and stayed out until he had set a better time. 'Sebastian's greatest strength is that he never gives up, just like Michael,' Noack said. 'He has an insatiable desire to learn and he doesn't repeat the same mistakes.'

Vettel (who has always politely rejected the 'Baby Schumi' tag) appears to have upped his game in 2011. Unlike 2010, when he was dubbed the 'Crash Kid' by McLaren team principal Martin Whitmarsh, 2011 has been almost blemish-free. Gone, too, is the occasional petulance which punctuated 2010, replaced by a seemingly unflappable coolness. Partly that is down to being put under little or no pressure, partly the twenty-four-year-old's increasing maturity. Not that everyone has been won over. Vettel is universally respected, widely liked, but perhaps not yet loved. Sure he is cool, he is young, he fits Red Bull's brand, but to some he remains oddly anodyne. Maybe it cannot be helped. Behind the easy-going, fun-loving exterior, the driver who gives his race cars racy names (current model: Kinky Kylie), quotes *Fawlty Towers* and takes his mechanics out for pizza, is an intensely private individual.

Vettel is extremely protective of his family and girlfriend Hanna, a fashion design student with a British father who he met at school in Heppenheim. His private life remains strictly off limits. It makes for an interesting comparison with our own karting prodigy, Lewis Hamilton, whose private life – the Pussycat Doll, the visits to Los Angeles – is under so much scrutiny and whose heart-on-sleeve behaviour tends to polarise opinion. 'It seems that Lewis has lost the control about his self, his priorities have shifted and maybe he looks too many times to the errors in others,' was Noack's observation. 'Maybe he has too many distractions. Sebastian loves and lives his job. That's what makes him so successful.'

Out on track the final race of the day is about to take place. It is being run in memory of Tommy Knoppen, a young Danish karter who died in an accident two years earlier. It is a tribute both to him and to the pull of Kerpen that the assembled field is so strong Schumacher has qualified only seventh. The forty-two-year-old recovered to finish fourth. Still no podium but you have to admire the energy. Behind the barriers the young karters, flushed from their own exertions, jostle for position. One day, perhaps, they too will follow in the footsteps of Kerpen's kings.

Sporting Champion: Sebastian Vettel – 4 Formula One World Drivers' Championships (2010, 2011, 2012, 2013).

ENGLAND – RUGBY WORLD CUP

JOHNSON THE DRIVING FORCE BEHIND
THAT DROP OF MAGIC

Mick Cleary, 24 November 2003

The garlands were heading Jonny Wilkinson's way from the moment the ball left his right foot for the clinching extra-time dropped goal in England's 20–17 victory over Australia. The real tributes, though, for this World Cup success should go to the big bear of a bloke, with blood trickling from a cut down his nose, who stepped forward shortly before 10.45 p.m. in rain-swept Sydney to collect the Webb Ellis Cup from Australian Prime Minister John Howard. Martin Johnson loomed large over the final as he has done over England's Rugby World Cup campaign. He is England's unbending talisman, a rallying point in times of crisis (and there were a few in this tournament) and a fount of down-to-earth common sense.

Sport is not about dressing-room rhetoric; it is about ever-changing realities. Johnson adapted to circumstance, through the World Cup and through the stomach-churningly tense events of the final game. England's captain is far more than a brooding symbol of defiance. He is also a smart footballer. Look past the bushy brow and hefty muscle and appreciate the subtle touches and fine decision-making. It was Johnson's final lung-busting piece of support play, driving the Wallabies on to the back foot, that helped tee up Wilkinson's last-gasp pot for glory. Matt Dawson made the initial thrust, Johnson kept the defence honest, and Wilkinson did the necessary. 'That all gave me more time than I'd had with my other dropped-goal efforts,' Wilkinson said. 'It was the easiest of the kicks.'

On a lap of honour that the players never wanted to end, a

salute to the massed white-shirted, drenched but delirious ranks, Johnson at one point draped his giant arm round the shoulder of Wilkinson. The warrior and the pin-up boy. You fancy that Wilkinson might yearn for Johnson's role away from the field of play – unobtrusive and unassuming. Wilkinson might need Jonno as his minder now as the superstar feeding frenzy starts. Once the bedlam at the Telstra Stadium had died down, Wilkinson headed back into the dressing room. There were a few mutual pats on the back before he sought out the sanctuary of the physio's room. 'I just wanted to detach myself from the madness for a while, take in a sense of calm,' Wilkinson said. He is a self-contained young bloke, rooted and obsessive about his trade. Do not be fooled by Wilkinson's soul-searching insecurities. He is every bit as tough a nut as Johnson, mentally and physically. The nation reached for the Valium when they saw Wilkinson slumped on the turf in obvious distress after clattering into Matt Giteau midway through the first half. 'I caught my head when Matt changed his angle late and I compressed my neck,' Wilkinson said. 'The pain went all the way down my right arm. It's known as a stinger and it's a problem I've had since I was sixteen. It's one of those things that shocks you and it's a case of lying there and hoping it turns out all right. This time the pain lasted longer than it normally does, about two to three minutes. I feared my final was over.' After treatment, he took up his position deep in the Australian twenty-two to face a Wallabies scrum. Bulky number eight David Lyons picked up and headed for Wilkinson. The England fly-half did not flinch, taking a step forward to make the tackle only for Neil Back to get to Lyons first. The retreat bugle will never sound when Wilkinson is around.

When Johnson does step aside from the captaincy, then a man of like no-surrender tendencies is waiting to take on the baton. Newcastle's director of rugby, Rob Andrew, feels that Wilkinson has been so wrapped up with this World Cup goal that an inhibiting weight of preoccupation will now lift from his shoulders. You caught a glimpse of that when that sweet, sweet drop went over. Wilkinson tends to bottle his emotions. Not this time.

Wilkinson missed three other dropped goal attempts, Mike Catt another. Not one of the squad or management tried to duck the fact that they had not played particularly well, especially in the second half when they failed to score a point. Australia, at 14–5, were there for the taking. England had struck a blow to the Wallabies' morale by scoring just before half-time when an arcing Lawrence Dallaglio break, carried on neatly by Wilkinson tracking on the inside, sent Jason Robinson scurrying and then skidding in at the corner.

England ought to have been even further ahead, lock Ben Kay blowing a gilt-edged chance in the twentieth minute when fumbling a pass with the line at his mercy. Long after the final whistle, he re-enacted the scene, diving over with ball safely in hand in a self-deprecating gesture. England fretted their way through the second half, allowing Australia to nibble away at their lead through the assured goal-kicking of Elton Flatley. Lote Tuqiri's sixth-minute try, a beautifully executed catch-and-take over Robinson's head from Stephen Larkham's pinpoint cross-kick, was supplemented by two second-half penalty goals from Flatley. His third was a masterclass of composure, the Wallabies centre nailing an angled 35-metre equalising penalty with the last kick of normal time. The penalty was awarded against the English scrum, the fifth of the night.

André Watson, the South African referee, was an utter disgrace at this phase of the game. The English front row destroyed their opponents and it was all they could do to keep the under-powered Wallabies' tight-head, Al Baxter, upright. Time and again Australia tried to collapse yet it was England who were penalised. 'It was very frustrating,' Trevor Woodman, England's loose-head, said. Watson, with his shrill, pompous manner, damn near cost England the game. As it was, England closed out the deal. Robinson made an all-important tackle on Tuqiri at one point, Will Greenwood on Mat Rogers at another. It was Rogers who cleared for touch from where England launched their last attack. There were only twenty-five seconds remaining as Wilkinson's dropped goal sailed through the posts. Once again England had toughed it out.

'I can go to my grave happy now,' said England's assistant coach, Phil Larder, who lost a World Cup final to Australia in 1995 when coaching Great Britain's rugby league team. 'Things got edgy when the scores closed. I'd have been suicidal if we'd lost. But when your destiny is wrapped up in people like Martin Johnson, you know it's in safe hands.' Johnson set the tone for the whole tournament with his unflagging desire to see the job done. In the final he had able lieutenants in key parts of the field in Dallaglio, who enjoyed his best game of the World Cup, scrum-half Matt Dawson and centres Greenwood and Mike Tindall. They all gave England go-forward and purpose. They played some rugby, too. The Australians did not have the last laugh on any front. England silenced an entire hemisphere – apart, that is, from their own raucous, celebrating hordes. They were all singing in the Sydney rain.

Sporting Champions: England – 1 World Cup (2003).

AUSTRALIA – RUGBY LEAGUE WORLD CUP

AUSTRALIA EXACT GLORIOUS REVENGE

Ian Chadband, 1 December 2013

With an inventive display of staggering power, pace and precision, Australia's rugby league titans climbed majestically back to the summit of their sport as they destroyed champions New Zealand 34–2 in the World Cup final. A world-record crowd for an international of 74,468 came to Old Trafford for an epic Antipodean showdown, but were treated instead to a supreme demonstration by the Kangaroos that they are among the very finest teams currently operating in any professional sport.

As a Champagne-drenched Cameron Smith lifted the cup, the tenth time that an Australian captain has hoisted the sport's ultimate trophy, he could reflect that his men would stand comparison with any of their illustrious predecessors. Because for an afternoon, with world-beating champions such as man-of the-match Johnathan Thurston, Cooper Cronk, Billy Slater and Smith himself all operating as if they knew this was an unrepeatable opportunity, the Australians were simply irresistible, combining an immaculate kicking game with attacking strength and flair as they ran in five tries.

Even more striking though was the Australians' utter bloody-minded determination to ensure their own line was not crossed. Even at the death, coach Tim Sheens could be seen growling at them not to slacken off as the Kiwis sought a meagre consolation. And they did not succumb, manically proud not to have conceded a try for five games since Josh Charnley went over for England near the end of the opening match of the tournament. It meant the Australian line had not been breached once in six hours forty-four minutes of physical battering. Quite incredible. 'They were outstanding, ruthless, saving their very best to the last,' conceded Stephen Kearney, the Kiwis' coach, admitting they were outclassed in every department.

Perhaps their exertions in the remarkable semi-final against England had told on them, but these Kangaroos would have won any which way. The statistics do not lie; since their World Cup final defeat five years ago, they have lost only one Test in twenty-five. And to think there had been a fond theory floating about at the Theatre of Dreams that this Australian side might choke a little, just as they did in their 2008 final when full-back Billy Slater's suicidal pass effectively sealed one of the biggest sporting shocks for a generation. Not a chance of it this time and how fitting that Slater, still not one hundred per cent fit following the knee injury that nearly kept him out of the final, should produce such a sweet redemption song, scoring twice and defending demonically under the high ball in a masterful performance.

But then, the big players, scenting this was their last shot at World Cup glory in the green and gold, were all tremendous, headed by Thurston, who could do no wrong with both his goal-kicking – seven out of seven – and his playmaking. Ten out of ten for that. In contrast, Sonny Bill Williams, around whom the contest had been sold as he sought to become the first player to win a World Cup in both rugby codes, was quite unable to deliver. He was hunted and ground down relentlessly and, despite still somehow managing to deliver a few offloads of inconceivable skill under pressure, was eventually hounded into a symbolic mistake, chucking a desperately hopeful pass near the Australian line in the seventy-second minute only for it to be picked off by Jarryd Hayne, who put in Brett Morris to score his second try. That fifth try represented the final, humiliating *coup de grâce* in a final that everyone had hoped would be a fitting climax to what has been a tournament of real enterprise and enjoyment. Instead, we got something almost as fine: a great team offering a performance that Smith described as the most complete he had been involved with.

The disappointment of the home team just failing to gain a place in the final was still palpable as the Manchester crowd evidently decided that England's conquerors deserved their backing. Boos rang out for the Australians in typical pantomime fashion, serving only to inspire them from the very start. Their first three tackles, murderous in their ferocity, signalled their intentions. The Kiwi prop Jesse Bromwich seemed so fazed, he dropped a straightforward pass and the Kangaroos were immediately all over their opponents. When the Kiwis soon lost one of their key weapons, as young wing sensation Roger Tuivasa-Sheck went off injured after seven minutes, they looked really up against it. Thurston's beautiful kick sailed over four Kiwi heads and sent Slater, catching and spinning balletically in mid-air, tumbling over the line.

After Cronk was unlucky to have a score ruled out by the video referee, he made up for the disappointment within minutes as he latched on to Darius Boyd's grubber. If the Kiwis entertained any hope of a second-half comeback, it was extinguished within forty-eight seconds of the restart as Slater finished off a four-man attack of swift, clinical simplicity. Like sharks, they poured in for the kill, with Morris demonstrating both skill and courage as he sprinted to touch down just before sliding down the grassy bank behind the try line and smashing into the advertising hoardings. Injured, he should not really have been on the pitch when he scored again minutes later. Yet that said everything about this team. 'We played simple footy, tough footy. It was about rolling our sleeves up and playing tough,' Smith said.

Sporting Champions: Australia – 10 World Cups (1957, 1968, 1970, 1975, 1977, 1988, 1992, 1995, 2000, 2013).

DECEMBER

DAVID STEELE – SPORTS PERSONALITY OF THE YEAR

MAN OF STEELE WITH A WINNING PERSONALITY

Ian Chadband, 12 December 2009

David Steele is a regular attendee of the BBC's *Sports Personality of the Year.* 'Go every year. Good do, it is,' he enthuses. One thing can be assured, though: whoever wins it will never eclipse this splendid sixty-eight-year-old granddad as the least likely but most warming winner in the event's history. Most years since the award's inception in 1954, the prize has been won by an athlete who epitomises British sporting excellence: say, a global champion or a once-in-a-generation footballer. Ah, but only once has it gone to a grey-haired, bespectacled symbol of national defiance in a losing cause.

Rewind to 1975 and a sporting landscape which matched the cheerless national struggle to escape an economic slump: Leeds fans rioting at the European Cup final, Don Revie's England fouling up their European Championship qualifying, their rugby counterparts unable to stop losing and failures aplenty in all the marquee sports. We were crying out for a hero but, amid the ruins of a first Ashes Test thrashing and the resignation of captain Mike Denness, never imagined a working-class saviour with grey thatch and silver specs. Here was a thirty-three-year-old from Stoke who looked forty, a printer by trade who had spent a dozen unheralded summers accumulating runs for unfashionable Northamptonshire, but whose dreams of playing for England had long departed. Steele could not stop Australia winning the series and did not even score a hundred, but his batting that summer, so full of sturdy application and grit as he averaged sixty, captured everyone's imagination. So did the man himself. 'They called me the bank clerk who went to war,' he recalls. 'Mind, the way the banks are going now, I wouldn't fancy putting that tag on me these days!'

Then, though, it fitted perfectly. Steele, the shock choice of new captain Tony Greig, seemed part English oak and part *Dad's Army*, the man who could stand up to the ferocity of Dennis Lillee and Jeff Thomson yet could not even find his way out of the Lord's Pavilion to make his debut knock. 'I went down one flight of stairs too many – but I got to the crease eventually!' Lillee was there to ask him: 'Where you been, Groucho?' A visit to the loo, per chance? 'Very nearly,' said Steele. 'Now get back to your mark and bowl, Dennis.' And did Thomson, on seeing the venerable looking debutant, really chip in: 'What we got here? Father bloody Christmas?' Sadly, Steele debunks that fond one. 'No, he didn't say nothing, Tommo. He just swore a lot.'

England slumped to forty-nine for four but the new number three was imperturbable in the rescue act, hooking Lillee fearlessly en route to fifty. Three more half-centuries followed in the series; where had he been all our lives? It was an irresistibly romantic tale. Famously careful with his money – he was nicknamed 'Crime' because crime doesn't pay – Steele's ideal distraction had been his benefit year with Northamptonshire, the best deal of which came when a local abattoir sponsored him. 'Yes, a lamb chop for every run up to fifty then after fifty, I was on steaks.' By the end of his best-ever summer, he'd earned 1,756 lumps. 'We had this list up in the kitchen and when we'd run out, we'd ring Harry at the abattoir and he'd say, "Aren't you finished yet?" I'd say, "No, we've still got another two hundred left". Kept us in meat for three years, that did.'

The country adored him. 'Well, we were in a bit of disarray and there's nothing an Englishman likes more than someone standing firm. The public got right behind me. A symbol of defiance? Well, I just felt I was doing my job. I was just a cricketer, just me. That summer, I'd got what I always wanted, the cap. The BBC award? The icing on the cake.' When he arrived for the ceremony at Shepherd's Bush, he was amazed to see two of his old mates from the Staffordshire leagues who told him they'd written to the *Radio Times* telling them why he should win. 'I thought, "Aye up, if they've invited them two, you must be number one, Steeley".' He was. When Lord Killanin, the Olympic president, presented the award, he hailed Steele for 'his courage, concentration and sportsmanship'.

A nation concurred. A maiden Test hundred followed against the formidable all-pace West Indies attack the next summer before he got discarded for the tour to India, supposedly because the selectors thought he would struggle against spin. Which Steele still thinks a load of old nonsense. It was not his last service for England, though; as a coach at Oakham School, he helped hone Stuart Broad's talent. Having retired from printing, he reckons he hasn't 'got time in the day' what with all his gardening, his presidency of the local Geddington cricket club, his after-dinner speaking and looking after his baby granddaughter Gracie May. Keeps him young. 'No, I don't look thirty-three anymore,' he laughs. 'Just thirty-five!' In the mind's eye, though, he will always look forty and always be Groucho hooking Lillee to the boundary. Still the best personality of all the Personalities.

Sporting Champion: David Steele – BBC Sports Personality of the Year (1975).

KAUTO STAR – KING GEORGE VI CHASE

OLD CHAMPION'S STAR IS BURNING
BRIGHTER THAN EVER

Paul Hayward, 27 December 2011

His jockey is salt-and-pepper grey and the hours are ticking to his twelfth birthday, but Kauto Star remains ageless. 'The weak don't last, and that's in any walk of life. The tough do,' said Ruby Walsh after their record fifth victory in the King George VI Chase at Kempton Park. The clock's hands have been working backwards this winter for surely the greatest steeplechaser since Arkle. As he stood in the saddle, punching the air in front of 20,000 adoring punters, Walsh might have expected his own hair to turn from grey back to brown. Everything about Kauto Star speaks of youth and vitality even as he approaches equine pensioner years.

'He might be eleven but he's been eight, the way he's been at home,' said his trainer, Paul Nicholls, who resisted pressure to retire the dark old star of his yard after he was pulled up at Punchestown in the spring. The burden of handling the most cherished horse since Desert Orchid has weighed heavily on jump racing's champion trainer, but now we see what Nicholls himself observed when Kauto Star began sparkling again during autumn. In the winner's enclosure, as the crowd rejoiced, Nicholls savoured his hour of vindication, sending his champion on a lap of honour of the parade ring and calling him 'awesome'. He said: 'On this form he deserves to be favourite for the Gold Cup. He was never right last year. In hindsight I think it took him a while to get over that fall [in the 2010 Gold Cup]. Ruby's a massive plus for him, as well. They know each other.

'When he's right like that he's as good as ever. He comes into this winner's enclosure and he's hardly having a blow. He used to be like that when he was at his best. Last year here he bled and was out on his feet. This crowd reaction shows what a great horse he is and how good he is for racing. Six times he's been here now: won five and third in 2010. I'll never have another like him. To have a chaser like that is astounding.'

Boxing Day at Kempton has treated its bleary crowds to some fine spectacles down the years. Desert Orchid, especially, arranged his own annual pilgrimage to a track once known unceremoniously as 'the old gravel pit'. But this was the greatest of King George memories. A fifth King George victory was beyond even Desert Orchid's super-agile jumping and high work ethic. The Cheltenham Festival is where jump racing really loosens its tweeds and dabs its eyes with hankies. That great Cotswolds amphitheatre is set up for triumph and tragedy as winter turns to spring. Here, Sunbury on Thames was transported to the lush turf beneath Cleeve Hill as the crowd shook off their Christmas torpor and raised a cheer reminiscent of the best Cheltenham conquests.

Written into the script was comeback drama, of a sort. With his white blaize and aristocratic Flat racer's head, Kauto Star was thought to be in slow decline when Long Run deposed him at Kempton and Cheltenham in 2010–11. He was still good enough to stay on the scene but no longer sufficiently sharp to cope with the young powerhouse. 'I promise you, if I'd had any sign in the autumn he wasn't quite right there's no way I'd have run him,' Nicholls said. 'I said to Clive [Smith, his owner], "The way he's going, he doesn't want retiring".' At his yard in Somerset, Nicholls assured this newspaper that Kauto Star's revenge win over Long Run at Haydock Park in the autumn had been no isolated flourish. On the hills around the village of Ditcheat visual evidence supported his conviction. The old horse bounced down lanes and steamed up hills as part of his daily two-hour workout.

Most ageing thoroughbreds lose their appetite for graft. Kauto Star always seems to want more.

'If we can get him like this again he'll go really well at Cheltenham. He's the one to beat, isn't he?' Nicholls said. Denman, his next-door neighbour, has retired, and Long Run now has two defeats to reverse. 'Kauto won't have Denman revving him up the arse all the way down the hill and that might help him,' Nicholls joked. 'He finished weak in the Gold Cup last year. He's finishing strong now. He was given a great ride, we were very positive with him and he galloped all the way to the line. He was awesome.' The author of that ride, Walsh, has established a remarkable empathy with this winner of nineteen races from thirty starts over fences. The trick, by all accounts, is a positive tactical approach without too much bossing from the saddle at fences. 'The winning time wasn't great. Maybe it was a bit tactical, but you have to play your cards, don't you?' Walsh said.

Kauto Star possesses a rare sense of his own high place in the animal kingdom. Seriously, this is a horse with a keen awareness of the drama going on around him, a four-legged beast with an aura and even an ego. A career that first took flight with a modest hurdle win in France eight years ago shows no signs of halting. In all Kauto Star has run forty times over obstacles and covered hundreds of miles of Somerset in training. He has seen Denman pass into retirement and outshone his fancied stable-companion Master Minded, who injured himself after a bad mistake in this race.

You can see why bookmakers still favour Long Run for Cheltenham, but that hardly mattered on this day of near-geriatric glory. 'Your head told you Long Run would catch up with us after Haydock, but your heart hoped he wouldn't,' Walsh said. 'He [Kauto] is learning. In another couple of years he'll be bomb proof.' He is a champion who just never knows when to leave. Long

Run's connections probably thought the stage was theirs after an impressive victory here in 2010, but Kauto Star was only taking a sabbatical. As Nicholls told us: 'His star's still burning bright.'

Sporting Champion: Kauto Star – 5 King George VI Chases (2006, 2007, 2008, 2009, 2011); 2 Cheltenham Gold Cups (2007, 2009).

ENGLAND – THE ASHES

JUBILATION AS ENGLAND RETAIN ASHES IN STYLE

Derek Pringle, 29 December 2010

England have retained the Ashes on Australian soil for the first time since 1986, an era that now seems washed in sepia, albeit with colourful flashes of Ian Botham's mullet. Their victory by an innings and 157 runs was a neat echo of the win Mike Gatting's side had on the same ground twenty-four years and a day ago, when Andrew Strauss, England's victorious leader here, and another Middlesex captain, was just nine years old. Since the War, only four England captains, Len Hutton, Ray Illingworth, Gatting and now Strauss, have left Australia with the Ashes in their possession, so the rarity value cannot be doubted. But Strauss has not yet matched the others by winning the series, too, and retaining the Ashes is not quite the same currency as winning them. But the first part of the equation had been threatening to come since Australia's batting showed how prone it is to collapse. That it took until 11.53 a.m. on the fourth morning of the fourth Test for the first goal to be achieved, after Matt Prior caught Ben Hilfenhaus off Tim Bresnan, was more due to England's blip in Perth than any revival by Australia.

Bresnan has been excellent in this match, fully justifying the management's decision to bring him in for a jaded Steve Finn. His four for fifty, as England dismissed Australia second time round for 258 (Ryan Harris did not bat after sustaining a stress fracture to his ankle), will not get his name on any boards, but as one of the chief reasons behind England winning here and retaining the Ashes, they are surely big enough to go up in lights in Pontefract. Bresnan's haul, plus another monolithic innings from Jonathan Trott, as well as another fine team effort overall from Strauss's side, at least ensures Aussie paws will stay off the urn for another two and a half years. It will have been gratifying, too, that the feat was achieved at the MCG, the mecca of Australian cricket, possessing a symbolic resonance that is hard to beat when avenging cricketing scores as old as this one.

When you contrast the scenes here, as the team did a noisy lap of honour, to those of four years ago, when Andrew Flintoff's England team were roundly booed by their own fans after capitulating in a similar fashion to Australia this time, you realise English cricket has travelled further than the 9,000 miles it takes to get here. England have deserved their success. Aside from their stumble in Perth, they have shown more variety and consistency in their bowling than Australia, and more class in general across the team. Four of their batsmen have made hundreds, several of them big ones, something Andy Flower emphasised in his team talks as being crucial to winning here.

Since they arrived nine weeks ago, England have prepared and played well. By comparison, Australia have been complacent in their build-up and chaotic with some of their selections. With no spinner worthy of the name, they have resorted to four pace bowlers and a part-time leggie, forcing them to gamble on both pitch and toss. It worked in Perth, after England's batsmen failed to cope with Mitchell Johnson's wonder spell, but spectacularly backfired in Melbourne after England's pacemen blew them away on the first day for ninety-eight.

With Australia resuming on 169 for six here, it was merely a case of getting the ball on a length and being patient, though with Chris Tremlett bowling Johnson with the eleventh ball of the day, a swift dispatch looked likely. But Brad Haddin and Peter Siddle ensured it was not a complete rout with an eighth-wicket stand of eighty-six. The pair saved a bit of face, too, when they took the score past 185, thus avoiding the shame of suffering Australia's biggest defeat on home soil, a stain that has stood since 1892. Haddin even managed some big hitting off Swann, though when Siddle tried to follow suit he was held at long-on by Kevin Pietersen.

The serious business of winning this match, and with it the retention of the Ashes, began with a Trott run-out in Australia's second innings, his second such intervention of the series. England's bowlers were looking fairly toothless when Trott swooped at extra cover to take advantage of a jittery run by Shane Watson. With that breach made and Phillip Hughes on his way, it was over to Bresnan and his timely spell of three wickets for two runs in eighteen balls, including Australia's captain Ricky Ponting. Failure to take possession of the Ashes urn normally costs captains their job and for a quarter of a century most who have fallen on their sword were English ones. Ponting has been one of Australia's greatest players, yet with three Ashes failures he has matched the ignominy suffered by Billy Murdoch in the nineteenth century. Ponting lost over a stone to get lean and mean enough for this series, but with 116 runs at an average of 16.4, his batting has withered with him. Australian cricket had become nostalgic of late but those days are past and the rebuilding, with a new if not better captain, will surely start soon.

Sporting Champions: England – 14 Ashes away series wins (1882–83, 1884–85, 1886–87, 1887–88, 1894–95, 1903–04, 1911–12, 1928–29, 1932–33, 1954–55, 1970–71, 1978–79, 1986–87, 2010–11).